Sharing Cities Shaping Cities

Sharing Cities Shaping Cities

Special Issue Editors
Giuseppe Salvia
Eugenio Morello
Andrea Arcidiacono

MDPI • Basel • Beijing • Wuhan • Barcelona • Belgrade

Special Issue Editors

Giuseppe Salvia
Politecnico di Milano
Italy

Eugenio Morello
Politecnico di Milano
Italy

Andrea Arcidiacono
Politecnico di Milano
Italy

Editorial Office
MDPI
St. Alban-Anlage 66
4052 Basel, Switzerland

This is a reprint of articles from the Special Issue published online in the open access journal *Urban Science* (ISSN 2413-8851) from 2018 to 2019 (available at: https://www.mdpi.com/journal/urbansci/special_issues/Sharing_Cities_Shaping_Cities).

For citation purposes, cite each article independently as indicated on the article page online and as indicated below:

LastName, A.A.; LastName, B.B.; LastName, C.C. Article Title. *Journal Name* **Year**, *Article Number*, Page Range.

ISBN 978-3-03897-988-3 (Pbk)
ISBN 978-3-03897-989-0 (PDF)

© 2019 by the authors. Articles in this book are Open Access and distributed under the Creative Commons Attribution (CC BY) license, which allows users to download, copy and build upon published articles, as long as the author and publisher are properly credited, which ensures maximum dissemination and a wider impact of our publications.

The book as a whole is distributed by MDPI under the terms and conditions of the Creative Commons license CC BY-NC-ND.

Contents

About the Special Issue Editors vii

Giuseppe Salvia, Eugenio Morello and Andrea Arcidiacono
Sharing Cities Shaping Cities
Reprinted from: *Urban Science* **2019**, 3, 23, doi:10.3390/urbansci3010023 1

Jacqui Alexander
Domesticity On-Demand: The Architectural and Urban Implications of Airbnb in Melbourne, Australia
Reprinted from: *Urban Science* **2018**, 2, 23, doi:10.3390/urbansci2030088 6

Mark Hammond
Spatial Agency: Creating New Opportunities for Sharing and Collaboration in Older People's Cohousing
Reprinted from: *Urban Science* **2018**, 2, 64, doi:10.3390/urbansci2030064 16

Giacomo Durante and Margherita Turvani
Coworking, the Sharing Economy, and the City: Which Role for the 'Coworking Entrepreneur'?
Reprinted from: *Urban Science* **2018**, 2, 83, doi:10.3390/urbansci2030083 29

Mina Akhavan, Ilaria Mariotti, Lisa Astolfi and Annapaola Canevari
Coworking Spaces and New Social Relations: A Focus on the Social Streets in Italy
Reprinted from: *Urban Science* **2019**, 3, 2, doi:10.3390/urbansci3010002 50

Mayo Fuster Morell and Ricard Espelt
A Framework for Assessing Democratic Qualities in Collaborative Economy Platforms: Analysis of 10 Cases in Barcelona
Reprinted from: *Urban Science* **2018**, 2, 61, doi:10.3390/urbansci2030061 61

Afif Fathullah and Katharine S. Willis
Engaging the Senses: The Potential of Emotional Data for Participation in Urban Planning
Reprinted from: *Urban Science* **2018**, 2, 98, doi:10.3390/urbansci2040098 74

Yiyun Sun
Sharing and Riding: How the Dockless Bike Sharing Scheme in China Shapes the City
Reprinted from: *Urban Science* **2018**, 2, 68, doi:10.3390/urbansci2030068 95

Giovanni Vecchio
Producing Opportunities Together: Sharing-Based Policy Approaches for Marginal Mobilities in Bogotá
Reprinted from: *Urban Science* **2018**, 2, 54, doi:10.3390/urbansci2030054 114

About the Special Issue Editors

Giuseppe Salvia is a research fellow at Politecnico di Milano, with a Ph.D. in Design. He is mainly interested in the way socio-technical innovations reconfigure practices and routines in order to understand and develop strategies for transitioning towards more sustainable patterns of consumption and production. He has been investigating contemporary phenomena related to the sharing economy; collaborative consumption; energy use; making, repair, fabbing, and DIY; and the acquisition and development of skills. Methodologically, Giuseppe uses ethnographical and co-design tools to explore how socio-technical innovations and practices occur and evolve. He has also collaborated on research projects focusing on design strategies for sustainable consumption, life cycle assessment, bio-inspired design approaches, materials innovation and sensory qualities. Giuseppe also teaches undergraduate and postgraduate courses in schools of product design and urban studies. He is the (co-)author of over 50 publications, an organizer of international conferences and events.

Eugenio Morello is an architect by education, an associate professor of urban design at Politecnico di Milano, and a coordinator and research scientist of the Laboratorio di Simulazione Urbana Fausto Curti, at the Department of Architecture and Urban Studies. Since 2017, he has been the Rector's Delegate for environmental sustainability and he is responsible for institutional projects aimed towards developing a sustainable campus. He is the principal investigator of the European H2020 projects for the co-design of nature-based solutions and novel urban services in Milan. Since 2015, he has served as a member of the board of the Urban Planning, Design, and Policy Ph.D. program. He is an instructor of the design studio 'Energy and Urban Planning', on energy transition and urban resilience solutions. His research interest is situated at the intersection of urban design and environmental quality and climate design. He investigates the integration of environmental aspects and energy transition solutions aiming towards the closing of energy and material cycles at the local scale. More recently, his research work has developed new insights into the topics of collaborative consumption and the sharing society and how these new paradigms can inform urban planning and urban design and co-design.

Andrea Arcidiacono is an associate professor and member of the board of the Ph.D. programme in Urban Planning, Design and Policy UPDP at the Department of Architecture and Urban Studies (DAStU), Politecnico di Milano. He is the vice-president of the National Institute of Planning (INU), director of the LabPPTE—Plans, Landscape, Territories, and Ecosystem at the DAStU, and scientific director of the national Land Take Research Centre (CRCS). He is a member of the editorial board of the Italian Journal "Urbanistica". His research interests include urban planning and design; landscape planning; open spaces design; ecosystem analysis and nature-based solutions for spatial planning; and policies for land take limitation. He is the DAStU principal investigator of the European programme LIFE 2014-2020 'European Programme for the Environment and Climate Action' (LIFE 2017), involved in the three-year funding programme: 'SOIL4LIFE', the project leader of the DAStU-POLIMI research group for studies and researches to support the design of the new Lombardy Regional Landscape Plan PPR, scientific director for the research activities funded through a regional competitive bid by Fondazione Cariplo 2014. He is the (co-)author of over 100 scientific publications.

Editorial

Sharing Cities Shaping Cities

Giuseppe Salvia *, Eugenio Morello and Andrea Arcidiacono

Department of Architecture and Urban Studies (DAStU), Politecnico di Milano, 20158 Milano, Italy; eugenio.morello@polimi.it (E.M.); andrea.arcidiacono@polimi.it (A.A.)
* Correspondence: giuseppe.salvia@polimi.it

Received: 31 January 2019; Accepted: 20 February 2019; Published: 22 February 2019

---

1. Contemporary 'Shapring': How is Sharing Shaping Urban Practices and Dynamics?

In recent years, 'sharing cities' has spread globally, starting in 2012 when Seoul declared its intent to pursue sharing economy strategies [1]. Other cities then followed, including Amsterdam, Boulder, and Rio de Janeiro. Their pursuits to become sharing cities also intended to face major contemporary urban challenges, including global urbanization [2] and resource depletion [3]. Sharing cities make use of (often smart) technologies to connect a larger number of users to idling assets, hence to be 'shared' by a wider population, rather than being individually owned. Within this trend, assets that are typically shared include vehicles and rides, bedrooms and accommodation, as well as tools and competences.

Environmental, social and business advantages are envisaged by many [4–6], often leading to significant financial investments by industries, public bodies and international organizations. Sharing cities is a locution which has emerged to express the marriage of the sharing economy in urban areas [7–9]. Davidson and Infranca [10] describe urban conditions as fundamental for the value proposition of the innovative elements of the current sharing hype.

The physical and social configuration of a city shapes the way in which sharing takes place: size and type of fabric, mobility and accessibility, availability of public spaces, social norms, habits and traditions and, therefore, the unit of analysis. Vice versa, how sharing shapes—rather than being shaped by—urban features may apply likewise and, in our view, deserves attention to reflect upon the changes that the contemporary sharing-based practices may bring about.

Cities are complex systems, crossed and shaped by flows of both material and immaterial resources. Sharing practices are impacting on the human connections and relationships to assets, shifting from ownership-based to access-based approaches. It is not the practice of sharing alone that is new [11], but rather the dynamics of no longer relying on previously formed relationships with sharers ([9], p. 88), thus expanding the network of interactions to geographically distributed 'strangers' [12]. The types of connections between engaged actors are shifting from more traditional dyadic forms (i.e., one-to-one) towards polyadic (i.e., one-to-many) or even rhizomatic patterns (i.e., many-to-many) [13,14]. Also, in our view, these patterns of spread connectivity represent a key element of the 'sharing' trend, i.e., the facilitated access to a multitude of distributed assets, resources and people. All this will have strong implications in transforming cities in the near future; this urban transition is going to take place regardless of urban planning practices and top-down decision making. It is the sole responsibility of urban planners to recognize the new design challenges offered by the sharing society and turn them into opportunities for regenerating urban space.

This Special Issue intends to contribute towards this direction, i.e., scoping the implications of sharing in shaping the urban context, a dynamic we call 'shapring' for convenience. To this end, a call for contributions to a research symposium was launched to respond to research questions regarding:

- Urban fabric: How is 'sharing' shaping cities? Does it represent a paradigm shift with tangible and physical reverberations on urban form? How are shared mobility, work, inhabiting, energy, and food provisions reconfiguring the urban and social fabric?

- Social practices: Are new lifestyles and practices related to sharing changing the use and design of spaces? To what extent is sharing triggering a production and consumption paradigm shift to be reflected in urban arrangements and infrastructures?
- Sustainability: Does sharing increase the intensity of use of space and assets, or, rather, does it increase them to meet the expectations of convenience for urban lifestyles? To what extent are these phenomena fostering more economically-, socially-, and environmentally-sustainable practices and cities?
- Policy: How can policy makers and municipalities interact with these bottom-up phenomena and grassroots innovation to create more sustainable cities?

More than 70 contributions from over 30 countries were submitted for double-blind peer review and a selection of 12 were presented in Milan in March 2018, hosted by Politecnico di Milano. Nearly 50 delegates (including researchers, practitioners and municipalities' representatives) debated on key themes and features characterizing the phenomenon from multiple perspectives and drawing on insights from fieldwork activities in Europe, Asia and Oceania.

Some of the presented contributions were further developed for submission to the Special Issue, which in our view constitutes a primary step-stone in the path which addresses how the socio-technical innovation brought about by sharing is affecting the reconfiguration of urban dynamics and spaces.

The full papers of this Special Issue investigate multiple forms of sharing, including novel ones for either domestic or working spaces; collaboration forms, platforms and commons; citizens' sharing practice and data. These are briefly summarized below.

2. Shaping Domestic Space for Accommodation

Housing and accommodation are amongst the most recurrently cited practices of the sharing economy, possibly also due to the hype and debated case of AirBnB. Illegal accommodation conditions (e.g., hygiene regulation, fire safety) and restricted housing access for locals (e.g., higher rent prices) are detrimental consequences of shared accommodation abuses.

Jacqui Alexander [15] reports emerging housing typologies in Melbourne in response to the demand for shared accommodation. A densification of sharing room standards is witnessed, often shrinking in size and reshaped in suboptimal conditions (e.g., room with no access to natural light) within supersized houses to escalate profit. Alexander conceptualizes novel forms for houses to be shared, meeting comfort standards and more importantly proposes strategic planning to assist in subverting the possibly pernicious effects of global disruption in favor of local interests.

Mark Hammond [16] interprets sharing accommodation as a process of citizen engagement in the house design process, beyond profession and technical skills. The author explores and applies the concept of 'spatial agency' in the development of co-housing spaces in the UK to be inhabited by older people. Although the investigation embraces a wider definition of the sharing economy, which is not necessarily related to the contemporary forms, the cases presented highlight two major implications of interest in architectural and urban studies aligned with the aim of this Special Issue, i.e., on the one hand, how the definition of indoor shared spaces and assets may reverberate in the reconfiguration of local communities, neighborhoods and the whole cities; on the other hand, the reshaped role of the architect who may enable—rather than define—the configuration of space that best fit with its inhabitants preferences.

3. Shaping Working Space and Offices

The sharing economy and practice are also related to novel forms and dynamics of working, demanding flexibility, adaptability, knowledge transfer, etc. Coworking spaces are spreading to meet such forms, as highlighted by two full papers investigating the Italian context, which raise reflections upon urban reconfiguration and developments.

Giacomo Durante and Margherita Turvani's study [17] contributes to the identification of a 'coworking bubble', due to a low performance output of such spaces in Italy. The factors are multiple, mainly depending upon the space managers and number of services provided. The implications spread across the cities and the novel forms of work which such spaces and their users may generate.

Mina Akhavan [18] and colleagues investigated the impact of Italian coworking spaces in their urban context, with a focus on the case of Milan. Coworking spaces appear to support situated urban regeneration, especially when in connection with contemporary forms of socializing in cities, as in the case of Social Street.

4. Shapring through Collaborative Platforms

Sharing also applies to collaborative communities who cooperate to make a change, often for local impact. Different forms of collaboration are present, specifically through platforms, cooperatives and professional mediators.

Mayo Fuster Morell and Ricard Espelt [19] describe the forms and dynamics of the platform collaborative economy, drawing on outcomes from fieldwork research. Three macro-models are identified (i.e., open commons, uniform, platform coops) and 10 case studies in the Barcelona collaborative economy ecosystem were analyzed according to six democratic common qualities, which constitute the Star Framework. The application of the framework helps to qualify the nature of existing cases and infers the possibility of an alternative economy based on solidarity and collaboration to be initiated and fostered in the future.

5. Shapring through Data

Sharing in urban contexts redefines territories and reshapes their syntax. Citizens make use of the city and assets by drawing on local knowledge, accomplishing daily practices, and uptaking socio-technical innovations to accomplish their routines. This determines how cities are made.

These urban dynamics are reflected by data exchanged by citizens with the digital and online services they use. The presenters of the citizens' sharing panel of the symposium reported their studies on how data sharing reveals or may reveal such novel urban forms, with the audience questioning whether this data may predict patterns.

Katharine Willis and Afif Fathullah [20] address how data on emotions and crowd-sourcing may be used to investigate how citizens experience places. Using physiological wearable devices, human body alterations are proxies for emotional variations. These are identified while Plymouth's citizens navigate in the city, thus depicting the emotional landscape and stress hotspots. Such an approach could be scaled up in the future through widely distributed devices (e.g., embedded in smartphones) and may inform urban planners and municipalities in particular about how the city is felt and where interventions may be required to enhance citizens' urban experience.

Sun [21] reports insights from a study on dockless bike sharing (DBSS) user experience in Beijing, China. Social and environmental sustainability are the key issues. Low is the access for low-income and older people. Furthermore, bike sharing seems to use new resources rather than existing ones. Optimal governance of DBSS is to be distributed and coordinated between governments (infrastructure and regulations), companies (qualities and maintenance) and citizens (education and culture).

Vecchio [22] addresses the role of policy to enhance urban mobility through demand matchmaking and shared means, as a way to access opportunities, namely, to overcome criminality and poverty in marginal areas. The evidence is built upon fieldwork data of travelers across the Colombian capital, Bogotà, in which the coproduction of mobility services is explored.

In response, policy measures are proposed as operational options that nonetheless require recognition and support by the institutions responsible for urban mobility planning.

6. Conclusions

The papers introduced above contribute to the effort of initiating structured, fieldwork-informed reflections about sharping, and the change to the urban fabric generated by the spreading of sharing-based practices. Although interpretations of sharing and the sharing economy were not necessarily consistent, relevant areas of investigation and territory were covered and raised the importance of additional investigations. The other areas that deserve attention include:

- Sharing as an urban phenomenon and the limitations in marginal contexts (either periphery or smaller cities), where sharing could provide benefits and reshape the urban configurations and dynamics.
- The potential of intensifying the use of existing assets by sharing is often contradicted by the replication of assets to ensure flexibility and adaptability, leading to a dualism between scarcity and abundance.
- The implementation of policies regulating interventions in the urban configuration for enabling forms of sharing that may benefit local citizens, thus limiting risks for gentrification or escalation of resource intensity.

Acknowledgments: The editors of the Sharing Cities Shaping Cities Special Issue wish to thank all the authors for providing insightful information and reflections on contemporary sharing landscape; the dept. of Architecture and Urban Studies (DAStU) of Politecnico di Milano and the European Commission for providing funding to the research symposium in which the Special Issue originated. The symposium was an initiative of and co-funded by the H2020 project 'Sharing Cities', which has received funding from the European Union's Horizon 2020 research and innovation programme under Grant Agreement N°691895.

Conflicts of Interest: The authors declare no conflict of interest.

References

1. Moon, M.J. Government-driven Sharing Economy: Lessons from the Sharing City Initiative of the Seoul Metropolitan Government. *J. Dev. Soc.* **2017**, *33*, 223–243. [CrossRef]
2. UNDESA. World Urbanization Prospects: The 2018 Revision. 2018. Available online: https://esa.un.org/unpd/wup/Publications (accessed on 21 February 2019).
3. Krausmann, F.; Gingrich, S.; Eisenmenger, N.; Erb, K.H.; Haberl, H.; Fischer-Kowalski, M. Growth in global materials use, GDP and population during the 20th century. *Ecol. Econ.* **2009**, *68*, 2696–2705. [CrossRef]
4. Botsman, R.; Rogers, R. *What's Mine is Yours. How Collaborative Consumption is Changing the Way We Live*; HarperCollins: London, UK, 2010.
5. McLaren, D.; Agyeman, J. *Sharing Cities*; The MIT Press: Cambridge, MA, USA, 2016.
6. Rifkin, J. *Age of Access: The New Culture of Hypercapitalism*; Putnam Publishing Group: New York, NY, USA, 2000.
7. Agyeman, J.; McLaren, D.; Schaefer-Borrego, A. Sharing Cities. Briefing for the Friends of the Earth Big Ideas Project. 2013. Available online: https://friendsoftheearth.uk/sites/default/files/downloads/agyeman_sharing_cities.pdf (accessed on 21 February 2019).
8. Agyeman, J.; McLaren, D. Sharing cities. *Environment* **2017**, *59*, 22–27. [CrossRef]
9. Cohen, B.; Muñoz, P. Sharing cities and sustainable consumption and production: towards an integrated framework. *J. Clean. Prod.* **2016**, *134*, 87–97. [CrossRef]
10. Davidson, N.M.; Infranca, J.J. The Sharing Economy as an Urban Phenomenon. *Yale Law Policy Rev.* **2016**, *34*, 215–279.
11. Price, J.A. Sharing: The Integration of Intimate Economies. *Anthropologica* **1975**, *17*, 3. [CrossRef]
12. Schor, J. Debating the sharing economy. *J. Self-Gov. Manag. Econ.* **2016**, *4*, 7–22.
13. Giesler, M. Consumer Gift Systems. *J. Consum. Res.* **2006**, *33*, 283–290. [CrossRef]
14. Ertz, M.; Durif, F.; Arcand, M. Collaborative Consumption: Conceptual Snapshot at a Buzzword. *J. Entrep. Educ.* **2016**, *19*, 1–23. [CrossRef]
15. Alexander, J. Domesticity On-Demand: The Architectural and Urban Implications of Airbnb in Melbourne, Australia. *Urban Sci.* **2018**, *2*, 88. [CrossRef]

16. Hammond, M. Spatial Agency: Creating New Opportunities for Sharing and Collaboration in Older People's Cohousing. *Urban Sci.* **2018**, *2*, 64. [CrossRef]
17. Durante, G.; Turvani, M. Coworking, the Sharing Economy, and the City: Which Role for the 'Coworking Entrepreneur'? *Urban Sci.* **2018**, *2*, 83. [CrossRef]
18. Akhavan, M.; Mariotti, I.; Astolfi, L.; Canevari, A. Coworking Spaces and New Social Relations: A Focus on the Social Streets in Italy. *Urban Sci.* **2019**, *3*, 2. [CrossRef]
19. Fuster Morell, M.; Espelt, R. A Framework for Assessing Democratic Qualities in Collaborative Economy Platforms: Analysis of 10 Cases in Barcelona. *Urban Sci.* **2018**, *2*, 61. [CrossRef]
20. Fathullah, A.; Willis, K.S. Engaging the Senses: The Potential of Emotional Data for Participation in Urban Planning. *Urban Sci.* **2018**, *2*, 98. [CrossRef]
21. Sun, Y. Sharing and Riding: How the Dockless Bike Sharing Scheme in China Shapes the City. *Urban Sci.* **2018**, *2*, 68. [CrossRef]
22. Vecchio, G. Producing Opportunities Together: Sharing-Based Policy Approaches for Marginal Mobilities in Bogotá. *Urban Sci.* **2018**, *2*, 54. [CrossRef]

© 2019 by the authors. Licensee MDPI, Basel, Switzerland. This article is an open access article distributed under the terms and conditions of the Creative Commons Attribution (CC BY) license (http://creativecommons.org/licenses/by/4.0/).

Article

Domesticity On-Demand: The Architectural and Urban Implications of Airbnb in Melbourne, Australia

Jacqui Alexander

School of Architecture, Monash Art Design and Architecture (MADA), Monash University, Caulfield East, Melbourne 3145, Australia; jacqui.alexander@monash.edu; Tel.: +61-410-269-095

Received: 14 July 2018; Accepted: 7 September 2018; Published: 12 September 2018

Abstract: The home-sharing platform, Airbnb, is disrupting the social and spatial dynamics of cities. While there is a growing body of literature examining the effects of Airbnb on housing supply in first-world, urban environments, impacts on dwellings and dwelling typologies remain underexplored. This research paper investigates the implications of "on-demand domesticity" in Australia's second largest city, Melbourne, where the uptake of Airbnb has been enthusiastic, rapid, and unregulated. In contrast to Airbnb's opportunistic use of existing housing stock in other global cities, the rise of short-term holiday rentals and the construction of new homes in Melbourne has been more symbiotic, perpetuating, and even driving housing models—with some confronting results. This paper highlights the challenges and opportunities that Airbnb presents for the domestic landscape of Melbourne, exposing loopholes and grey areas in the planning and building codes which have enabled peculiar domestic mutations to spring up in the city's suburbs, catering exclusively to the sharing economy. Through an analysis of publically available spatial data, including GIS, architectural drawings, planning documents, and building and planning codes, this paper explores the spatial and ethical implications of this urban phenomenon. Ultimately arguing that the sharing economy may benefit from a spatial response if it presents a spatial problem, this paper proposes that strategic planning could assist in recalibrating and subverting the effects of global disruption in favor of local interests. Such a framework could limit the pernicious effects of Airbnb, while stimulating activity in areas in need of rejuvenation, representing a more nuanced, context-specific approach to policy and governance.

Keywords: Melbourne sharing economy; Melbourne Airbnb; architectural and urban effects of Airbnb; socio-spatial effects of Airbnb; Airbnb and housing typologies; Airbnb and domestic design; Airbnb and planning; Airbnb and policy innovation; Airbnb and governance

1. Introduction

In its short lifespan, home-sharing platform Airbnb has revolutionized tourism by developing a framework that enables a global pool of applicants to rent homes on-demand, in shorter increments of time, and at a premium [1]. In turn, this phenomenon is transforming the way we use, access, and design domestic space, and is disrupting the social dynamics of cities around the world. While there is an emerging body of literature examining Airbnb and its impacts on housing markets in first-world, urban environments, its effects are contingent on local particularities, including social, political, economic, and morphological systems, and they are therefore difficult to generalize. Moreover, Airbnb's impact on dwellings and dwelling typologies—as distinct from property—remain underexplored. As such, this paper investigates "on-demand domesticity" through a case study analysis of Melbourne, Australia. There, the uptake of Airbnb has coincided with the high-density apartment boom to produce some significant social transformations, but also unique formal reverberations, as evidenced by a number of domestic mutations emerging in the city's suburbs. Through an analysis of available spatial data, this paper discusses the intersection of the three categories of Airbnb listings—entire home, private room, and shared room—with the domestic landscape of Melbourne, highlighting the need for development and planning strategies to address this new kind of quasi-commercial, quasi-residential use and the array of challenges it has already wrought. Ultimately, this paper argues that if Airbnb presents a spatial problem, it might benefit from a spatial solution. Rather than defaulting to generic caps or blanket bans on listings as implemented by other global cities, this research proposes that strategic planning could be deployed as a means to recalibrate and subvert global disruption in favor of local interests.

The sharing economy has exploded in the last decade in the context of increasing resource limitations, postindustrial economies, neoliberal austerity and privatization, and property speculation and accumulation [2]. Less production and fewer resources have forced consumption to be reconceptualized to enable a high turnover of existing products, and property is no exception. Airbnb is an example *par excellence* of what is known in business terms as 'collaborative consumption' [3]: a model designed to maximize value from latent assets (in this case, housing) through short-term leasing, or "sharing" [1]. While still arguably in its infancy, the origins of the sharing economy can be traced back to the arrival of Web 2.0 at the turn of the 21st century, when the social web [4] began to facilitate new global communication and "virtual communities" and promised increasing horizontality through "user-generated content" [4]. The first wave of sharing made possible by the internet was largely content and image-based, exemplified by not-for-profit organizations like Wikipedia (2001) and Creative Commons (2001) and later, free but sponsored social media sites like Facebook (2004). Importantly, as Belk points out, these platforms operated outside of "expectations of reciprocity" [5] or payment for service. By 2007, the smartphone had delivered personal GPS, opening up new possibilities for the real-time sharing of resources and services. In the wake of the global financial crisis's conditions and politics of austerity [6], there was much need and enthusiasm for the peer-to-peer sharing of goods and services via platform cooperatives [7]. But the global debut of home-sharing platform, Airbnb, in 2008 and its ride-sharing counterpart, Uber, in 2009, marked the beginning of a new kind of peer-to-peer model that is inherently transactional—one in which everything is able to be commodified [8], including domestic space.

In Australia, the uptake of Airbnb has been rapid, enthusiastic, and largely unregulated [1]. Endorsed by both the public and private sectors—with government organizations like Tourism Victoria [9] and corporate giant Qantas [10] forging recent partnerships with the platform—it is now responsible for contributing over $400 million each year to the Victorian state economy alone [1,11]. Significantly, Airbnb's arrival in Australia in 2012 coincided with the beginning of a strategic market-led apartment building program in the eastern states, designed to accommodate the growing population and avert a recession following the decline of mining investment [12]. Unlike other parts of the world which have struggled to regain their footing following the 2008 collapse, Australia has experienced a continuous period of economic prosperity, largely as a result of this population growth and high-density housing boom [13], which has seen the rapid transformation of east coast cities, including Melbourne, Sydney, and to a lesser extent, Brisbane. While apartment building has stimulated growth in the construction industry as intended [14], increasing supply has done little to alleviate the housing affordability crisis [13] which until now has continued to escalate in Melbourne and Sydney. In Australia, America, and the UK, rising property prices have been fueled by global investment in 'stable' assets. Tax offsets like capital gains tax exemptions and negative gearing have incentivized development but have also pitted owner-occupiers against investors, inflating house prices and driving up rents [13], which in Melbourne reached record highs in 2017 [15]. Airbnb and other home-sharing platforms have been blamed for exacerbating the crisis, with investors buying up apartments to lease exclusively as short-term rentals for a higher return.

Melbourne is a particularly pertinent city for interrogating the architectural and urban effects of Airbnb, not simply because of its already pressured housing market, but because of its laissez-faire approach to business and property development, which has enabled both Airbnb usage, and until recently, the design quality of apartments, to carry on unregulated. While Sydney has recently implemented caps on the number of days Airbnb properties can be listed and enabled bi-laws to be passed by strata owners corporations [16], Airbnb activity in Melbourne remains unrestricted. The popularity of short-term holiday rentals in Sydney has posed challenges in terms of rental affordability, housing supply, and nuisance activity. However, because the design quality of apartments has been regulated since 2002 in New South Wales [17], the overall standard of residential construction is higher than in Victoria, and so the effects of disruption on the built fabric of the city are less overt. By comparison, while multi-residential development in Victoria is also subject to planning permissions from the local or state authority, until recently there were no planning guidelines to protect the internal amenity of individual apartments, such as minimum room sizes. Victoria's "Better Apartment Design Standards" [18] were only introduced in 2017 after years of poor quality development and mounting pressure from the architecture profession whose input is still not mandatory in the design of multi-residential development. This gap in the planning process has resulted in a glut of homogenous dwellings in the inner city which lack basic amenities such as natural light to bedrooms, cross-ventilation, and private outdoor space [19]. Considered unlivable by many residents, these kinds of apartments have found a new market on Airbnb, and are often let year-round as holiday rentals [1].

In contrast to Airbnb's opportunistic use of existing housing stock in other global cities, in Melbourne, there is some evidence to suggest that the relationship between short-term rentals and the construction of new homes has been more symbiotic—perpetuating, and in some cases, even *driving* housing models. As such, this research paper asks the following: what tangible effects is Airbnb having on the built fabric of Melbourne, and how might we establish a policy framework to effectively address the challenges and opportunities that this disruption presents for the city?

2. Materials and Methods

Primary geospatial data sourced from InsideAirbnb.com provides a useful starting point for understanding how Airbnb is disrupting the spatial dynamics of metropolitan Melbourne. This data has been modelled according to listing type (entire home, private room, and shared room), relative to urban infrastructure, and in consideration of existing housing typologies in the urban, inner, and middle rings where Airbnb activity exists. Building on a discussion of issues explored in a short opinion piece for Architecture Australia [1], this paper interrogates anomalies and hotspots within this dataset by isolating and reviewing Airbnb listings of interest. By examining spatial data in combination with interior and exterior photography included in the listings, it has been possible to identify and locate specific sites of interest as case studies for further analysis. Publically available architectural marketing and planning drawings have been sourced, and case studies have been visited to develop a clear picture of the spatial context. One such case study—the supersized house, which perhaps best demonstrates the reverberations of Airbnb on domestic form—has been analyzed in detail in order to understand the regulatory processes which enabled its development. Planning submission drawings have been closely scrutinized in relation to the National Construction Code (NCC) and local planning schemes to determine existing grey areas and loopholes that have facilitated the construction of new shared practices and typologies. Finally, a context-specific, strategic planning approach to regulation to constrain and target disruption in a way that is useful for the city has been tested through an action-based, speculative design-research project.

3. Results

When modelled, data suggests that Airbnb is taking available housing stock off the market where it is in high demand: in the city center close to employment and public transport [1]. This trend is consistent with many other global cities such as London [20], Amsterdam [21], and New York [22] that have since taken steps to cap the number of days Entire Homes can be listed, or in the case of Berlin, ban them all together [23].

Due to the current lack of regulation in Melbourne, Entire Homes, which exist in large concentrations in the inner city (Supplementary Material 1), can be let exclusively as holiday rentals, and are often listed by professional hosts with multiple properties. Entire Homes constitute the majority of Airbnb rentals in Melbourne—around 57% (Table 1)—which on average have very low occupancy rates [1]. As we have seen in parts of central London and elsewhere, large swathes of vacant property, either as a result of the ebbs and flows of tourism or as untenanted investments, have implications for housing affordability and supply, but can also pose broader urban challenges for local businesses, street life, and security, particularly at certain times of year [1,24].

Table 1. Percentage Breakdown of Airbnb listings in Metropolitan Melbourne by listing category. Data sourced from *InsideAirbnb.com*, 2016.

Entire Homes	Private Rooms	Shared Rooms	Total
56.85%	41.1%	2.04%	100%
6361	4600	229	11,190

The distribution of both Entire Homes and Shared Rooms in Melbourne closely corresponds with the intensity of new apartments in the central business district (CBD) and the inner city. Shared Rooms only constitute about 2% of all listings (Table 1), but they present a variety of other social and regulatory challenges [1]. These listings tend to be concentrated in a small number of isolated new developments in the western end of the CBD close to existing backpacker's accommodation and in the northeastern corner of the CBD near RMIT University—an area which has traditionally catered to large populations of international students (Supplementary Material 2). Developments such as these, which pre-date the implementation of minimum design standards, are characterized by 'buried' bedrooms and inadequate floor, storage, and outdoor space. The Shared Room listings operating within them are often overcrowded, with two-bedroom apartments accommodating up to eight guests [1] and being marketed as longer-term housing options for international students, contract workers, and new migrants. When they are used this way—effectively functioning as informal hostels—these properties do not comply with the health and hygiene regulations required for this building classification [25]. Moreover, with four to a room, these apartments significantly exceed the assumed occupational load upon which fire engineering assessments for residential towers are based (two people for the first bedroom and one for every other bedroom) [25]. Given the prevalence of Shared Room listings within particular developments, this kind of en-masse overloading could have grave consequences for fire safety and emergency egress—issues which have been brought to the fore following recent fires at the Lacrosse Building in Melbourne and Grenfell Tower in London [1].

More promising is the distribution of Private Rooms in Melbourne, which represent around 41% of listings (Supplementary Material 3; Table 1) [1]. While Private Rooms are still prevalent in the inner-city, their pattern is more diffuse in the inner and middle suburbs, which is in line with Australia's predilection for very large houses but shrinking households [1]. *Private Rooms* in Melbourne commonly take the form of a spare room or bungalow in a family home or share-house occupied by other residents. They are more likely to be peer-to-peer, promoting efficient use of latent space and minimizing periods of vacancy. With strategic planning, this kind of Airbnb usage in Melbourne might yield very positive outcomes, increasing the number of people within the housing stock and dispersing the economic benefits of the tourist economy [1].

However, without regulations, even the Private Room model is susceptible to exploitation, as demonstrated by one particular supersized house identified in the inner suburbs of Melbourne, which has seemingly mobilized the home as a machine for maximizing profit (Figure 1a). This 18-bedroom, 18-bathroom, post-nuclear house leases its rooms year-round on Airbnb for approximately AUD$70.00 per night. At maximum occupancy, the house is capable of generating around AUD$8800 p/w in rent, or around 14 times the average income for a rental property in the area.

Figure 1. (**a**) Supersized 18 bedroom, 18 bathroom Airbnb house in an inner suburb of Melbourne, Australia. Drawing by Jacqui Alexander. (**b**) Existing conditions plans and elevation drawings as documented in the original planning submission, with a total of nine bedrooms. Drawing by Jacqui Alexander.

Typologically, this uncanny domestic model sits somewhere between a suburban detached house and a hotel. Private Rooms are accessed via long corridors, with a large communal kitchen accommodating four industrial-sized fridges and not one but *two* island benches, a communal laundry, gymnasium, living room, and lounge. The reconceptualization of the private space of the home as a shared, commercial space is evident in the interior photographs, which are complete with exit signs, fire extinguishers, security cameras in common areas, and tactile indicators, suggesting that the house was subject to public-use regulations. Further investigation confirms that the home is not new, but a significantly remodeled older property, likely constructed in the 1970s. In 2009, a development application to partially demolish, expand, and remodel the home was approved, but prohibited the use of the land as a "backpackers' lodge, hostel, nurses' home, residential aged care facility, residential college or residential hotel without further consent of the responsible authority" [26]. The permit conditions have been obtained but it has not been possible to locate the endorsed plans. A subsequent planning application lodged two years later reveals that the existing house at the time of submission had a total of nine bedrooms (Figure 1b), and permission was being sought to double the yield to 18 bedrooms. Additional research reveals the house is now listed on the Public Register of Rooming Houses in Victoria [27], establishing its current classification under the building code.

In Victoria, a rooming house is simply defined as: "a building where one or more rooms are available to rent, and four or more people in total can occupy those rooms" [27] However, these buildings have a long history as affordable accommodation for people who do not meet the minimum income threshold or do not have the required rental history to enter the mainstream market. They are commonly operated by church groups, private housing providers, or registered individuals. According to Consumer Affairs Victoria, a rooming house resident is someone whose "room in a rooming house is their *only or main residence*" [27] and who does not need to sign a tenancy agreement to live there. While the supersized house is primarily marketed to tourists via Airbnb who would not typically meet the definition of a 'rooming house resident', it appears to occupy a grey area by incentivizing stays of six months or more with discounted rates, while also accommodating short-term stays.

4. Discussion

The supersized house can be read as an urban artefact—an extreme example of the way in which the sharing economy can shape cities in the absence of adequate regulatory and planning controls. It raises some interesting questions in relation to housing provision, legislation, equity, and affordability. Airbnb is clearly filling a gap in Melbourne's housing market for short- and medium-term tenancies, as demonstrated with both Private and Shared Room listings. Is this example merely elevating the caliber of rooming houses that currently exists and charging accordingly? Or is it disingenuous to register and advertise oneself as a rooming house if the intended market is primarily tourists? According to the Tenants Union of Victoria's (TUV) 2016 report, the median weekly rental cost for rooming houses in Melbourne is $195.00 (approximately $28 per day) [28] or roughly half the rate of the supersized house. Taking into consideration their respective target markets and price points, there is little grounds to compare these two models in practice. The question remains: what happens when candidates seeking *actual* rooming house accommodation contact this provider? While Airbnb has effectively made homes available for public use, access remains at the discretion of the host, and as such, risk is managed in other ways, including prohibitive fees, rating systems that can engender bias, or outright exclusion [29].

Moreover, will this house set a precedent for more supersized share-houses, and what effect will that have on rents? This particular case study is located in an inner suburb with a long history of affordable, informal student share-housing. It is prudent to note that when this domestic case study was identified in 2016, the host was operating a total of 81 Airbnb listings in Melbourne, many of which were Private Rooms in similarly overblown, newly-built residential constructions, in or around the same neighborhood. Further research is required to understand the planning processes and building classifications which enabled these other developments.

Does the planning process and building code need to change to allow for new shared typologies that can be more appropriately regulated according to their use? Whether or not the supersized house is ethical or equitable, it is certainly opportunistic and highlights the current inadequacy of both the National Construction Code (NCC) and the statuary planning processes in addressing the bourgeoning shared practices and typologies that Airbnb and other home-sharing disruptors have wrought. But while it can be argued that the provision of poor-quality apartments in Melbourne has been perpetuated by their popularity as short-term rental accommodation, there is also evidence to suggest that in the Australian context, Airbnb's Private Room model might play a useful role in intensifying the suburbs, promoting more efficient use of space in existing large homes and dispersing the economic benefits of the tourist economy [1].

If we agree that Airbnb presents a spatial problem, it might benefit from a spatial response. Rather than default to blanket bans and caps, this research advocates that through design and strategic planning, we can recalibrate the patterns of disruption through the following strategies: limiting its capacity for inequity and stimulating local economies where productive (Figure 2a). In the context of Melbourne, this would mean restricting Entire Home usage in the inner city, where competition for housing is high, and incentivizing Private Room letting in middle suburbs in need of rejuvenation, intensification, and greater housing diversity. Currently, a significant obstacle in promoting peer-to-peer home sharing in Melbourne's middle suburbs is the radial train and limited tram network, making it difficult to move around, especially with the added encumbrance of luggage [1]. However, the Melbourne Metro Tunnel currently under construction and the proposed Airport Rail Link—both earmarked for completion by 2026—present an opportunity to revolutionize tourism in Melbourne in a way that could benefit visitors and citizens (Figure 2b). The Airport link which is planned to operate between Tullamarine and Albion Station could unlock the western suburbs, attracting tourists on inbound services to the city and decentralizing tourism [1]. Through strategic planning, Private Room rental could be promoted in the suburbs to optimize spare bedrooms in large homes, intensifying distributed neighborhoods and stimulating local business (Figure 2c).

As well as maximizing efficiencies in existing properties, Private Room letting could help *drive* housing innovation in these suburbs by encouraging small-scale, grassroots infill development that could cater to temporary guests but also the growing numbers of empty-nester and single parent households, as well as families with dependents [30]. Currently in Victoria, infill types like granny flats must only house dependents and must be removed when the family member moves out or moves on. By following New South Wales' lead in making granny flats a permanent and more broadly accessible housing option, the state government could strategically incentivize the development of additional autonomous accommodation on single allotments to support home-sharing in the broadest sense. Local controls in combination with Airbnb's property review mechanism could lift the design quality of new dwellings, and the increased densities could help the council to fund infrastructure and amenity improvements for residents.

(a)

Figure 2. *Cont.*

Figure 2. (a) The top ten most popular suburbs in Melbourne for Airbnb rentals (2017). Nine of the ten are considered "inner urban"; the other, Brunswick, is "inner suburban". These suburbs are all well-serviced by train and public transport networks. The current inefficient radial rail network is a primary obstacle in decentralizing Airbnb use in the city and dispersing its economic benefits. (b) The government's current plan to develop an airport rail link by 2026 could revolutionize tourism in Melbourne, connecting Melbourne's east and west through a new continuous route and making the western suburbs accessible for tourists on inbound services to the city. (c) Ten suburbs with Airbnb potential have been identified, which will become more accessible to tourists via two new major transport infrastructure upgrades: the airport rail link and the Melbourne Metro Tunnel. Western suburbs such as West Footscray are earmarked for rejuvenation in the Maribyrnong structure plan and could benefit from home-sharing intensification. On the other hand, established southeastern suburbs like Ormond, which has very large houses but shrinking households, could optimize space through private-room rental.

While the findings in this paper are highly particular to the social, economic, political, and urban context in Melbourne, this research seeks to demonstrate that a strategic, "glocal" approach to Airbnb regulation—one which considers the interplay of global and local forces—could be leveraged to achieve positive urban outcomes for citizens. Can we establish rules of engagement for Airbnb activity in Melbourne to catalyze better and more diverse housing provision? For Melbournians, infill development may come as a welcome alternative to densification via the current controversial high-rise, high-density model [31], delivering infrastructure that would endure long after the tourists have left the scene [1].

Supplementary Materials: The following are available online at http://www.mdpi.com/2413-8851/2/3/88/s1.

Acknowledgments: The author would like to thank Monash University for support in the development of this research.

Conflicts of Interest: The authors declare no conflicts of interest.

References

1. Alexander, J. Disruptive Domesticity: Housing Futures and the Sharing Economy. *Arch. Aust.* **2018**, *107*, 108–112.
2. Self, J.; Bose, S.; Williams, F. *Home Economics*; The Spaces: London, UK, 2016; pp. 11–23.
3. Botsman, R.; Rodgers, R. *What's Mine is Yours: The Rise of Collaborative Consumption*; Harper Collins: New York, NY, USA, 2010.
4. O'Reilly, T. Open Source Paradigm Shift. *O'Reilly Media*, June 2004.
5. Belk, R. Sharing Versus Pseudosharing in Web 2.0. *Anthropologist* **2014**, *18*, 7. [CrossRef]
6. Tonkis, F. Austerity Urbanism and the Makeshift City. *City* **2013**, *17*, 312–324. [CrossRef]
7. Scholtz, T. *Uberworked and Underpaid: How Workers are Disrupting the Digital Economy*; Polity: Cambridge, MA, USA, 2016.
8. Thom, J. Belong Anywhere, Commodify Everywhere: A Critical Look into the State of Private Short-Term Rentals in Stockholm Sweden. Master's Thesis, KTH, Stockholm, Sweden, 2015.
9. Mannix, L. While Uber is Illegal, Airbnb gets Government Help. *The Age*, 6 December 2015. Available online: http://www.theage.com.au/victoria/while-uber-is-illegal-airbnb-gets-government-help-20151206-glgm6j.html (accessed on 14 January 2016).
10. Qantas: Feel at Home Earning Qantas Points with Airbnb. Available online: https://www.qantaspoints.com/earn-points/airbnb (accessed on 9 September 2018).
11. Galloway, A.; White, A. Airbnb Melbourne: $400million a year Injected into Victorian Economy. *Herald Sun*, 2017. Available online: https://www.heraldsun.com.au/news/victoria/airbnb-melbourne-400m-a-year-injected-into-victorian-economy/news-story/c97afe034dae2344f8f204876eb03284 (accessed on 2 August 2017).
12. Australian Property Observer. Australia's Housing Boom Finished, But So Is the Drag from Mining: HSBC'S Paul Bloxham. Available online: https://www.propertyobserver.com.au/forward-planning/advice-and-hot-topics/78116-the-housing-boom-is-over-but-so-is-the-mining-drag-hsbc-s-paul-bloxham.html (accessed on 9 September 2018).
13. Daley, J.; Coates, B.; Wiltshire, T. *Housing Affordability: Re-Imagining the Australian Dream*; Grattan Institute, University of Melbourne: Melbourne, Australia, 2018.
14. Australian Construction Industry Observer. Two Up and Two Down—Trends forecast the Australian Construction Market Report. May 2018. Available online: https://www.acif.com.au/forecasts/summary (accessed on 9 September 2018).
15. Kirsten, R.; Zhou, C. Melbourne Renting: Rent at Record Highs and Rising Faster than Income and Vacant. *Domain*. 2018. Available online: https://www.domain.com.au/news/melbourne-renting-rent-at-record-highs-rising-faster-than-incomes-and-vacant-20170209-gu7wpm/ (accessed on 10 January 2018).
16. Australian Broadcasting Corporation. Available online: http://www.abc.net.au/news/2018-06-05/airbnb-changes-as-nsw-government-reaches-compromise/9836648 (accessed on 9 September 2018).

17. New South Wales Planning & Environment Department. State Environmental Planning Policy No. 65—Design Quality of Residential Flat Development (SEPP 65) Sydney. 2002. Available online: https://legislation.nsw.gov.au/inforce/08f04365-88c2-4fe5-b56a-f76fdd390b10/2002-530.pdf (accessed on 20 February 2018).
18. Victorian Office of Environment, Land, Water and Planning. Better Apartments, Design Standards. Available online: https://www.planning.vic.gov.au/__data/assets/pdf_file/0024/9582/Better-Apartments-Design-Standards.pdf (accessed on 20 February 2018).
19. Alexander, J. Airbnb Urbanism. *Future West J. Aust. Urban.* **2016**, *1*, 54–61.
20. Airbnb: Responsible Hosting in the United Kingdom. Available online: https://www.airbnb.com.au/help/article/1379/responsible-hosting-in-the-united-kingdom (accessed on 9 September 2018).
21. Lomas, N. Amsterdam to Airbnb-Style Tourist Rentals to 30 Nights a Year per Host. *Tech Crunch*, 10 January 2018. Available online: https://techcrunch.com/2018/01/10/amsterdam-to-halve-airbnb-style-tourist-rentals-to-30-nights-a-year-per-host/ (accessed on 9 September 2018).
22. Editorial: New York Deflates Airbnb. *The Economist*, 27 October 2016. Available online: https://www.economist.com/news/business/21709353-new-rules-may-temper-airbnb-new-york-its-future-still-looks-bright-new-york-deflates (accessed on 9 September 2018).
23. Payton, M. Berlin Stops Airbnb Renting Apartments to Tourists to Protect Affordable Housing. *The Independent*, May 2016. Available online: http://www.independent.co.uk/news/world/europe/airbnb-rentals-berlin-germany-tourist-ban-fines-restricting-to-protect-affordable-housing-a7008891.html (accessed on 9 September 2018).
24. Catherine, C. *Speculative Vacancies 08: The Empty Properties Ignored by Statistics, Prosper Australia*; Prosper Australia Research Institute (PARI): Melbourne, Australia, 2015.
25. Australian Building Codes Board. *National Construction Code Series 2017*; Volume 2: Building Code of Australia Class 1 to Class 10 Buildings; Australian Government and State and Territories of Australia: Canberra, Australia, 2013; pp. 71–77.
26. Moreland City Council. *Planning Permit No. MPS/2008/523*; Moreland City Council: Coburg, Germany, 2009.
27. Victorian State Government Department of Consumer Affairs. Public Register of Rooming Houses. Available online: https://www.consumer.vic.gov.au/housing/renting/types-of-rental-agreements/sharing-in-a-rooming-house/public-register-of-rooming-houses (accessed on 28 February 2018).
28. Lina Caneva. Rooming House Tenants pay High Price for Living in Poverty. Available online: https://probonoaustralia.com.au/news/2016/10/rooming-house-tenants-pay-high-price-living-poverty/ (accessed on 28 February 2018).
29. Edelman, B.; Luca, M.; Svirsky, D. Racial Discrimination in the Sharing Economy: Evidence from a Field Experiment. *Am. Econ. J.* **2017**, *9*, 1–22. [CrossRef]
30. Bennet, A. Housing Diversity: Adapting 1.0 Infrastructure for 3.0 Lives. *Arch. Aust.* **2018**, *107*, 21–22.
31. Worrall, A. Respected Melbourne Planning Expert Michael Buxton Retires from RMIT. *Domain*, 13 May 2018. Available online: https://www.domain.com.au/news/respected-melbourne-planning-expert-michael-buxton-retires-from-rmit-20180512-h0zwq1/ (accessed on 9 September 2018).

© 2018 by the author. Licensee MDPI, Basel, Switzerland. This article is an open access article distributed under the terms and conditions of the Creative Commons Attribution (CC BY) license (http://creativecommons.org/licenses/by/4.0/).

Article

Spatial Agency: Creating New Opportunities for Sharing and Collaboration in Older People's Cohousing

Mark Hammond

Manchester School of Architecture, Manchester Metropolitan University, Manchester M15 6BR, UK; m.hammond@mmu.ac.uk

Received: 2 June 2018; Accepted: 27 July 2018; Published: 2 August 2018

Abstract: Older people's cohousing enables individuals to share spaces, resources, activities, and knowledge to expand their capability to act in society. Despite the diverse social, economic, and ethical aims that inform the creation of every cohousing community, there is often a disconnect between the social discourse developed by cohousing groups and the architectural spaces they create. This is a consequence of the building development process in cohousing, in which groups of older people are tasked with making decisions with considerable spatial implications prior to any collaboration with an architect. The concept of "spatial agency" offers an alternative model for the creation of cohousing, in which the expansion of architectural practice beyond aesthetic and technical building design enables social and spatial considerations to be explored contemporaneously. This study uses a two-year design-research collaboration with a cohousing group in Manchester, UK, to test the opportunities and constraints posed by a "spatial agency" approach to cohousing. The collaboration demonstrated how spatial agency enables both the architect and cohouser to act more creatively through a mutual sharing of knowledge, and, in doing so, tests new opportunities of sharing that are currently outside the cohousing orthodoxy.

Keywords: ageing; cohousing; architecture; co-design; spatial agency; sharing; design-research; critical autoethnography; Bourdieu

---

1. Introduction

The cohousing model is a residential typology consisting of individual dwellings with collectively owned facilities, with most communities seeking to develop strong social bonds between residents through shared management, labour, and leisure activities. There is a growing cohort of "older people" (commonly defined as those aged 50 and over) seeking to develop cohousing as a way of responding to the opportunities and challenges posed by their experiences of ageing. Older people's cohousing uses the sharing of spaces, resources, activities, and knowledge as a way of increasing the agency of those who reside in cohousing communities and developing new relationships between the older individual and the cities they inhabit. Many communities seek to address wider social issues through their sharing practice, such as environmental destruction [1], unaffordability of housing [2], and societal paternalism [3]. Cohousing developments are resident-led and most employ participatory design approaches, with residents having a significant influence on the forms of sharing that are practiced within their community. Despite this, architectural responses to cohousing rarely reflect the diversity of cohousing groups and their different collective aims, with most adopting an orthodox set of shared spaces.

This study develops an alternative understanding of the architect's role in older people's cohousing based on Awan, Schneider, and Till's concept of "spatial agency" [4]. Spatial agency seeks to apply architectural knowledge in contexts beyond the design of technical and aesthetic form, positioning the architect as one of many agents of change. This new form of practice was investigated through a two-year design-research collaboration with an older people's cohousing group in Manchester, UK, in which spatial agency was used to challenge the cohousing orthodoxy and identify opportunities for new forms of sharing within a cohousing community and within the wider city.

2. Ageing, Sharing, and Cohousing

An ageing population is set to be one of the main demographic shifts of the next century. Whilst this is a positive development that generates many opportunities in society, discussion of urban ageing often focuses on the problems of a large older population, such as the "burden" that older people place on healthcare, pension, and housing systems [5]. This pervasive deficit perspective leads to the marginalisation of older people in urban society. Older people are " ... relatively disempowered from the option of managing community and neighbourhood change", as housing, economic, and cultural opportunities disproportionately favour the needs of younger professionals [6] (p. 334).

One such form of marginalisation for older people is the emergence of the "sharing economy", or "collaborative consumption". Whilst there is a great deal of ambiguity surrounding these terms [7] (p. 4), it can be broadly defined as a socio-economic model based on the peer-to-peer exchange of services or the maximization of under-utilised assets [8] (p. 121). Prominent web-based models for "sharing", such as AirBnB and Uber, have been successful in making goods and services more accessible for many people. The movement from ownership-based consumption to access-based consumption has increased the affordability of some resources or services, whilst online infrastructure enables people to commercialise their own assets or labour with a much larger pool of individuals than previously possible. Despite these benefits for many people, the sharing economy enables exclusionary practices that adversely impact individuals based on race and income, and, in doing so, reproduce existing societal inequalities [7] (pp. 6–8). In terms of age, web-based sharing platforms are disproportionally used by younger people; 18–29 year-olds are 700% more likely to use Uber (USA) than those aged 65 and over [9] (p. 13), and just 5% of properties listed on AirBnB are posted by people aged 60 and over [10]. Whilst some have noted the potential for web-based platforms could offer potential benefits for older people, such as the provision of in-home care support, these are still in their infancy [11].

The opportunities for older people posed by peer-to-peer sharing can only be fully understood through a broader definition of the sharing economy. Rather than limiting the definition to a web-based, profit-driven model of sharing, it is important to recognise that the coordinated acts of peer-to-peer exchange can exist outside of virtual mechanisms, and that these exchanges are often driven by social and emotional rewards rather than economic or material benefits [12–14]. By expanding the definition of the sharing economy to offline and non-profit platforms, it is possible to identify a number of practices through which older people can improve their quality of life through shared, social interaction. For example, the "Men's Sheds" initiatives in the UK enabled older men to share their tools with each other. The aim of this is not to provide older men with access to assets they do not own, but to enable members to " ... sharing skills and knowledge, and of course a lot of laughter" [15]. Similarly, the "homeshare" model offers older people a way of maximising the value of an under-used asset (an empty bedroom), but with social support as a primary motive as opposed to financial income. Tenants rent a bedroom at a below market rate in return for undertaking some domestic tasks (like cleaning and gardening) and offering companionship to the older person they live with [16,17].

The understanding of sharing as a means of creating new social relationships is one of the core elements of "older people's cohousing". Whilst cohousing takes many forms, all seek to use the sharing of spaces, resources, activities, and knowledge to achieve more than they could in isolation, and to increase their agency to affect social change within the city.

The cohousing model emerged in northern Europe in the 1970s and commonly consists of privately owned residences and collectively owned communal spaces [18]. There is a range in the size and forms taken by cohousing communities, although 20–30 dwellings are cited by many practitioners as an optimal size [19–21] Cohousing communities are often resident-led and managed, with the explicit aim of generating social bonds between residents. A recent development in the field of cohousing is "older people's cohousing", which has become an established sub-section of the cohousing movement in the last 15 years [19,22–24]. The increasing interest in older people's cohousing can be linked to the transitions of aspirational baby boomers into older age, who seek " ... an alternative to living alone, but reject conventional forms of housing for older people as paternalistic and institutional." [23] (p. 107). For many, changing residential environment in later life offers a "...meaningful avenue for the elderly to extend themselves into the future, to find meaningful new stimulation and roles, and to enhance their satisfaction during later life" [25] (p. 211). This is, however, predicated on the financial, physical, and social capability to initiate such a change; barriers have thus far limited older people's cohousing to relatively wealthy and healthy individuals. One of the key benefits of older people's cohousing is the ability to be open about their own experiences of ageing, and, therefore, access mutual support in response to the changing physical capabilities and emotional experiences of growing older [24]. Other studies have also identified how cohousing can lead to increased participation in civic and political processes [26] and increases the social capital of cohousers within the cities and neighbourhoods that they reside in [27].

It is important to distinguish between cohousing as a form of housing development, and cohousing as a set of relationships enabled by the environment it is situated in. Sharing not only informs the day-to-day experiences within a cohousing community but often contributes to the transformation of the neighbourhoods and cities in which they are located.

The day-to-day experiences within a cohousing community usually focus on opportunities for informal social interaction, facilitated by the sharing of communal facilities. Communal kitchens and dining rooms are ubiquitous in cohousing, enabling groups to regularly share meals together [18–20,28]. Many cohousing groups establish informal club or activity groups to use these spaces, such as a walking group or book clubs. For older people, the mutual support derived from such a rich social network also provides resilience to negative macro-level conditions, like ageism, in society or the medicalisation of support needs amongst their cohort [24].

Although there are some examples of cohousing communities that become inward facing [29] (pp. 2030–2031), many seek to develop strong relationships with the communities and cities they are situated in [30] (p. 324). For example, the "Solinsieme" community in St. Gallen, Switzerland use their communal space to host events for the wider community, including lectures and games nights [31–33]. Cohousing has also attracted political support for the contributions it makes to cities, with cities like Hamburg supporting cohousing in areas with highly transient populations to encourage stability and community resilience [34] (pp. 407–409).

In addition to these immediate interactions with neighbours (both inside and outside their respective communities), many cohousing groups seek to effect change on a wider city or societal level. These are often as a response to a perceived social injustice, or to demonstrate that alternative models of living are possible. Examples of these include communities, such as LILAC in Leeds, UK, whose mutual ownership model was developed in response to the increasingly unaffordable housing in the UK [2]. Sharing is often used as a means of achieving a higher level of environmental sustainability than is possible in an individual home, with communities, such as the Lancaster Cohousing in the UK, installing district heating system and hydroelectric power installations [1]. For older people, cohousing can offer a means of mitigating against predicted drops in state care provision through mutual social support [22,35].

One of the key challenges within cohousing is the difficulty of the development process. Although there is a lack of comprehensive data sources, it has been suggested that just one in 10 cohousing groups ever progress to the construction phase [36]. It is not uncommon for the cohousing development to exceed 10 years [37], with a DIY ethic, lack of property development expertise, and difficulties procuring land all cited as challenges for prospective cohousing groups [36]. These issues are particularly pertinent in relation to older people's cohousing, where a prolonged development process might account for a significant portion of the individuals remaining years.

3. Architecture and the Creation of Cohousing

Whilst most definitions of cohousing attempt to describe a series of spaces, facilities, relationships, and practices [18,19], cohousing can also be understood as a medium through which individuals define these parameters for themselves. Rather than a fixed model of shared living, cohousing offers older people the opportunity to create and negotiate their own social, ethical, and environmental vision, and, in doing so, increases their capabilities to affect change in their immediate housing community and the wider city. The diversity of motives behind cohousing demonstrates the need for each cohousing community to define their own understanding of sharing, which is based on the collective capabilities and desires of residents. This requires the creation and negotiation of a social vision alongside the spatial environment through which it is practiced. As a result, the cohousing model is notable for the near-universal adoption of participatory design practices in the development process [19] (pp. 19–20).

There is a lack of critical understanding of participatory design within the cohousing field beyond the notion that cohousers should be "involved" in the design process to some extent [20] (p. 201). This is usually manifest as a series of workshops led by an architect to propose the architectural form of the site and building, based on a brief, site, and budget that had been pre-agreed by the cohousing group [38]. The architect's role is limited to the aesthetic and formal design, informed by their own tastes and design expertise, which are augmented to some extent with the views of the cohousing group they work with. Whilst this is cited as an important way of bringing the cohousing group together and making sure that the community meets the requirements of the clients [39] (p. 235), this design process can be seen as limiting. In this design process, cohousing groups are tasked with creating a collective identity and social ethos, but are disempowered from exploring the spatial implications and possibilities of these ideas. By the time an architect has been employed, the social definition of the community is no longer malleable, as it is manifest in budgets, design briefs, and site selections. This results in communities with a strong conceptual ethos, which are often not represented spatially. For example, the Older Women's Cohousing (OWCH) community in London, UK has developed a strong feminist and anti-ageism identity, manifest in a building that is " ... beautiful and suited to community living, but not particularly radical." [40] (p. 29).

Overcoming these limitations demands a new understanding of the architect/cohouser relationship, in which the social discourse within a cohousing group is developed in parallel with the spatial discourse through which it is enabled. This requires a reconceptualisation of the linear development process, in which architects only contribute to the final building design phase.

Awan, Schneider, and Till's model of "spatial agency" is critical of the interpretation of architecture as the aesthetic and technical task of building design [4] (p. 30). In response to this, they argue that architects should seek new forms of practice that engage with the social, political, and ethical aspects of society [41]. They propose that architects take on the role of spatial agents, a transition predicated on two fundamental shifts in architectural practice: First, it calls for the " ... inclusion of others, amateurs, in the processes" of design; and second, it dismisses the idea that " ... the building as the sole source and representation of expertise" held by the architect [4] (p. 43). This requires the architect to reject their role as the autonomous creator of purely aesthetic or technical form [4] (pp. 27–28), and instead understand that their role is " ... not the agent of change, but one among many agents." [41] (p. 97).

By breaking the link between architectural practices and the creation of a building, spatial agency enables an alternative understanding of the architect's relationship to cohousing. Rather than separating the social discourse within a community (defined by the cohousing group) from the spatial or architectural production of the community (defined primarily by the architect), spatial agency provides a means of developing both in unison. This creates an opportunity to identify and test new opportunities for sharing that a cohousing group would be unlikely to consider had they not collaborated with a designer. By challenging the idea of the architect solely as a building designer, spatial agency also opens the opportunity for architects and cohousing groups to collaborate at a much earlier stage of development than is seen in most cohousing developments.

In 2014, I began collaborating with Manchester Urban Cohousing (MUCH) in Manchester, UK; a group of older people who were attempting to establish a cohousing community. The group were in the very early stages of setting up their cohousing group, and the group did not have a site, brief, or finances in place. Despite this, the group saw the value in collaborating with an architect to better understand what they could achieve and how it might shape the definition of their collective values. As a result, I took on the role of a spatial agent with the group, supporting the development of a shared, creative, and spatial discourse that would underpin their later aspirations to create a cohousing community. Over the course of a two-year design-research collaboration, we sought to identify the limitations and opportunities presented by spatial agency in cohousing, and how it could help to create innovative forms of sharing both within and outside the confines of a cohousing community.

4. Methodology: Exploring the Potential of Spatial Agency through Design-Research

MUCH was formed in response to a series of conversations between seven friends about what they wanted to do in retirement. The group discovered cohousing after it was featured in a newspaper, which led them to spend four years discussing and researching the model.

My collaboration with MUCH began in January 2014 and finished in April 2016. During this time, the initial group of seven members grew, stabilising at 14 members for the majority of the collaboration. The majority of the group had either retired, reduced their working hours, or had plans to retire in the next couple of years. None of the group came from architectural backgrounds, and none of the group had experience in property development.

The collaboration aimed to establish and test how the group could share spaces, resources, activities, and knowledge, both within their cohousing community and with the wider city. Informed by the concept of spatial agency, the interactions between MUCH and myself took place much sooner than an architect would normally work with a cohousing group, focusing on the early project definition stage, rather than designing the actual building that the group would construct. The purpose of these interactions was to help create a social and spatial discourse about the forms of sharing that would be possible in their community, and eventually produce a design brief based on these ideas. The collaboration adopted a non-linear structure of reflexive, iterative, and generative practices, embracing the transformative potential of "contingency", a key quality of spatial agency [42]. As a result, the collaboration with MUCH involved participation in a wide range of situations where opportunities could emerge, but, equally, could not be known in advance. Practically, this involved attending or delivering 37 individual practices; meetings, workshops, design charrettes, training events, and site visits. Through these practices, we identified challenges and limitations within the cohousing development process and proposed how spatial agency could contribute to resolving these limitations. The collaboration with MUCH was recorded through contemporaneous field notes, photos, and audio recordings, with additional reflections gathered through a structured focus group after our collaboration.

The collaboration with MUCH took the form of "research through practice". Research through design is a process through which issues and questions emerge because of design practices, and are tested through the application of new practices [43] (p. 96). My practices as a spatial agent were, therefore, both the research methodology and the object of enquiry. This approach enabled the generation and communication of knowledge that would not be possible as either a non-participant observer or through retrospective case-study analysis. Whilst practice-led research is well established in the architectural field [44], the approach presents a number of methodological challenges, such as the replicability of creative processes in which the researcher is an active participant. The approach employed in this study recognises that any number of variables could have changed the trajectory of the collaboration, but that this does not undermine the validity of the insight it provides, as " . . . there are forms of knowledge peculiar to the awareness and ability of a designer" [45] (p. 5), which can only be accessed through the undertaking of creative enquiry [42]. With regards to these constraints and opportunities, this study does not claim to provide a general evaluation of the effectiveness of spatial agency compared to other architectural approaches. Instead, it presents examples of how spatial agency enables older people to act creatively and provide critical analysis through which the architect-cohouser relationship can be better understood.

One of the challenges of research through design is that knowledge is often embedded within the traditional architectural outputs; buildings, models, and drawings [42,43]. By adopting the spatial agency position that building design is not the sole expression of architectural knowledge, this study used critical autoethnography as a means of documenting and reflecting on the interactions within the processes of design, as opposed to analysing the designed outcomes.

Autoethnography is a narrative-based enquiry in which a subject is studied through the experiences of the author. Although written from an autobiographical perspective, the methodological orientation is ethnographic as it seeks to understand the interactions between the author and other individuals, in this case within the act of co-design [46] (p. 48). This approach offers a unique insight into the cohousing development process, as the majority of the research to date has focused on retrospective case study analysis undertaken by researchers who were not involved in the development process. The result of this is a focus on outcomes within the existing cohousing literature, rather than the interactions through which these outcomes were created.

Rather than simply describing the interactions between the architect and cohouser, critical autoethnography demands that a theoretical position is used to analyse the experiences of the author, and therefore provide insight that can be applied to a wider set of situations that other practitioners might face. This critical analysis should not be static, but allow the author to " ... openly discuss changes in their beliefs and relationships over the course of fieldwork" as their experiences help shape their understanding of the people and contexts they operate within [47] (p. 384). In my collaboration with MUCH, the critical analysis is informed by Pierre Bourdieu's theories of practice [48], which are used to identify the limits to creativity and how they can be overcome.

Through a critical autoethnographic account of two workshops, this paper identifies the limitations and opportunities posed by spatial agency. The first workshop was a self-directed design game, in which the self-imposed limits that the MUCH members adopted were identified through a creative exercise. The second workshop was a narrative based workshop, in which participants used narrative to critique the cohousing orthodoxy and create innovative forms of sharing within and outside their proposed community. These two workshops demonstrate how spatial agency can allow creative ideas about sharing to emerge through a propositional critique of the cohousing orthodoxy, but also the creative limits that prevent these from emerging as part of the normal development process when architectural input only occurs much later.

5. Workshop One: Design Game

The MUCH group requested that I design a workshop for their public recruitment event, with the goal of providing an opportunity for prospective members of their group to be creative and get to know each other. I proposed a short design game, in which the 22 participants would be tasked with creating a cohousing community in groups of five to six people, using model making and wooden blocks to produce their design (see Figure 1). The designs would be self-directed by each group without my involvement, thus they demonstrated both the group's creativity to define shared practices and also the limits of their creativity, which we could build on in later workshops. During the workshop, I circulated between the groups to discuss the decisions each group made. At the conclusion of the workshop, each group presented their design to the rest of the attendees.

Figure 1. Manchester Urban Cohousing (MUCH) members participating in the design game workshop.

The workshop demonstrated one of the limits to defining new forms of sharing; the reliance on past experiences as the basis for proposing new ideas. This was representative of Bourdieu's suggestion that " ... it is yesterday's man who inevitably predominates us, since the present amounts to little compared with the long past in the course of which we were formed and from which we result" [48] (p. 79). Many of the propositions developed by the MUCH members were explicitly based on their own past experiences, either directly through their own interactions or indirectly through various forms of media. For example, one of the group wanted to reduce their maintenance burden, noting that they wanted the shared interactions within the community to be focused on leisure rather than labour. This idea was manifest in their design, which included a self-cleaning ceramic façade. One member of the group explained that the idea had been based on a holiday to Vienna, where he visited Otto Wagner's ceramic fronted art nouveau apartments. This demonstrates how past experiences can be the basis of creativity, as the individual transposed his knowledge of an architectural case study in a novel way, rather than as a simple facsimile of the original.

Whilst "yesterday's man" provided the impetus for creativity in this example, there were other situations where the opposite was true. Bourdieu also argues that our reliance on past experiences to inform future practices generates a "sense of limits", in which all actions reproduce the "established order" rather than genuinely innovative ideas [48] (p.164). He proposes that individuals place a self-imposed demand for realism in their actions, which causes past experiences to be reproduced and perpetuates certain ideas as being "sensible" and "reasonable" [48] (p. 79). The "sense of limits" that I observed within the workshops was derived from two interrelated constraints. First, there were examples in which groups regulated their actions to make "sensible" propositions. Second, there were a number of situations in which the participants had ideas and desires that they were unable to propose in spatial forms.

The self-regulating tendencies of the groups were evident in the way they dismissed ideas outside of the cohousing orthodoxy. Whilst a number of people identified unusual ideas for sharing space, including a brewery and a community cinema, these ideas were dismissed as unrealistic by others and not included in their final designs. The designation of these ideas as unreasonable was because they had never seen a housing community with a community cinema attached to it, but this in itself should not have made the idea unreasonable. A small cinema space could take up a similar sized space as an art room or craft workshop; ideas that can be seen in various existing cohousing communities. The barrier to creativity in this situation was that the participants had not seen one in the past, and thus could not confidently envision what spatial form it would take or whether it would be affordable. As a consequence, this self-regulation (if unchallenged) has the potential to close off opportunities for new shared spaces and activities that might enable a cohousing group to create positive relationships and contributions to their wider neighbourhood.

Another theme was that the group raised conceptual ideas that they were unable to propose because they could not conceive the forms they would take. For example, one group proposed a shared laundry space as a means of reducing their carbon footprint. Whilst the shift from individual to shared washing and drying machines would have contributed to their aims, the group decided they wanted to investigate a natural clothes drying system within the design of their building. The problem they faced was their inability to conceive how this would work. The group raised vague ideas about " ... some type of 'dry greenhouse'", but they were unable to progress with the idea any further without the support of a designer. This highlights one of the key contributions that spatial agency can have in cohousing-the potential to overcome the limitations to our own creativity by testing ideas that would otherwise be discarded. The cohousers were proposing exciting ideas but were unable to evaluate the realism of their ideas or convert many of their concepts into spatial propositions. These ideas would be unlikely to make it into their design brief if they had no means of testing their feasibility.

During a structured reflection on the workshop, the MUCH members identified how negotiating different ideas into the same formal design was a challenge. One member of the group noted that:

" ... it drove us to think 'how would we manage that?' What it throws up is that you can't move forward with those tensions in the group. We need a framework to overcome these issues ... otherwise you spend the time thinking 'nobody is listening to me anymore'."

In response to this, we decided to create a workshop in which each MUCH member had the opportunity to express their ideas individually. The aim of this was to make clear and discuss the different aspirations held within the group. We agreed that we needed to develop an alternative means of expressing creativity that did not rely on traditional architectural design skills, and I worked with two MUCH members to design a workshop in response to this.

6. Workshop Two: Narrative Workshop

One of the challenges of the design game workshop was that it tasked the participants to act as "architects". Whilst this did demonstrate the wide range of capabilities within the group, it also placed the onus on them to propose the spatial manifestation of their desired shared practices, something that paradoxically acted as a barrier to creativity. Discussing this with the group, it was suggested that it would be interesting to explore other mediums of creativity that might allow them to be propositional without having to express their ideas architecturally. I proposed using storytelling as a way of overcoming these challenges and was asked to design a workshop in collaboration with one of the MUCH members.

During the narrative workshop, I asked each MUCH member to tell a story describing a single day in their imagined cohousing community. Participants were asked to suggest what they would do, thinking about situations inside their home, the cohousing community, and in the wider neighbourhood they would live in. To help the group develop these stories, we gave everyone a scenario within which to frame their narratives, such as a Sunday in summer, a cold and rainy Tuesday, or Christmas Eve. Following this, the whole workshop was repeated with a single change; the cohousers were asked to tell a story based on the same scenario, but when they were 20 years older.

Much like the previous design game workshop, this exercise both enabled creative ideas to emerge and highlighted the limits of the group's creative potential. It quickly became clear that, rather than proposing a radical vision of cohousing, the participants used the workshop to critique and elaborate on the existing cohousing orthodoxy. The workshop showed how a sense of limits was perpetuating the inclusion of common sharing practices seen in cohousing within their narrative, but equally generated opportunities for the cohousers to interrogate the impact of these norms within specific situations.

For example, one member of the group based her narrative around her children visiting her over Christmas, as they currently did at her present home. Unexpectedly, the participant generated an additional constraint in her narrative She imagined that the cohousing community would have a guest room (which is a common shared asset within the cohousing orthodoxy), but in her narrative this room was overbooked. Her story proposed that her family had to stay at a hotel nearby, which she argued was not ideal, but that she could not imagine another way of doing it. Through her narrative, the MUCH member had effectively critiqued a "sensible" element of the cohousing orthodoxy as insufficient to her needs, but also identified her own inability to propose an alternative proposition. In a short discussion that followed the story, another cohouser said that they go away at Christmas so the narrator's children they could stay in her flat instead of a hotel. It would have been easy for the participants to simply suggest that the community would need more shared guest rooms, but by expressing their desired experiences a creative, social alternative emerged.

Other stories developed by the MUCH members expanded upon elements of the cohousing orthodoxy, imagining a different relationship between the cohousing community and wider neighbourhood. One of the stories described how the MUCH members were holding a meal for socially isolated older people in the community. The story described how the meal would take place in a large communal dining room, a space that is ubiquitous in the cohousing orthodoxy, and demonstrated how this type of space could enable the MUCH group to enact the kind of social change that they could not achieve in their current individual houses. This shows that whilst the individual still retained a sense of limits by proposing a standard cohousing element, they also acted creatively by reinterpreting its use to match their social and ethical dispositions. On one level, this story might affect how the dining space could be designed, considering a different use of the space. Equally, the story identified a social vision that could be explored in a multitude of different ways within the design process.

When the workshop transitioned into telling a story that imagined the community in 20 years, it became evident that the group were having a more difficult time imagining what their community would be like. Many of the stories seemed to suggest that the community would start to look inwards and that individuals might not have such strong relationships with the wider community. Some suggested that shared spaces and activities might be used less as people became less active, whilst others proposed that they would be used more because people were less able to attend other events outside of their immediate community. It was noticeable that the stories at this stage had much less clarity and posed fewer definitive uses and interactions than the previous sets of stories. This highlighted the challenge facing the group; the need to imagine and respond to situations that were unknown to them at the time, such as the capabilities and desires they might have later in their life.

7. Discussion

The examples discussed in this paper demonstrate how co-design processes enable older people to investigate and test how sharing might shape their urban environment, and how different spatial constraints can influence what forms of sharing are possible. Although the focus of the collaboration with MUCH was not the development of traditional architectural plans, spatial agency did enable the exploration of how sharing and collaboration might shape the form of their community. A central component of this was the interrogation of the shared/private split within the community, with the group exploring models with much smaller private dwellings in favour of more elaborate shared facilities. Although the group agreed to adopt a fairly orthodox split between private and shared spaces, spatial agency created opportunities for this decision to be made consciously, and with the implications of different options properly investigated. The process of spatial agency did, however, influence the group's ideas about what form shared spaces should take. Whilst the cohousing orthodoxy is for a single, centralised "common house" where all collective activity is centred, the MUCH group recognised the opportunities posed by having a diversity of shared spaces. Rather than pre-determining the functions of these spaces, they felt it more important to create spaces with different spatial characteristics that they could appropriate for different uses as they emerged. This position was in recognition that the group's needs would inevitably change as they grew older, but that the types of shared activities the group might want to undertake in the future are unknown to them at present.

In addition to these specific spatial investigations, the process of creating an inclusive, creative process was an equally important element of my role as a spatial agent. One of the ways that older people are marginalised in society is through a widely held stereotype that they lack creativity [49] (p. 25). This should not be understood as a failure of older people to be creative, but the consequence of systemic conditions in which older people's creativity is diminished or ignored. The two workshops described in this paper show how adopting a spatial agency approach can help to develop a shared discourse from which older people are empowered to be creative, and through which novel opportunities for sharing emerge. By challenging the delineation of the social and spatial qualities of cohousing, we were able to identify and respond to our own internalised limits that led us to accept the existing cohousing orthodoxy. This, in turn, led to the development and testing of new ideas for sharing spaces and activities, both inside and outside their proposed community, that would not have otherwise be considered.

One of the ways that MUCH could express themselves in these workshops was the rejection of normative ideas about ageing within their cohousing community. Although there was some discussion about physical decline and building accessibility, the group were primarily driven by a positive vision of themselves in older age, in which they would not be defined by their physiology. This was an explicit response to the medicalisation of other housing options for older people, such as private "sheltered" housing, of which they had reservations. One of the MUCH members referred to the processes we developed as a form of "future-scoping";

"I think one of the challenges for all of us, and you, is to come up with our own ageing, and not be influenced by images of what older people look like. We are using each other to future-scope ourselves, in space. That's really exciting! ...It's been a real challenge because we all have these different ideas about our futures, and the shape and space needs to mirror and enable that."

The capability to imagine possible futures is a key element of the cohousing development process, and is particularly important for older people in making decisions about the homes and communities they wish to grow older in, which are impacted by their "...uncertainty about their future selves." [50] (p. 48). The spatial agency approach offered opportunities to explore possible futures because the focus was not purely limited to defining the architectonic form the community would take. Rather than placing the onus on the individual to imagine whether staying or leaving their home would provide them with a better future, a spatial agency approach to cohousing enables the individual to explore and construct a future they actually desire, and to examine whether this vision is achievable.

Through the sharing of space, assets, knowledge, and practices, cohousing enables older people to increase their ability to reshape neighbourhoods, cities, and everyday experiences. Despite the interest in cohousing in the UK, few new cohousing communities have come to fruition. Cohousing groups face a number of challenges, not least the direct competition with better resourced commercial developers, particularly in desirable urban locations [23] (p. 119). It is perhaps time to question whether the 25 dwelling, single-site cohousing community that is promoted within mainstream cohousing discourse is viable, and instead move to investigate innovative responses. Spatial agency provides a suitable platform for architects to contribute to this and support the emergence of new ideas that challenge some of the norms within cohousing. Whilst the inclusion of architectural expertise at such an early stage of the development process presents a number of challenges, including how such a collaboration can be funded, it also provides a unique opportunity to generate creative solutions to some of the issues that cohousing groups face.

Funding: This research received no external funding.

Acknowledgments: The author would like to thank the members of Manchester Urban Cohousing for their contributions, insight and support during the course of our collaboration.

Conflicts of Interest: The authors declare no conflict of interest.

References

1. Lancaster Cohousing. Lancaster Cohousing: Our Vision. Available online: http://www.lancastercohousing.org.uk/About/Vision (accessed on 2 May 2015).
2. LILAC. Briefing Sheet: Affordability. Available online: http://lilac.coop/wp-content/uploads/2018/07/lilac-briefing-sheet-affordability.pdf (accessed on 2 August 2018).
3. OWCH. Housing for Women. Available online: http://www.owch.org.uk/housing-for-women (accessed on 2 May 2017).
4. Awan, N.; Schneider, T.; Till, J. *Spatial Agency: Other Ways of Doing Architecture*; Routledge: London, UK, 2011; ISBN 9780415571937.
5. Handler, S. A Research & Evaluation Framework for Age-friendly Cities. Available online: http://hummedia.manchester.ac.uk/institutes/micra/A%20Research%20and%20Evaluation%20Framework%20for%20Age-friendly%20Cities_web%20version.pdf (accessed on 2 August 2018).
6. Phillipson, C. The "elected" and the "excluded": Sociological perspectives on the experience of place and community in old age. *Ageing Soc.* **2007**, *27*, 321. [CrossRef]
7. Frenken, K.; Schor, J. Putting the sharing economy into perspective. *Environ. Innov. Soc. Transit.* **2017**, *23*, 3–10. [CrossRef]
8. Richardson, L. Performing the sharing economy. *Geoforum* **2015**, *67*, 121–129. [CrossRef]
9. Pew Research Centre Shared, Collaborative and On Demand: The New Digital Economy. Available online: http://www.pewinternet.org/2016/05/19/the-new-digital-economy/ (accessed on 01 May 2018).
10. Airbnb. Airbnb Fast Facts. Available online: https://2sqy5r1jf93u30kwzc1smfqt-wpengine.netdna-ssl.com/wp-content/uploads/2017/08/4-Million-Listings-Announcement-1.pdf (accessed on 1 February 2018).
11. Miller, J.; Ward, C.; Lee, C.; D'Ambrosio, L.; Coughlin, J. Sharing is caring: The potential of the sharing economy to support aging in place. *Gerontol. Geriatr. Educ.* **2018**. Advanced online publication. [CrossRef] [PubMed]
12. Huber, A. Theorising the dynamics of collaborative consumption practices: A comparison of peer-to-peer accommodation and cohousing. *Environ. Innov. Soc. Transit.* **2017**, *23*, 53–69. [CrossRef]
13. Belk, R. You are what you can access: Sharing and collaborative consumption online. *J. Bus. Res.* **2014**, *67*, 1595–1600. [CrossRef]
14. Hamari, J.; Sjöklint, M.; Ukkonen, A. The sharing economy: Why people participate in collaborative consumption. *J. Assoc. Inf. Sci. Technol.* **2016**, *67*, 2047–2059. [CrossRef]
15. UK Men's Sheds Association. What Is a Men's Shed? Available online: https://menssheds.org.uk/about/what-is-a-mens-shed/ (accessed on 11 February 2018).
16. Fox, A. Homeshare—An inter-generational solution to housing and support needs. *Hous. Care Support* **2010**, *13*, 21–26. [CrossRef]
17. Homeshare UK. What Is Homeshare? Available online: https://homeshareuk.org/about-homeshare/homeshare/what-is-homeshare/ (accessed on 7 January 2018).
18. Meltzer, G. *Sustainable Communities*; Trafford: Victoria, BC, Canada, 2005; ISBN 9781412049948.
19. Durrett, C. *The Senior Cohousing Handbook*, 2nd ed.; New Society Publishing: Gabriola Island, BC, Canada, 2009; ISBN 9780865716117.
20. Williams, J. Designing Neighbourhoods for Social Interaction: The Case for Cohousing. *J. Urban Des.* **2005**, *10*, 195–227. [CrossRef]
21. Holtzman, G. Introduction to Cohousing and the Australian Context. Available online: http://synthesisstudio.org/wordpress/wp-content/uploads/Introduction-to-Cohousing-and-the-Australian-Context__GiloHoltzman_2010.pdf (accessed on 4 April 2014).

22. Brenton, M. Senior Cohousing Communities—An Alternative Approach for the UK? Available online: https://www.jrf.org.uk/sites/default/files/jrf/migrated/files/senior-cohousing-communities-full.pdf (accessed on 11 March 2017).
23. Scanlon, K.; Arrigoitia, M.F. Development of new cohousing: Lessons from a London scheme for the over-50s. *Urban Res. Pract.* **2015**, *8*, 106–121. [CrossRef]
24. Glass, A.P.; Vander Plaats, R.S. A conceptual model for aging better together intentionally. *J. Aging Stud.* **2013**, *27*, 428–442. [CrossRef] [PubMed]
25. Kahana, E.; Kahana, B. Environmental Continuity, Futurity and Adaption of the Aged. In *Ageing and Milieu: Environmental Perspectives on Growing Old*; Rowles, G.D., Ohta, R.J., Eds.; Academic Press: London, UK, 1983; pp. 205–230. ISBN 9780125999502.
26. Berggren, H.M. Cohousing as Civic Society: Cohousing Involvement and Political Participation in the United States. *Soc. Sci. Q.* **2017**, *98*, 57–72. [CrossRef]
27. Ruiu, M.L. The Social Capital of Cohousing Communities. *Sociology* **2016**, *50*, 400–415. [CrossRef]
28. Fromm, D. *Collaborative Communities*; Van Norstrand Reinhold: New York, NY, USA, 1991; ISBN 9780442237851.
29. Tummers, L. The re-emergence of self-managed co-housing in Europe: A critical review of co-housing research. *Urban Stud.* **2016**, *53*, 2023–2040. [CrossRef]
30. Ruiu, M.L. Differences between Cohousing and Gated Communities. A Literature Review. *Sociol. Inq.* **2014**, *84*, 316–335. [CrossRef]
31. Homes and Communities Agency. HAPPI Study Trip 5: Germany and Switzerland. Available online: http://cfg.homesandcommunities.co.uk/sites/default/files/happi_trip_5_report_final.pdf (accessed on 2 March 2017).
32. Feddersen, E.; Ludtke, I. *Living for the Elderly: A Design Manual*; Birkhauser: Basel, Switzerland, 2009; ISBN 9783035608441.
33. Jubilar. Solinsieme: How it was Conceived. Available online: https://blog.jubilares.es/solinsieme-como-se-gesto/ (accessed on 1 February 2018).
34. Ache, P.; Fedrowitz, M. The Development of Cohousing Initiatives in Germany. *Built Environ.* **2012**, *37*, 395–412. [CrossRef]
35. Loppukiri Cohousing Briefly in English (Overview). Available online: http://www.loppukiriseniorit.blogspot.fi/p/blog-page_1790.html (accessed on 22 August 2013).
36. Crabtree, L. Build It Like You Mean It: Replicating Ethical Innovation in Physical and Institutional Design. In *Material Geographies of Household Sustainability*; Lane, R., Gorman-Murray, A., Eds.; Routledge: Abingdon, UK, 2016; pp. 157–174.
37. OWCH. OWCH Development. Available online: http://www.owch.org.uk/owch-development (accessed on 12 November 2016).
38. UK Cohousing Network. The Cohousing Toolkit. Available online: https://cohousing.org.uk/files/toolkit_march_2012.pdf (accessed on 2 August 2013).
39. Durrett, C.; McCamant, K. *Creating Cohousing*; New Society Publishers: Gabriola Island, BC, Canada, 2011.
40. Arrigoitia, M.F.; Scanlon, K. Co-designing Senior Co-housing. *Urban Des. Gr. J.* **2015**, *28–30*, 28–30.
41. Schneider, T.; Till, J. Beyond Discourse: Notes on Spatial Agency. *Footprint* **2009**, *4*, 97–111.
42. Rendell, J. Architectural research and disciplinarity. *Archit. Res. Q.* **2004**, *8*, 141–147. [CrossRef]
43. Murray, S. Design Research: Translating Theory into Practice. In *Design Research in Architecture*; Fraser, M., Ed.; Ashgate: Chichester, UK, 2013; pp. 95–116.
44. Hill, J. Architects of Fact and Fiction. *Archit. Res. Q.* **2015**, *19*, 249–258. [CrossRef]
45. Cross, N. Design Research: A Disciplined Conversation. *Des. Stud.* **1999**, *15*, 5–10. [CrossRef]
46. Chang, H. *Autoethnography as Method*; Left Coast Press: Walnut Creek, CA, USA, 2008; ISBN 978-1598741230.
47. Anderson, L. Analytic Autoethnography. *J. Contemp. Ethnogr.* **2006**, *35*, 373–395. [CrossRef]
48. Bourdieu, P. *Outline of a Theory of Practice*; Cambridge University Press: Cambridge, UK, 1977; ISBN 978-0521291644.

49. Swift, H.J.; Abrams, D.; Marques, S. Threat or Boost? Social Comparison Affects Older People's Performance Differently Depending on Task Domain. *J. Gerontol. Ser. B Psychol. Sci. Soc. Sci.* **2012**, *68*, 23–30. [CrossRef] [PubMed]
50. Peace, S.; Holland, C.; Kellaher, L. *Environment and Identity in Later Life*; Open University Press: Bristol, UK, 2006; ISBN 978-0335215119.

 © 2018 by the author. Licensee MDPI, Basel, Switzerland. This article is an open access article distributed under the terms and conditions of the Creative Commons Attribution (CC BY) license (http://creativecommons.org/licenses/by/4.0/).

Article

Coworking, the Sharing Economy, and the City: Which Role for the 'Coworking Entrepreneur'?

Giacomo Durante * and Margherita Turvani

Dipartimento di Progettazione e pianificazione in ambienti complessi (DPPAC), Università IUAV di Venezia, Santa Croce 1957, 30135 Venezia, Italy; margheri@iuav.it
* Correspondence: gdurante@iuav.it

Received: 16 July 2018; Accepted: 30 August 2018; Published: 3 September 2018

Abstract: Sharing economy platforms enabled by information and communication technologies (ICTs) are facilitating the diffusion of collaborative workplaces. Coworking spaces are emerging as a distinctive phenomenon in this context, not only fostering knowledge transfer and facilitating innovation, but also affecting the urban and socio-economic fabric contributing to urban regeneration processes at both the local scale and the city scale. Although the positive impacts of coworking on the urban environment are documented, there is still little or no evidence of the economic viability of coworking businesses, and a "coworking bubble" has been evoked. Given the lack of data, a national survey was set up of Italian coworking businesses, aimed at assessing the relevance of internal organizational factors (size, occupancy, profitability, services provided) for the sustainability of coworking businesses. By presenting the results of the survey, we argue that the sustainability and viability of the coworking model is highly dependent on internal factors, strictly related to the entrepreneurial action of coworking managers.

Keywords: sharing economy; sharing platform; coworking; coworking space; coworking business; collaborative workplaces; urban regeneration; entrepreneurial action

1. Introduction

Globalization and information and communication technologies (ICTs) are continuously transforming the relationship between geographical locations, spaces and economic activities [1], shaping urban and regional geographies [2]. Within this general trend, the rise of sharing/collaborative forms of the economy is now accompanied by a debate regarding the range of their potential benefits in terms of economic growth [3] and sustainable development [4,5].

The technological innovation driven by ICTs matches important changes in urban areas and the labour market. Traditional productive areas are being abandoned and traditional businesses (manufacturing) are relocating to other areas. High skilled workers—in terms of internet and digital skills—find their own way to enter the market, given the fact that their new competencies are not covered by traditional enterprises and the shrinking traditional sectors. These choices happen in a situation of individual scarcity of financial and banking capital, and necessitates innovative solutions for these new enterprises, made up mostly by individual freelancers, start-ups and micro-enterprises. Within this framework, work and workplaces are being radically modified [6], giving rise to collaborative workplaces, such as hacker spaces, maker spaces, fabrication laboratories (Fab Labs) and coworking spaces.

Coworking is often regarded as the "new model of work", a typical case of the sharing and collaborative economy [7]. Its appearance and diffusion have been related to the more general growth of the so-called "creative class" [8] in the knowledge and creative industries. The rationale for coworking is found in the need of knowledge workers and freelancers to work in a community, sharing not only know-how and skills, but also a physical space. Coworking spaces (CSs) are shared workplaces made up by open space desks and other facilities and services offered and organized by coworking businesses (CBs), run by coworking managers, providers or proprietors.

CSs exhibit both access to a shared physical space and the sharing of intangible assets [9]. CBs create advantages for the working community by boosting knowledge transfer, opening new job opportunities and offering shared physical assets.

The diffusion of coworking is the result of the interest from CS utilizers (CUs) toward the services supplied by CBs. In fact, CBs offer an array of innovative services that differ from traditional enterprises, targeting the needs of both "lone eagles" [6] (i.e., individual freelance workers) and new kinds of enterprises, most notably start-ups. To do so, CBs are required to meet the new market demands of highly-skilled workers and knowledge-intensive activities.

It has been claimed that new collaborative workspaces are largely located in a few creative cities that are acting as "coworking hotspots" [6] (p. 11). Coworking is thus an urban phenomenon that shows its potential in terms of the regeneration and revitalization of urban environments. It contributes to job creation [10,11], to the reuse of former industrial buildings turned into vacant spaces [12,13], to the development of creative districts by enhancing the "innovation ecosystem" of cities [14], to the transformation of public spaces [15], and to the attraction of other types of activities inside the urban area [11].

Ponzini and Rossi [16] argue that the growth of the urban creative class and Florida's creative city theory, whereby the competitiveness of cities depends on the emergence of creative activities, fueled a variety of interventions and urban policies targeting both the urban physical fabric and the economic fabric. Among them, the opening of new spaces for the creative class, such as CSs, is viewed by some authors as a sort of "urban panacea", promoting successful urban regeneration policies. However, against this widespread idea of considering coworking as a positive phenomenon, some authors have suggested the presence of a "coworking bubble" [6,17,18], casting a shadow on the sustainability of the coworking model.

In 2017, we conducted research in Porto Marghera (Venice, Italy), a former chemical industrial site and now one of the largest Italian brownfields, which is undergoing a slow process of urban regeneration, especially in the northern part.

In this context, the search for new business opportunities as well as the challenges posed by the reuse of vacant spaces located on the former industrial site, led some local entrepreneurs to consider coworking as a possible alternative for the relaunch of their underused areas and vacant buildings.

Given the lack of data on the economic viability and operating conditions of Italian CBs, required by Venetian entrepreneurs to evaluate different investment possibilities for their area, we wanted to answer to the following research questions: (1) where are Italian CBs located? (2) Are CBs economically viable? (3) Is the intensity of use of CS the key to their economic viability? (4) What are the internal factors and operational conditions ensuring the efficiency and the success of a CB? (5) Are CSs cheaper than traditional office spaces?

The aim of this paper is twofold: on the one hand, it wants to contribute to situating coworking in the urban debate, deepening its potential for the renewal of urban areas; on the other hand, it seeks to understand whether coworking represents an effective response to the needs of new enterprises, and to what extent coworking promoters are capable of supplying solutions to such needs.

In the first desk research phase, we produced a national coworking census, mapping Italian CBs to explore their location. Secondly, to find evidence regarding the economic viability of coworking, we conducted a national survey of CBs. The survey was carried out in spring 2017, submitting a questionnaire to the coworking managers of Italian CBs. Finally, we compared the prices for access to CSs to those for the rent of traditional office spaces. We argue that the economic viability of CBs—and therefore their ability to produce positive effects on urban fabrics and more generally on cities—is highly dependent on internal factors, strictly related to the choices of coworking promoters and managers. We highlight the important role of the coworking promoter/manager, whose organizational and marketing choices can determine the success of the CB, and secondarily trigger spillover effects for the urban and economic fabrics.

The paper is organized as follow: in the Section 2 we situate coworking in the broader sharing economy debate. In the Section 3, we explore the possible impacts of this phenomenon on the city, with reference to the relevant literature. In the fourth Section 4 we introduce the scope, the methodology and the description of our survey. The main results and key findings of our survey are presented in the Section 5. A discussion (Section 6) and conclusion (Section 7) follow.

2. Coworking in the Sharing Economy Debate

The sharing economy is emerging as a global trend now diffused in different economic activities, such as retail, logistics, transportation, tourism, and in various spheres such as the labour market organization, finance, and office spaces [19]. Their common feature is that they facilitate access to goods and services, on the demand and supply side, through digital platforms [20]. Being a widespread phenomenon, the sharing economy is affecting the entire economy. The increasing number of activities involving sharing practices is shaping cities [21], and rural areas are also now experiencing some of the transformative effects of the sharing economy [22].

The spread of sharing practices has been facilitated by the advent of ICTs and digitisation, enabling both the creation of digital sharing platforms and the possibility of working from different locations. However, the sharing economy, in contrast to Friedman's idea of a globalized world becoming flat [23], has proved to be affected by the spatial dimension, and represents an urban phenomenon that "directly affects the urban economy at both the neighbourhood and city-wide levels" [21] (p. 259). In the same way, the emergence of ICTs and digitisation also changed the idea of work, transforming communities and workplaces [2] and leading to what has been called the "third wave of virtual work" [24]. The first wave was characterized by the increased use of personal computers and emails, creating the possibility to work as self-employed freelancers; the second wave occurred when companies started to take the cost advantages related to virtual work, despite the disadvantages related to their inferior commitment to one employee. These workers started to feel the need to be part of a community and to "renew social contacts" [25] (p. 576) between them. This demand is producing the "third wave of virtual work", whereby virtual workers "physically reunite and retether to specific spaces" [24], giving rise to a new kind of "localized spaces for collaborative innovation" [14] (p. 1), such as CSs. Within this process, sharing economy platforms are facilitating the participation of individuals in communities, offering new possibilities for virtual workers not only to physically gather, but also to cooperate easily and to take advantage of less expensive online services, such as e-commerce, e-marketing, e-procurement, e-assistance.

CSs can be generally defined as "shared workplaces utilised by different sorts of knowledge professionals, mostly freelancers, working in various degree of specialisation in the vast domain of the knowledge industry" [18] (p. 194). In practical terms, CSs are open space offices furnished with desks and internet connections—and often also meeting rooms, private office spaces and other equipped rooms—that are rented to freelancers, professionals, start-ups or micro-businesses.

Since the opening of the first CS in 2005 in San Francisco [18,26], CSs have been increasing worldwide at an impressive pace. As reported in 2012, their number doubled each year since 2006 [27], and is still growing; the same happened to the number of coworking members worldwide [28–32].

The phenomenon of coworking is generally analysed within the sharing economy debate [9,18,20,22], as it involves both "the access of shared physical assets (office, infrastructure, cafeteria, etc.) and the sharing of intangible assets, such as (information, knowledge, etc.)" [9] (p. 6). Some authors say that CSs reflect "the collective-driven, networked approach of the open-source-idea translated into physical space" [33] (p. 202). Others claim that coworking can be associated with the sharing economy, as the latter is also characterized by the possibility to access under-utilized resources and physical assets [34,35], for the purpose of maximizing the utilization of "'surplus' or 'idle' capacity" of those assets [36]. Even if the boundaries of the sharing economy are difficult to define precisely and in the relevant literature "there is no 'shared' consensus on what activities comprise the 'sharing economy'" [19] (p. 6), some authors tried to produce a classification of sharing economy activities and platforms. According to Richardson, the phenomenon can be better understood "as a series of performances, rather than a coherent set of economic practices" [20] (p. 127). The performances identified are: the enactment of a community, the access to common resources, and the collaboration between participants [20]. From our perspective, coworking is characterised by all these performances. Following another approach, Codagnone and Martens divide the existing sharing platforms into three categories: "(a) recirculation of goods (second-hand and surplus goods markets); (b) increased asset utilization (production factors markets); and (c) service and labour exchanges" [19] (p. 10). According to these authors, coworking can be associated with initiatives falling inside the second and third categories, as CSs facilitate respectively the recirculation of idle assets, vacant or underused spaces, and the creation of new job opportunities through networking.

3. Coworking and Urban Area Renewal

While many authors have written about the definition of coworking and CS [6,14,18,26,37], few have discussed the effects of shared work practices on the evolution of cities and the potential of CSs to transform the urban fabric. Only recently, the potential role of CSs in stimulating urban regeneration processes and "micro-scale physical transformations" [15] (p. 3) has been discussed, viewing coworking as a means of providing an effective alternative for the reuse of former industrial or under-utilised buildings [38].

According to this view, the urban regeneration potential of CSs is twofold. Firstly, the reuse of vacant or underused buildings is contributing to the recycling of idle urban assets, thus contributing to the realization of a circular economy, centred on the reuse of assets that have completed their life cycle, giving them new life and minimising energy and material waste. CSs, seen as the answer to the new organizational needs of knowledge workers, fit into the challenges posed by the re-cycling of the urban fabric [39], moving from deindustrialization to a new phase of economic growth. It is worth noting that CSs, in order to differentiate themselves from traditional office spaces, "tend to emphasize their idiosyncratic, bespoke 'Post-Fordist' design aesthetics" [32] (p. 10) and their location in former industrial buildings responds to such desires. Many CSs have already opened inside industrial era buildings [32]. There are indeed several examples of this trend: Betahaus in Berlin's Kreuzberg, a space of 3000 sqm now converted into a hub for creative start-ups; Ponyride in Detroit, a formerly derelict building now home of a business incubator and collaborative workspaces [40]; the 311 coworking space in Verona (Italy), opened in 2015 on formerly industrial land close to the city centre, a collaborative open space of 2000 sqm [41]. These examples show the potential of CBs—and in general of shared service accommodation—in "reusing and revaluing decaying properties" [12] (p. 118). Furthermore, the opening of CBs is also impacting positively on the quality of the surrounding neighbourhood, increasing the attractiveness of the area by occasionally improving public spaces and generating socio-economic and micro-regeneration effects [15]. Secondly, according to other authors, coworking is capable of producing some "soft" impacts on the city. The emergence of new forms of creative production has favoured the concentration of creative activities in some places [42], benefitting from urban density and the generation of proximity spill-overs [43]. Some authors study "the creative city" or the "knowledge-based city" [44,45] and the appearance of innovation districts [46] shaping the urban economy. This phenomenon is seen as very positive, and politicians are looking with more and more interest to the potential of creative activities to foster the competitiveness of cities, by leveraging the "urban creative class" [16] (p. 1052). In line with this, CBs represent a strategic model, acting "as interfaces with the creative milieu in the city and beyond" [47] (p. 133), and boosting innovation processes in the city at the individuals and community levels [48]. Kojo and Nenonen, studying the evolution of CBs, identified regional development as one driver for the evolution of coworking [49], while Buksh and Mouat say that the presence of knowledge workers has "wider economic and social benefits across the city fringes and regional centres" [2] (p. 22).

Of course, the effects of CBs on the urban environment arising from the two approaches described above are deeply intertwined, as the concentration of creative activities is "the result of both material and immaterial transformations" [42] (p. 63).

Despite coworking being celebrated as a positive urban phenomenon, able to enhance competitiveness, foster innovation and contribute to urban regeneration, some authors have evoked the presence of a "coworking bubble". Back in 2012, Cashman observed that Spain, despite the economic crisis and the high level of unemployment, exhibited the most pronounced growth of CSs [17]. According to other authors, the bubble could be explained by both the precariousness of the knowledge workers, "pushed to become freelancers" and "to seek asylum in CS" [6] (p. 17), and the low profitability of CBs, frequently forced to seek public subsidies [50]. In the debate on urban regeneration policies, coworking is considered by some authors as a sort of "urban panacea". From our perspective, coworking is an entrepreneurial activity that could also represent an innovative way to reuse vacant buildings and regenerate urban areas. As we have described, while some authors explored the influence of CSs on the urban environment, their contributions focus more on the effects of creative activities, rather than exploring the preconditions for the appearance of "urban creative concentrations" [42]. More particularly, in the case of CSs, there is little or no evidence of the role played by internal factors and operational conditions in contributing to the sustainability of the coworking model. To fill this gap, we decided to investigate these aspects, submitting a questionnaire to Italian coworking managers/promoters.

4. Materials and Methods

The purpose of the research into Italian CBs, conducted in early 2017, was to collect data about the ongoing experiences in Italy to understand their conditions of operability, economic sustainability, space uses and organization in different urban contexts.

This research was set up to answer to the questions posed by some entrepreneurs, who are looking at coworking as a possible business to relaunch vacant or underused areas located in the Venice mainland, inside Porto Marghera, a former chemical industrial hub and now one of the biggest Italian brownfields, also included in the Italian National Priority List [51]. In this context, coworking might offer a possible innovative solution to facilitate an urban regeneration process and the reuse of vacant buildings, as suggested by Ginelli for the Milan case [52], considering also the track record of successful experiences of reuse and soft regeneration associated with collaborative workspaces and coworking [40,53].

Investors are looking at the possibility to start a coworking business in the area, and our work was aimed at responding to their need to evaluate the advantages and disadvantages of the coworking model, looking at ongoing experiences to evaluate the economic viability of coworking, in order to develop different investment scenarios for their area. In order to offer precise indications to local entrepreneurs, given the lack of meaningful data about the Italian operational context of CBs, we investigated the internal and external factors conducive to the growth of such businesses, the importance of entrepreneurial actions and the contractual forms of successful initiatives, setting up a national survey of CBs.

The survey was designed to understand the conditions for the success of a CB. On the one hand, the economic viability and sustainability of a CB is dependent on external factors: its location, the activities and amenities in the surrounding area, the accessibility of the structure. These are all preconditions for the occurrence of "urban creative concentrations" [42], and hence factors affecting the success and the outcomes of a CB. On the other hand, the viability of a CB is related to internal factors, such as the availability of enough space to meet the demand, the differentiation of the working environment into different ambiances suitable for different purposes, the quality of the services provided, which is then reflected in the physical layout of the space; but also organisational factors, such as the types of contracts offered, the price paid to rent a desk, the flexibility of the opening hours and days, and more generally the atmosphere perceived by the CUs.

Our research aimed to explore some relevant factors of the success of CBs, looking at their location, internal factors and operational conditions.

The research was carried out in three different phases. The first phase was the creation of a coworking census at the national level, and the mapping of Italian CBs, aimed at evaluating the dimensions of the Italian coworking phenomenon and at exploring the location of CBs. CBs were mapped using the results from Google Maps search engine with the keyword "coworking".

The second phase aimed at understanding the operational conditions of CBs already in business. In this phase, an online questionnaire was sent to Italian coworking managers and providers. The research questions guiding the preparation of the questionnaire were: (1) how important is entrepreneurial action for the success of the CB? (2) Are there any specific distinctive features of successful CBs? (3) What kind of contracts and services do CBs offer to their CUs?

The preparation of the questionnaire was anticipated by two site visits to CSs in Italy, one in Mestre (Venice mainland) and one in Verona. The first location was chosen because it is part of the biggest network of affiliated CBs in Italy; the second location was 311 in Verona, which—as already mentioned in the introduction—represents a relevant case study, considering that it opened in a former industrial building and contributed to the revitalization of the surrounding area. Along with the site visits, we carried out desk research into the websites of coworking providers (both single and affiliated CBs), to understand how they are organised and to provide a taxonomy of the different supplementary rooms and services offered by CBs. The taxonomy was useful to better tailor the questionnaire.

The questionnaire was made up of 37 questions—comprising multiple choice questions, dichotomous questions and semantic differential questions—covering the most important organizational and economical aspects of CBs. The questionnaire was sent by email to the coworking managers of 413 coworking spaces of the 495 that were recorded during the first phase of the research; a total of 82 coworking managers did not provide a valid email address.

We collected 128 complete questionnaires with a response rate of 31%.

CS, the shared working environment, is what characterizes a CB. Therefore, we grouped the respondents according to the rate of occupation of the open space desks. This variable may be a proxy for the economic sustainability and is the principal internal factor and operational condition affecting the viability of CBs. This choice is in line with the survey carried out by Deskmag, an online magazine about coworking, that shows that most of the revenue of a coworking space comes from the rent of open space desks [54]. Open space desk occupation is directly connected to the economic viability of the CB, as each user pays to rent a desk first and this allows CUs to use the other possible facilities. CBs were grouped in three categories based on the reported rate of occupancy of the offered open space desks during the previous six months. The three categories were: low performance, comprising CBs where the percentage of occupancy was less than 50%; medium performance, with a level of occupancy between 50% and 75%; and high performance, with occupancy of more than 75%. We analysed these three groups of CBs in relation to the other variables that we investigated in the questionnaire, such as the dimensions of their coworking space, the length of their period of activity, the number of open space desks, the types of the contracts offered to users, the profitability and the level of cost associated with each type of contract, the presence of individual office rooms and the level of saturation associated, the possibility to use meeting rooms, the different kinds of services provided, and the opening times.

In the third phase, we focused on the rental expenses for the use of a coworking spaces. As coworking spaces are often regarded as a cheap way for freelancers to rent a work space that they could not otherwise afford in a traditional office, we collected information about the price per square meter of different Italian CSs. Then, we compared them with the data on office spaces rental values provided by the Italian Revenue Agency. The purpose was to test whether Italian CSs are cheaper than traditional offices.

5. Results

The results are presented in three separate sections. In the Section 1, we provide some insights based on our national census of CSs. In the Section 2, we present the key findings regarding the questionnaire survey, focusing on the physical arrangement of CSs (i.e., the factors which characterise the layout of a coworking space) and on the organizational and managerial aspects. In the Section 7 we compare the rent prices of CSs with rent prices of traditional office spaces.

5.1. Mapping Italian Coworking Businesses

The census of Italian CBs registered the presence of 495 CBs. In Figure 1, Italian CBs are aggregated by municipality and displayed in relation to the inhabitants of each municipality, distinguishing CBs located in municipalities with more than 250,000 inhabitants. The map shows that CBs are located predominantly in the north of Italy. Despite coworking being a phenomenon generally associated with big cities, Italian CBs are also located in small cities and towns. In fact, cities with more than 250,000 inhabitants account for the 37% of the mapped CBs, while the 46% are situated in municipalities with less than 100,000 inhabitants. The biggest concentration of CBs is in Milan and its metropolitan area, accounting for the 20% of total Italian CBs.

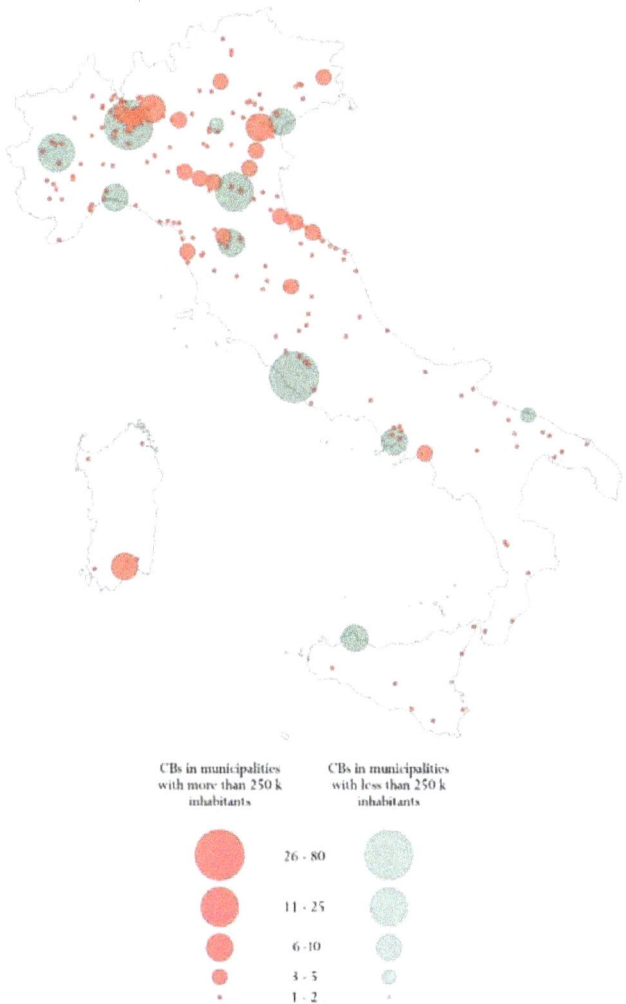

Figure 1. Map of CBs by municipality.

5.2. Results of the National Survey on Coworking Businesses

The indicator according to which we chose to evaluate the performance of CBs was the occupancy rate of open space desks. Based on this variable, we grouped the CBs into three performance categories.

This resulted in 76 CBs associated with low performance, 24 with medium performance, and 28 with high performance (see the percentages in Figure 2).

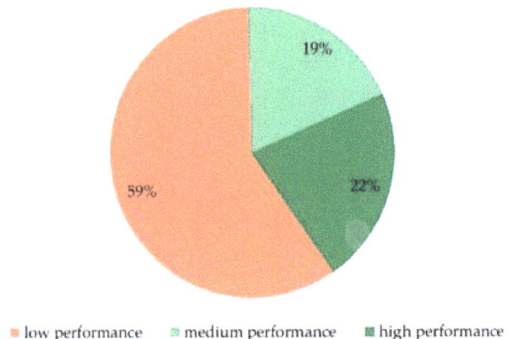

Figure 2. Share of respondents by performance category.

These results were then cross-referenced with the information regarding the other variables investigated, highlighting some differences between high performance, medium performance and low performance CBs.

5.2.1. Longevity and Dimension

The first variable we investigated was the timespan the CB had been in activity. As shown in Figure 3, a significantly wider share of high-performance CBs had been in business for three years or more than the low-performance CBs. The low-performance CBs were characterised by a shorter time-span of activity than high-performance CBs. The data showed that the share of CBs that opened less than one year before the survey was 28% for low-performance CBs and 7% for high-performance CBs.

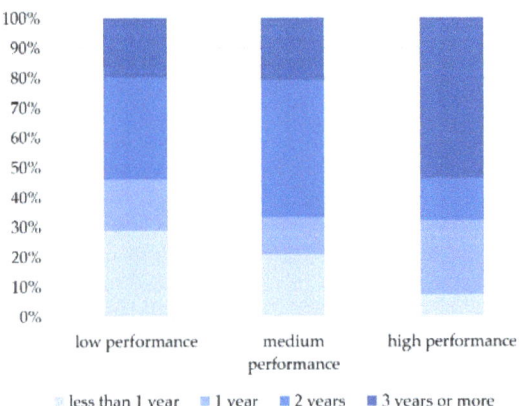

Figure 3. Timespan of activity by performance category.

The second aspect we considered in relation to performance was the dimension of the CS provided in each CB. As summarized in Figure 4, a considerable share of high-performance CBs are characterised by a large CS: one in four high-performance CBs is bigger than 800 sqm, while only

4% of low-performance CBs are bigger than 800 sqm. Beside this, it is worth noting that almost half of the Italian CBs (49%) were found to be small.

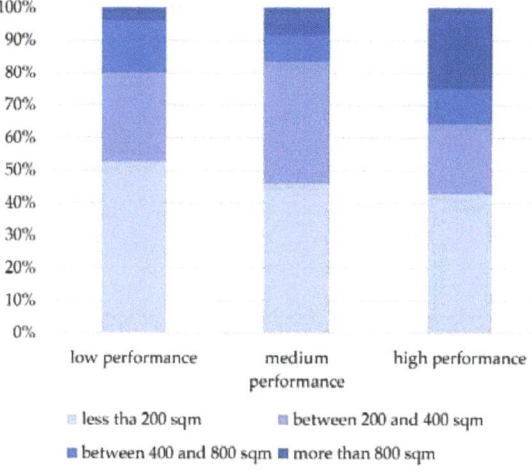

Figure 4. Dimension of CSs by performance category.

As shown in Table 1, the average floor space occupied by open space desks also reflected this difference, even considering the trimmed mean and discarding outlier values, which resulted mainly from the presence of very large CSs affecting the average values. The standard deviation of the dimensions of the CS of high-performance CBs was also higher than that of the medium-performance CBs and low-performance CBs, underlining the fact that the floor space occupied by open space desks in high-performance CBs is also more variable.

Table 1. Mean, trimmed mean and standard deviation of the dimension of open space by performance category (sqm).

	Low Performance	Medium Performance	High Performance
Mean	95	127	210
Trimmed mean 20%	80	98	159
Standard deviation	87	150	269

According to the results for the dimension of the CSs, high-performance CBs turned out to have on average a higher number of open space desks (see Table 2).

Table 2. Mean, trimmed mean and standard deviation of the number of desks in open space by performance category (units).

	Low Performance	Medium Performance	High Performance
Mean	15	19	36
Trimmed mean 20%	13	15	26
Standard deviation	13	23	55

5.2.2. Flexibility and Profitability of Contracts

A third aspect investigated was the flexibility of the contracts offered to the users of the open space, represented by the different types of contracts (daily, weekly, monthly or annual) offered by each CB. As shown in Figure 5, the share of high-performance CBs offering four kinds of contract was substantially lower than the contracts offered by low-performance CBs: more than a half of the CBs turned out to offer only one kind of contract. Regarding the types of contracts offered (see Figure 6), the main differences between high-performance and low-performance CBs was the proportion of CBs offering daily contracts and weekly contracts, while the difference in proportion offering monthly contracts and annual contracts was much smaller.

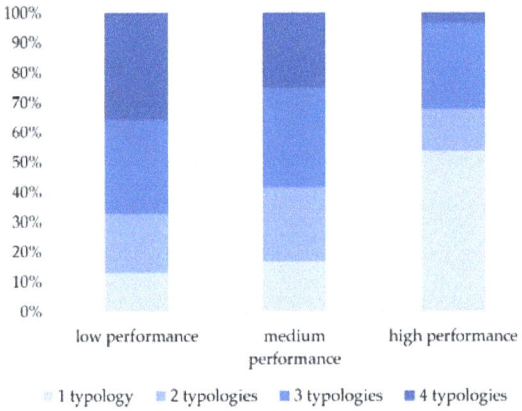

Figure 5. Number of contracts offered by performance category.

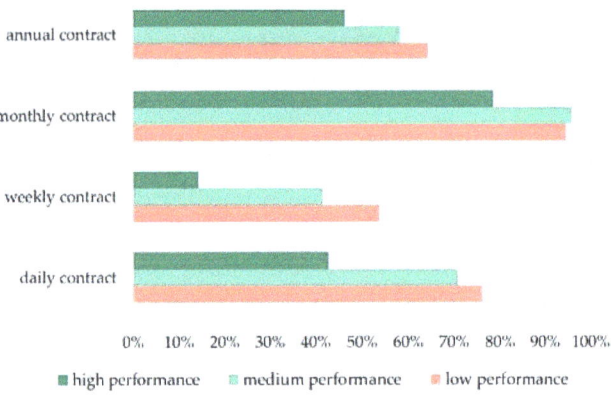

Figure 6. Types of contracts offered by performance category (percentages calculated from the total number of answers received for each type of contract).

We investigated the profitability associated with the renting contracts. It was measured by asking coworking managers to indicate a percentage range of profit associated with each type of contract in the previous six months.

The profitability of daily contracts was generally low, and only a few low-performance CBs presented a high share of profitability (Figure 7).

Weekly contracts turned out to be the worst contract in terms of profitability for every performance category. Also, 30% of low-performance CBs and up to the 57% of high-performance CBs did not even offer weekly contracts.

Monthly contracts (Figure 8) was the most profitable in each category of CBs. High profitability (80–100%) was obviously more frequent for high-performance and medium-performance CBs. In coherence with this data, a low level of profitability (0–20%) appeared more recurrently for low-performance CBs.

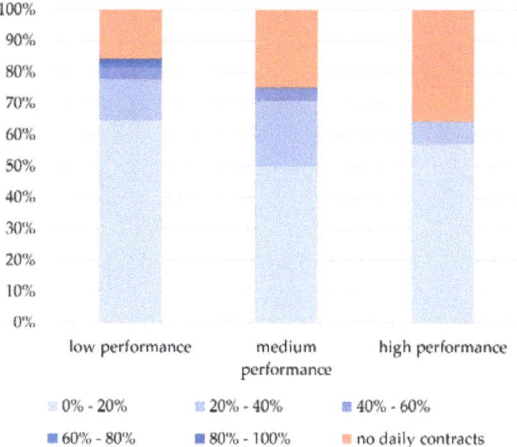

Figure 7. Shares of profitability associated with daily contracts by performance category (last six months).

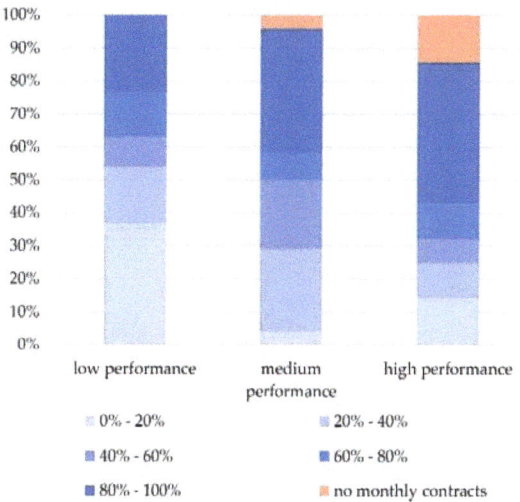

Figure 8. Shares of profitability associated with monthly contracts by performance category (last six months).

The situation with regard to annual contracts (see Figure 9) was similar.

We then asked coworking managers which kind of contract is the most profitable. Monthly contracts turned out to be the most profitable for medium-performance and high-performance CBs, followed by daily contracts. For low performance CBs, daily contracts were reported to be the most profitable (Figure 10).

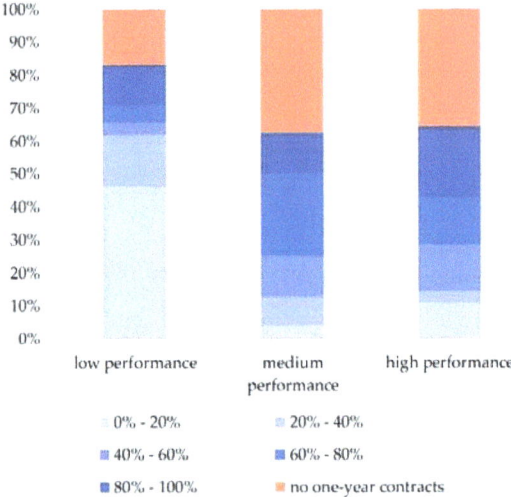

Figure 9. Share of profitability associated with annual contracts by performance category (last six months).

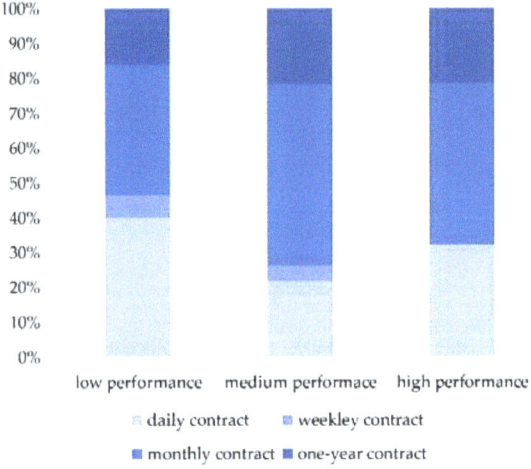

Figure 10. Most profitable contracts by performance category.

In terms of administrative costs, some contracts were costlier than others. The respondents reported that the costliest contract is the daily contract (see Figure 11), and this was found to be a common result in all three performance categories.

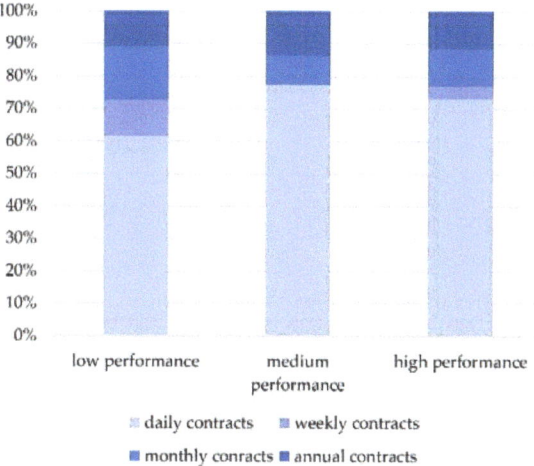

Figure 11. Costliest contracts by performance category.

5.2.3. Occupancy and Services Provided

As discovered during the visit to CSs and using the information found on coworking providers' websites, a common feature of CBs is the presence of individual office spaces.

This trend was confirmed by the data collected during the survey, as 69% of the respondents declared that their CSs were equipped with individual office spaces.

By comparing the occupancy of individual office spaces in the six months immediately prior to the survey (see Figure 12), high-performance CBs were found to have a better level of occupancy, followed by medium-performance CBs, while low-performance CBs showed significantly lower percentages of occupancy.

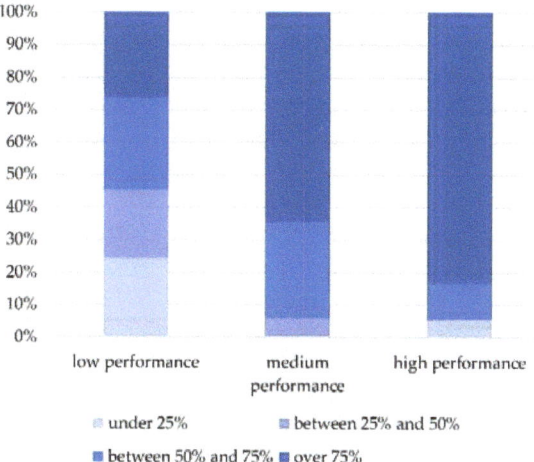

Figure 12. Shares of occupancy of individual office spaces by performance category (last six months).

The presence of meeting rooms is another key element of CSs. High-performance CBs were found to have the highest number of meeting rooms (Figure 13). In fact, 29% of high-performance CB managers reported that their space is equipped with three or more meeting rooms, while only 12% of low-performance CBs arranged their spaces in the same way, as most of them were generally equipped with only one meeting room.

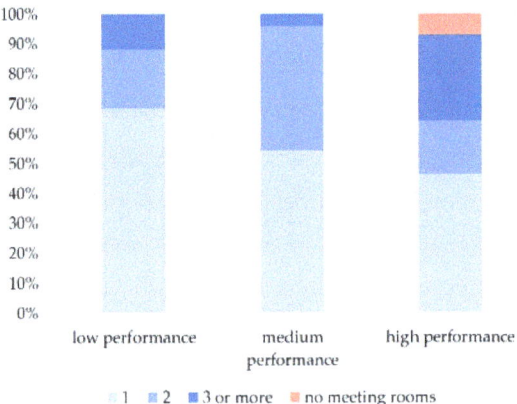

Figure 13. Number of meeting rooms by performance category.

Some services, such as a fast internet connection and printers were found to be provided by almost every CB (Figure 14). For other services the analysis highlighted some differences between high-performance, medium-performance and low-performance CBs: the presence of a bar/restaurant and a kitchen could be observed more in high-performance and medium-performance CBs; the presence of a relaxation space, parking lots, a garden and vending machines was more frequent in medium-performance CBs; bicycle racks and landlines were services offered more commonly by high-performance CBs.

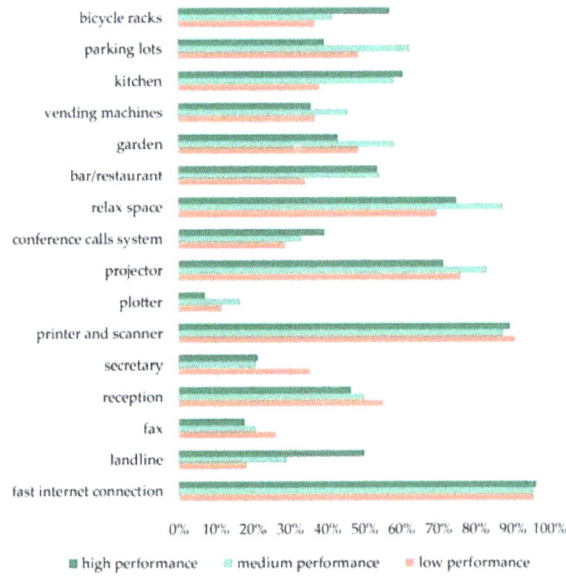

Figure 14. Services offered by performance category (percentages calculated from the total number of answers received for each service).

5.2.4. Timetable

The coworking managers were asked to indicate the opening hours and days of their CSs.

A significant number of high-performance CBs reported being open every day, while low-performance CBs tend to offer fewer opening days (Figure 15). The same situation was observed for the opening hours (Figure 16).

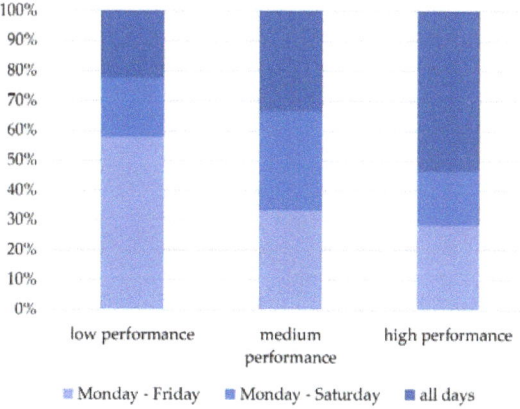

Figure 15. Opening days by performance category.

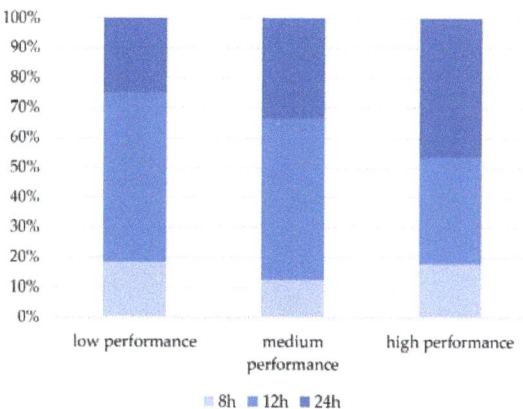

Figure 16. Opening hours by performance category.

5.3. Comparison of Coworking and Traditional Office Rent Prices

We now turn to the comparison of rental prices between traditional offices and coworking spaces, since in the literature the success and the diffusion of these new types of workplaces is related not only to better services, but also to their being a cheaper alternative to the traditional office. By looking at some of the coworking providers' websites, we collected data on the open space surface and the relative monthly fees, considering the minimum monthly fee for renting a desk in an open space. Using this information, we then calculated the price per square meter, and we compared this value to that for traditional offices in the same area. The monthly rental price per square meter for offices can be found at the Italian Revenue Agency (Agenzia delle Entrate) webGIS, offering minimum and maximum prices for different areas [55]. We used the latest data available (year 2016, I semester), considering the mean between the maximum and minimum values. Other related useful information pertained to the quality of available spaces, as in some areas there are different prices according to the state of maintenance of the office spaces.

Figure 17 below shows that the price per square meter of CSs were much higher than those associated with traditional offices in every location we considered.

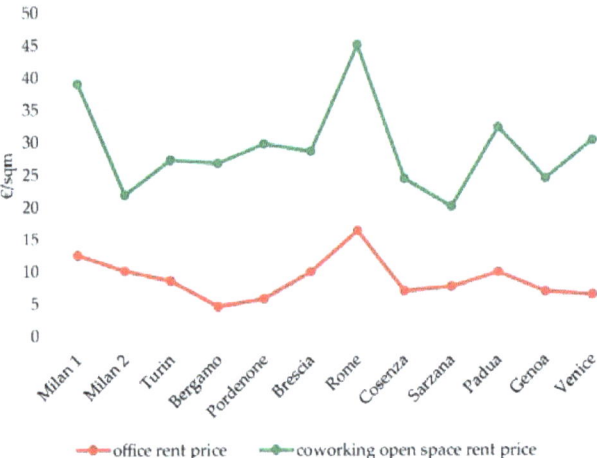

Figure 17. Comparison between average prices per square meter of CSs and traditional offices.

6. Discussion

In this paragraph, we discuss the results of the national survey, and we compare them with data from a selection of surveys and forecasts conducted by Deskmag. These are global surveys aimed at exploring the general trends of coworking worldwide, and the only studies on coworking also providing some data about the organization of CSs and the profitability of CBs, which are useful for coworking promoters starting a new business or that are already in business.

In line with the survey carried out by Deskmag in 2012 [27], which registered a relevant increase in CBs located in rural areas, our mapping of Italian CBs shows that there is a significant share of CBs located outside big municipalities, even though coworking maintains its urban character in large "hotspot" cities, as suggested by Moriset [6]. The spread of CBs to many small municipalities or medium-sized towns reflects the distribution of the population in Italy, where only few municipalities have more than 250,000 inhabitants [56]. Agglomerations at different scales, among smaller municipalities, around medium-sized cities and in large urban areas create opportunities for creative activities in many different locations, and the territorial distribution and concentration of CBs reflect those opportunities.

The main result of our survey is that the success of any CB, in terms of the intensity of occupancy of the provided desks, which is directly related to the profitability of the CB, is highly dependent on internal factors. These are physical factors: the high level of occupation of open space desks that characterises high-performance CBs is associated with the dimensions of the CS, showing that large CSs are the most attractive. This result is also in line with the latest coworking forecast provided by Deskmag [30], which shows that CSs are becoming bigger, and the increasing size is associated with higher profitability, as also reported in a previous survey by Deskmag [27]. High-performance CBs also show a higher level of occupancy of individual offices. The presence of these spaces, according to Deskmag's latest survey [29], is one of the new elements in a CS, as CBs are expected to show a higher share of individual offices [30]. In our survey, CBs with a medium and high level of performance are those offering more services to coworking users. The factors contributing to the attractiveness of CSs are also organisational: the success of any CB appears to be related to the opening times and to the variety of contractual forms. High-performance CBs offer a lower number of contractual forms, mainly monthly and annual contracts, lowering the turnover of CUs and consequently increasing the intensity of use in time. Of course, these contracts are more profitable exactly because they guarantee a higher occupancy rate, leading to a selection of coworking members through time.

The second important result of the survey is to show the role of coworking managers and coworking promoters, confirming the relevance of strategic choices and investments, which might be related to the mission of the proprietors of CSs, and to the interaction with proactive users. As observed by the investigation of Spinuzzi [26], CBs differentiate themselves from the others by arranging the CS in different ways, according to their location, design, flexibility and professionalism. These differentiators are highly reliant on the choices of the coworking managers "who structure, design, furnish, and run their sites based on their understanding and model of coworking" [26] (p. 418). According to Parrino, the choice of coworking manager could also facilitate the exchange of knowledge between CUs, by providing online platforms, networking events and coaching [57].

Another important factor affecting the success of a CB turned out to be its longevity, as high-performance CBs turned out to have been in the business for three or more years. Again, this finding confirms the results of Deskmag's second global survey, which showed that "72% of all coworking spaces become profitable after more than two years in operation" [54]. The rationale of this finding could be that, provided the high risks distinctive of this type of business, the fact that highly-skilled digital workers and new enterprises require innovative services and solutions, and the scarcity of financial capital associated with these activities, the oldest cohort of CBs are the most effective and the most able to overcome risk and obstacles to their successful operation.

A third result pertains to the comparison of the price paid in traditional and CB spaces: although coworking is often considered a cheap alternative to traditional offices, our data show that CUs spend more to rent a desk in a CS. This result indicates that CUs might prefer to pay for the "liquidity" of their choices and short-term perspectives in their own personal business. They are willing to pay more to have flexibility, to have more services, and to have fewer constraints, especially avoiding the length of office lease agreements, which according to Italian law last for at least six years.

7. Conclusions

Coworking is considered by many authors to be an activity falling under the umbrella of the sharing economy. It is characterized by the tendency of highly-skilled workers to physically gather in some locations to take advantage of proximity and knowledge exchange, a process facilitated by digital platforms. In this way, coworking involves sharing both physical assets (office, common spaces) and intangible assets (knowledge, skills). Coworking is also generally regarded as a positive urban phenomenon, fuelling regeneration processes and enhancing competitiveness, even if some authors evoke the presence of a "coworking bubble".

Following the interest of some local entrepreneurs in the coworking model as a possible innovative way to relaunch their vacant properties located in the former industrial site of Porto Marghera (Venice, Italy), our study investigated coworking as an entrepreneurial activity, which opens up the possibility to offer new market opportunities enabled by digitization and urban regeneration. We claimed that the lack of data on the dimensions of the coworking phenomenon in Italy, on the one hand, and about the organizational and economic aspects of CBs on the other hand, made any generalization about the sustainability of coworking untenable. Sharing the concerns regarding a "coworking bubble" and of the low sustainability of CBs, we decided to investigate the economic viability of Italian CBs, looking at the role of internal factors and exploring how those factors can contribute to the sustainability of the coworking model. In fact, although in the last few years a lot of literature has been produced around the concept of coworking, the factors contributing to the success of CBs seem to be overlooked. This is why we collected data on various determinants, physical and intangible, that might enhance the success and the viability of coworking as an innovative model of regeneration, creating value for decaying properties and vacant buildings.

A national survey was carried out in three phases: firstly, we conducted a national census of Italian CBs, mapping the results at the municipal scale; then we submitted an online questionnaire to coworking managers and providers, investigating the arrangement of the space, the services provided and their profitability; finally, we compared the rent prices of CSs and traditional offices, to understand whether the preferences of CUs are related to the greater affordability of CSs.

The major contribution of our work is that we recognized that coworking is an entrepreneurial activity, emerging to answer to the needs of highly-skilled workers and new kinds of enterprises, such as start-ups. These new enterprises are different from traditional enterprises as they are characterised by high level human capital and scarce financial resources, and thus they need different kinds of services. We found that CUs are willing to pay more to get access to CSs precisely because of the opportunities and services inside CSs. These opportunities are the result of the entrepreneurial action of coworking promoters, in their attempt to respond to the necessities of flexible jobs.

The other contribution of this paper is the proposal of a rough ranking of efficiency in Italian coworking initiatives. Based on our findings, the largest businesses, by practicing simpler contractual schemes, reach higher utilization and, after a few years of operation, better financial performance. The role of the coworking manager is emphasized and it is strictly related to the success of the CB: the entrepreneurial ability of coworking promoters in attracting CUs and in making the right investment choices is the enabling condition for CBs to become viable, strengthening the affiliation between CUs and the CB, and sustaining a working community. Following Richardson [20], we consider coworking as being characterised by a series of performances—the enactment of a community, the access to common resources and the collaboration between participants—and we believe that the occurrence of these performances is deeply affected by the choices of coworking managers.

We suggest that further research should look at the characteristics of CUs, to investigate whether the success of CBs is also related to the typology, structure and operating conditions of start-ups or other businesses using their CS. In fact, CUs might differ not only in the type of business they are undertaking, but they could also have access to different financial resources, changing the way they are building their business and thus also the services they expect to find inside a CS. Therefore, it would be interesting to set up a survey of CUs, and to match the results to those from the survey of CBs.

The alleged presence of a "coworking bubble" and the fact that CBs were found to be often unprofitable [54] or to rely on public subsidies [50], suggests a move away from the emphasis on the creative class acting as an "urban panacea" for urban regeneration and competitiveness. Instead, we shed light on the role of the "coworking entrepreneur", whose choices create the operational conditions for the economic viability of CBs and the attractiveness of CSs, consequently producing some positive urban effects. In fact, coworking can produce a positive effect on the urban environment and for the people involved only if they become more stable forms of work organization in the city, lasting in time and surviving as business activities capable of interacting with the socio-economic urban fabric. At a broader scale, the emerging forms of sharing activities and collaborative workplaces are leading to a "spatial reconfiguration of jobs in cities" [58], creating new networks of microbusinesses that are replacing the traditional industrial clusters and in which coworking spaces are acting as physical platforms [18]. It is also changing "the way cities generate jobs through entrepreneurship" [59], and in this sense the "coworking entrepreneur" should be regarded as an urban innovator, whose choices are capable of producing urban concentrations of creative activity and consequently shape the urban and socio-economic fabric of our cities.

Author Contributions: G.D. and M.T. contributed to the design and implementation of the research, to the analysis of the results, and to the writing of the manuscript. G.D. contributed to the production of maps and figures.

Funding: This research was funded in the frame of the European Social Fund 2014–2020 Programme: Programma Operativo Regionale della Regione Veneto—Fondo Sociale Europeo 2014–2020—Obiettivo generale "Investimenti in favore della crescita e l'Occupazione—Reg. 1304/2013—Asse "Occupabilità"—DGR n. 2121 del 30/12/2015.

Conflicts of Interest: The authors declare no conflict of interest.

References

1. Giddens, A. *The Consequences of Modernity*; Polity Press: Cambridge, UK, 1990; ISBN 978-0745609232.
2. Buksh, B.; Mouat, C.M. Activating smart work hubs for urban revitalisation: Evidence and implications of digital urbanism, for planning and policy from South-East Queensland. *Aust. Plan.* **2015**, *52*, 16–26. [CrossRef]
3. Celikel, E.B.; Abadie, F.; Biagi, F.; Bock, A.; Bontoux, L.; Figueiredo Do Nascimento, S.; Martens, B.; Szczepanikova, A. The European Collaborative Economy: A research agenda for policy support. *Eur. Comm.* **2016**. [CrossRef]
4. Heinrichs, H. Sharing Economy: A Potential New Pathway to Sustainability. *GAIA* **2013**, *22*, 228–231. [CrossRef]
5. Martin, C.J. Initial steps towards a research agenda for the sharing economy and socio-technical transitions. Working paper. *Studies* **2015**, *31*, 27–41. [CrossRef]
6. Moriset, B. Building new places of the creative economy. The rise of coworking spaces. In Proceedings of the 2nd Geography of Innovation International Conference 2014, Utrecht, The Netherlands, 23–25 January 2014.
7. Botsman, R.; Rogers, R. *What's Mine is Yours: How Collaborative Consumption is Changing the Way We Live*; HarperCollins Business: New York, NY, USA, 2011; ISBN 978-0007395910.
8. Florida, R. *The Rise of the Creative Class: And how It's Transforming Work, Leisure, Community and Everyday Life*; Basic Books: New York, NY, USA, 2002; ISBN 978-0465042487.
9. Bouncken, B.R.; Reuschl, J.A. Coworking-spaces: How a phenomenon of the sharing economy builds a novel trend for the workplace and for entrepreneurship. *Rev. Manag. Sci.* **2016**. [CrossRef]
10. Moretti, E. *The New Geography of Jobs*; Houghton Mifflin Harcourt: Boston, MA, USA, 2012; ISBN 978-0547750118.
11. Montgomery, J. Creative industry business incubators and managed workspaces: A review of best practice. *Plan. Pract. Res.* **2007**, *22*, 601–617. [CrossRef]
12. Fiorentino, S. Re-making urban economic geography. Start-ups, entrepreneurial support and the Makers Movement: A critical assessment of policy mobility in Rome. *Geoforum* **2018**, *93*, 116–119. [CrossRef]
13. Durante, G.; Turvani, M. Esperienze di coworking nel rilancio di are urbane dismesse o sotto-utilizzate. *Urban. Inf.* **2018**, *273–274*, 88–89.
14. Capdevila, I. Typologies of Localized Spaces of Collaborative Innovation. Working paper 2013. Available online: https://papers.ssrn.com/sol3/papers.cfm?abstract_id=2414402 (accessed on 15 June 2018).
15. Mariotti, I.; Pacchi, C.; Di Vita, S. Coworking Spaces in Milan: Location Patterns and Urban Effects. *J. Urban Technol.* **2017**. [CrossRef]
16. Ponzini, D.; Rossi, U. Becoming a Creative City: The Entrepreneurial Mayor, Network Politics and the Promise of an Urban Renaissance. *Urban Stud.* **2010**, *47*, 1037–1057. [CrossRef]
17. Cashman, A. 2000 Coworking Spaces Worldwide. Available online: www.deskmag.com/en/2000-coworking-spaces-worldwide-617 (accessed on 23 June 2018).
18. Gandini, A. The rise of coworking spaces: A literature review. *Ephemera* **2015**, *15*, 193–205. Available online: http://www.ephemerajournal.org/contribution/rise-coworking-spaces-literature-review (accessed on 15 June 2018).
19. Codagnone, C.; Martens, B. Scoping the Sharing Economy: Origins, Definitions, Impact and Regulatory Issues. Institute for Prospective Technological Studies Digital Economy Working Paper 2016/1, JRC100369. *Eur. Comm.* **2016**. [CrossRef]
20. Richardson, L. Performing the sharing economy. *Geoforum* **2015**, *67*, 121–129. [CrossRef]
21. Davidson, N.M.; Infranca, J.J. The Sharing Economy as an Urban Phenomenon. *Yale Law Policy Rev.* **2016**, *34*, 215–279. Available online: http://digitalcommons.law.yale.edu/ylpr/vol34/iss2/1?utm_source=digitalcommons.law.yale.edu%2Fylpr%2Fvol34%2Fiss2%2F1&utm_medium=PDF&utm_campaign=PDFCoverPages (accessed on 23 June 2018).
22. Finck, M.; Ranchordás, S. Sharing and the City. *Vanderbilt J. Transl. Law* **2017**, *49*, 1299. Available online: https://papers.ssrn.com/sol3/papers.cfm?abstract_id=2741575 (accessed on 2 July 2018). [CrossRef]
23. Friedman, T.L. *The World Is Flat: A Brief History of the Twenty-First Century*; Farrar Straus & Giroux: New York, NY, USA, 2005; ISBN 978-0374292881.
24. Johns, T.; Gratton, L. The Third Wave of Virtual Work. January–February 2013 Issue. *Harv. Bus. Rev.* **2013**. Available online: https://hbr.org/2013/01/the-third-wave-of-virtual-work (accessed on 2 July 2018).

25. Kubatova, J. The Cause and Impact of the Development of Coworking in the Current Knowledge Economy. In Proceedings of the 15th European Conference on Knowledge Management, Santarem, Portugal, 4–5 September 2014; pp. 571–577.
26. Spinuzzi, C. Working Alone Together: Coworking as Emergent Collaborative Activity. *J. Bus. Tech. Commun.* **2012**, *26*, 399–441. [CrossRef]
27. Deskmag. 2nd Annual Global Coworking Survey. Available online: http://reseau.fing.org/file/download/128857 (accessed on 2 July 2018).
28. Deskmag. 2017 Coworking Forecast. Available online: https://www.dropbox.com/s/phvl8cnw6p2k6hp/2017%20GCS%20%20Coworking%20Forecast.pdf?dl=0 (accessed on 3 July 2018).
29. Deskmag. First Results of the 2017 Global Coworking Survey. Available online: https://www.dropbox.com/s/8kfdsrtel6hpabd/First%20Results%20Of%20The%202017%20Global%20Coworking%20Survey.pdf?dl=0 (accessed on 3 July 2018).
30. Deskmag. 2018 Coworking Forecast. Available online: https://www.dropbox.com/s/rjbmdo4wp4aeccx/2018%20Complete%20Coworking%20Forecast.pdf?dl=0 (accessed on 3 July 2018).
31. Foertsch, C. 2016 Coworking Forecast. Available online: http://www.deskmag.com/en/2016-forecast-global-coworking-survey-results (accessed on 2 July 2018).
32. Waters-Lynch, J.; Potts, J.; Butcher, T.; Dodson, J.; Hurley, J. *Coworking: A Transdisciplinary Overview*; Working Paper 2016; RMIT University: Melbourne, Australia, 2016. [CrossRef]
33. Lange, B. Re-scaling Governance in Berlin's Creative Economy. *Cult. Unbound* **2011**, *3*, 187–208. [CrossRef]
34. Cohen, B.; Kietzmann, J. Ride On! Mobility Business Models for The Sharing Economy. *Organ. Environ.* **2014**, *27*, 279–296. [CrossRef]
35. Frenken, K.; Meelen, T.; Arets, M.; van de Glind, P. Smarter Regulation for the Sharing Economy, The Guardian. Available online: https://www.theguardian.com/science/political-science/2015/may/20/smarter-regulation-for-the-sharing-economy (accessed on 23 June 2018).
36. World Economic Forum. Collaboration in Cities: From Sharing to 'Sharing Economy', White Paper. 2017. Available online: https://www.weforum.org/whitepapers/collaboration-in-cities-from-sharing-to-sharing-economy (accessed on 23 June 2018).
37. Garrett, L.E.; Spreitzer, G.M.; Bacevice, P.A. Co-constructing a sense of community in coworking spaces. *Acad. Manag. Proc.* **2014**, *1*, 821–842. [CrossRef]
38. CBRE. U.S. Shared Workplaces. The Rise of the Shared Workplace in the Sharing Economy. 2016. Available online: https://www.cbre.us/global/agile-real-estate/how-the-sharing-economy-is-influencing-the-workplace# (accessed on 3 July 2018).
39. Fabian, L.; Munarin, S. *Re-Cycle Italy: Atlante*; LetteraVentidue: Siracusa, Italy, 2017; ISBN 978-88-6242-200-0.
40. Wood, B. The Co-Working Hubs Re-Energising Our Cities. Available online: https://thespaces.com/the-co-working-hubs-re-energising-our-cities/ (accessed on 15 June 2018).
41. Megna, F. Quando l'alleanza tra Giovani e Adulti Genera Valore Imprenditoriale. Il Caso Verona 311. Available online: https://www.tempi.it/alleanza-giovani-adulti-valore-imprenditoriale-verona-311#.Wzd_fdIzY2w (accessed on 30 June 2018).
42. Bruzzese, A. Creative production and urban regeneration in Milan. In *Milan. Productions, Spatial Patterns and Urban Change*; Armondi, S., Di Vita, S., Eds.; Routledge: Abingdon, UK, 2018; pp. 60–72. ISBN 978-1-138-24479-5.
43. Glaeser, E. *Triumph of the City: How our Greatest Invention Makes Us Richer, Smarter, Greener, Healthier and Happier*; Penguin Press: New York, NY, USA, 2011; ISBN 978-1594202773.
44. Landry, C. *The Creative City. A Toolkit for Urban Innovators*, 2nd ed.; Routledge: Abingdon, UK, 2008; ISBN 978-1844075980.
45. Musterd, S.; Murie, A. (Eds.) *Making Competitive Cities*; Wiley-Blackwell: Hoboken, NJ, USA, 2010; ISBN 978-1405194150.
46. Hanna, K. Spaces to Think: Innovation Districts and the Changing Geography of London's Knowledge Economy. *Centre Lond.* **2016**. Available online: https://www.centreforlondon.org/publication/innovation-districts/ (accessed on 25 June 2018).
47. Merkel, J. Coworking in the city. *Ephemera* **2015**, *15*, 121–139. Available online: http://www.ephemerajournal.org/contribution/coworking-city (accessed on 3 July 2018).

48. Capdevila, I. Co-working spaces and the localised dynamics of innovation in Barcelona. *Int. J. Innov. Manag.* **2015**, *19*. [CrossRef]
49. Kojo, I.; Nenonen, S. Evolution of co-working places: Drivers and possibilities. *Intell. Build. Int.* **2014**. [CrossRef]
50. Coiffard, X. Le Coworking Créateur de Richesse? Available online: http://angezanetti.com/le-coworking-createur-de-richesse/ (accessed on 3 July 2018).
51. ISPRA. Contaminated Sites of National Interest (SIN). Available online: http://www.isprambiente.gov.it/en/topics/soil-and-territory/copy_of_contaminated-sites/contaminated-sites-of-national-interest-sin (accessed on 1 July 2018).
52. Ginelli, E. Adaptive reuse of vacant office building in Milan. In Proceedings of the 41st IAHS World Congress, Algarve, Portugal, 13–16 September 2016.
53. Moffat, S. Coworking: The Regeneration Effect. Available online: https://medium.com/@SophyMoffat/coworking-spaces-the-regeneration-aec0bbe40eae (accessed on 29 June 2018).
54. Foertsch, C. How Profitable Are Coworking Spaces? Available online: http://www.deskmag.com/en/how-profitable-are-coworking-spaces-177 (accessed on 1 June 2018).
55. Geopoi. Available online: wwwt.agenziaentrate.gov.it/geopoi_omi/index.php (accessed on 3 July 2018).
56. Cabodi, C.; de Luca, A.; Di Gioia, A.; Toldo, A. *Small and Medium Sized Towns in Their Functional Territorial Context*; Case Study Report; TOWN 2014, Version 15; ESPON & University of Leuven: Leuven, Belgium, 2014.
57. Parrino, L. Coworking: Assessing the role of proximity in knowledge exchange. *Knowl. Manag. Res. Pract.* **2015**, *13*, 261–271. [CrossRef]
58. Armondi, S.; Bruzzese, A. Contemporary Production and Urban Change: The Case of Milan. *J. Urban Technol.* **2017**. [CrossRef]
59. Ferenstein, G. The Economic Impact of WeWork On Cities. Available online: https://www.forbes.com/sites/gregoryferenstein/2018/05/13/the-economic-impact-of-wework-on-cities/#683158254479 (accessed on 7 July 2018).

© 2018 by the authors. Licensee MDPI, Basel, Switzerland. This article is an open access article distributed under the terms and conditions of the Creative Commons Attribution (CC BY) license (http://creativecommons.org/licenses/by/4.0/).

Article

Coworking Spaces and New Social Relations: A Focus on the Social Streets in Italy

Mina Akhavan *, Ilaria Mariotti, Lisa Astolfi and Annapaola Canevari

Department of Architecture and Urban Studies—Politecnico di Milano, Milan 2013, Italy;
ilaria.mariotti@polimi.it (I.M.); lisa.astolfi@mail.polimi.it (L.A.); annapaola.canevari@polimi.it (A.C.)
* Correspondence: mina.akhavan@polimi.it; Tel.: +39-022-399-3928

Received: 11 October 2018; Accepted: 10 December 2018; Published: 24 December 2018

Abstract: The late 2000s witnessed a wide diffusion of innovative workplaces, named coworking spaces, designed to host creative people and entrepreneurs: the coworkers. Sharing the same space may provide a collaborative community to those kinds of workers who otherwise would not enjoy the relational component associated with a traditional corporate office. Coworking spaces can bring several benefits to freelancers and independent workers, such as knowledge transfer, informal exchange, cooperation, and forms of horizontal interaction with others, as well as business opportunities. Moreover, additional effects may concern the urban context: from community building, with the subsequent creation of social streets, and the improvement of the surrounding public space, to a wider urban revitalization, both from an economic and spatial point of view. These "indirect" effects are neglected by the literature, which mainly focuses on the positive impact on the workers' performance. The present paper aimed to fill the gap in the literature by exploring the effects of coworking spaces in Italy on the local context, devoting particular attention to the relation with social streets. To reach this goal, the answers (236) to an on-line questionnaire addressed to coworkers were analysed. The results showed that three quarters of the coworkers reported a positive impact of coworking on the urban and local context, where 10 out of 100 coworking spaces developed and/or participated in social streets located in Italian cities, but also in the suburban and peripheral areas.

Keywords: coworking spaces; social street; social relations; local communities

1. Introduction

In the context of a rising sharing economy and the growing knowledge of workers, the last two decades have witnessed the worldwide spread of the phenomenon of new workplaces known as "coworking spaces" (hereinafter CSs) [1]. One of the main strengths of CSs is they build a sense of community amongst the people working there (Coworkers-CWs), which may enable them to benefit from knowledge transfer, informal exchange, cooperation, and forms of horizontal interaction with others, as well as business opportunities [2–7]. Some studied have discussed the urban effects of CSs, including: (i) the improvement of the surrounding public space; (ii) the wider urban revitalization (from an economic and a spatial point of view); (iii) community building, with the subsequent creation of social streets (hereinafter SoSts) [8].

First founded in Italy, the concept of SoSts is a bottom-up approach to create communities at the neighbourhood level with the aim of shifting from online virtual meetings (on Facebook) to offline face to face gatherings in public spaces (such as the streets). Recently, CSs have shown interest in collaborating with such informal organizations to tackle social isolation and to create communities between coworkers and the residents living in the same neighbourhood.

Though the first CS was introduced in 2005, it is only in the past few years that we have seen a growing interest amongst scholars of varied disciplines to study and explore this concept as an alternative workplace, with respect to the traditional office space (see the Section 2.1). The term coworking was used more frequently before, often in contributions concerning business trends (Botsman & Rogers, 2011; Ferriss, 2009; Hunt, 2009). Regarding the SoSt, created in 2013; apart from some surveys that track the spread of these communities in Italy, no particular study has conducted a structured study to explore the importance and effects of the SoSt at a local urban scale. Both the phenomena of the CSs and SoSt are still nascent and need exploration through more in-depth studies that focus on relevant case-studies.

Within this framework, the present paper aims to contribute to the emergent literature on CSs and to fill the gap on the topic of collaboration between such workplaces with community-making organizations such as the SoSt. In particular, this study explores the local urban effects of CSs in Italy, with a particular focus on their interactions with the SoSts in Milan. Accordingly, to reach this goal, the results of the qualitative and quantitative research is described. On the one hand, data on CSs in Italy comes from the FARB research project—exploring the new workplaces, coworking spaces and makerspaces, in Italy—which has developed:

- an original georeferenced database on all CSs in Italy, with detailed information concerning the office spaces, provided services, etc.
- an on-line questionnaire to coworkers, with 236 responses.

Data on the SoSts, on the other hand, was mainly collected through desk research and on-site field data for specific cases in Milan.

The effects of CSs at the local level may include: (i) the extension of daily and weekly cycles of use (i.e., evening and night activities, weekend activities); (ii) the episodic participation in strengthening community ties (i.e., SoSts); (iii) the revitalization of existing retail and commercial activities; and (iv) the strengthening mini-clusters of creative and cultural productions [8]. The results of the empirical analysis showed that three quarters of the CWs reported a positive impact of the CS on the urban and local context, where 10 out of 100 CSs developed and or collaborated with SoSts streets located in several Italian cities, as well as in urban, suburban, or peripheral areas.

The remainder of this paper is structured as follows. Section 2 outlines the origins and main aspects of the two phenomena: CS and SoSt. The empirical insights on CSs in Italy, and on the relationship between the SoSt in the Lambrate neighbourhood (Milan) are presented in Section 3. The conclusion (Section 4) summarizes the findings, whilst introducing future lines of research.

2. Literature Review

2.1. New Forms of Workplace: The Rise of Coworking Spaces

Technological advancements and information and communication technologies (ICTs) have led to opportunities for changing the forms and nature of work, i.e., how, when, and where to perform various work activities [9]. Therefore, many individuals tend to work remotely as independent or freelance workers to make use of the autonomy and flexibility in space and time [10]. However, as shown in some studies, such workers may experience the feeling of isolation [11,12]. The knowledge economy is based on a highly skilled labour force and knowledge workers, and it has led to the rise of a creative class (Florida, 2002), which is drawn to the opportunities and amenities found in urban centres, and the demand for more collaborative and decentralized working trends [2]. These are some of the reasons that have given rise to the need for new forms of workplaces, such as coworking spaces, which are equipped with the necessary technological infrastructures, the ICTs, that favour high flexibility and hybridization, where people can work outside regular traditional office working hours. In this regard, some scholars argue that the borders between private homes, productive spaces, and socializing sites are becoming less evident [13,14].

Here, it is worth underlining the difference between such new emerging workplaces and the phenomenon of 'third places,' introduced by the sociologist Oldenburg [15], as informal social meeting places that are separate from the two conventional environments of the home (the first place) and the productive workspace/office (the second place). He argues that third places, such as community centres, cafes, bars, malls, libraries, parks, etc., are anchors of communities that may facilitate and foster broader, more creative interaction; hence, they are important for societies, public involvement, and the creation of a sense of place. In this regard, Martins [16] (p. 142) also adds that "The coffee shop, the pub or the park are more than spaces for pursuing creative lifestyles; they are part of a complex network of spaces that are used, and essential, for digital production". Others have asserted that such public spaces, which are not planned as official working environments, are increasingly being occupied as spaces for work [17].

Some scholars position new types of workplaces, such as CSs, within the wider collection of '*third spaces for work, learning and play*', which may facilitate formal productive activities within informal social interactions, often accompanied with direct/indirect learning programmes and the use of new technologies [18]. Unlike traditional third places such as libraries and bars, CSs are designed and planned specifically as facilitators for work by providing the basic necessities such as desk, technological needs (namely wifi), meeting rooms, and other equipment in order to develop their own network. CSs, therefore, offer geographical proximity and non-hierarchical relationships, which may create socialization and, consequently, business opportunities [2].

Since the birth of CSs in 2005, in the US, such sharing workplaces have spread worldwide over the last decade, and the coworking movement is reported to have roughly doubled in size each year since 2006 (Figure 1). In the growing literature on CSs, it is stressed the role of coworking in establishing a community; ensuring a quality of working behaviour as '*working-alone-together*', which involves a shared working environment and independent working activities [2,19–21].

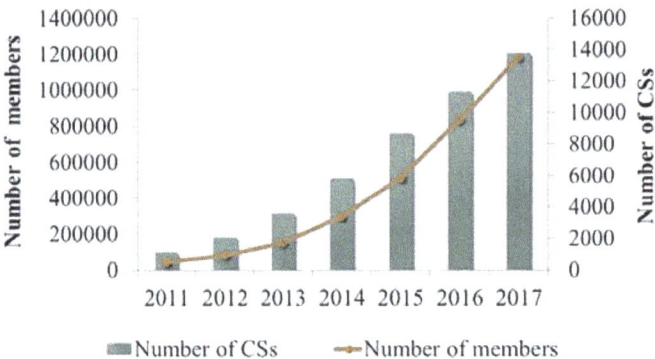

Figure 1. The number of CSs and their members (coworkers) worldwide (2011–2017). Source: own elaboration based on data from: 2017 Global CoWorking Survey, www.deskmag.com.

In the more recent literature, CSs are regarded as potential "serendipity accelerators" [3] (p. 8) designed to host knowledge workers, the creative class, and entrepreneurs, who endeavour to break isolation and to find a convivial environment that may favour meeting and collaboration [3]. Besides, CSs is considered as a "phenomenon that happens in shared, collaborative workspaces in which the emphasis is on community, relationship, productivity and creativity" [22] (p. 4). In other words, it provides localized spaces where independent professionals work while sharing resources and their knowledge with the rest of the community [23].

Furthermore, as mentioned beforehand, trends such as the rise of the digital economy, advancements in information and communication technologies, growth in entrepreneurship, freelance and teleworkers demands new workplaces and collaborative coworking culture, which enables the formation of an economy that may support community and innovation [24]. In this regard, Merkel [25] (p. 122) underlines that "as flexibly rentable, cost-effective and community-oriented workplaces, coworking spaces facilitate encounters, interaction and a fruitful exchange between diverse work, practice, and epistemic communities and cultures". Nevertheless, studies have also argued the fact that simple physical proximity of coworkers may not necessarily promote interaction and collaboration towards a sense of community [26], yet instead other factors such as social animation, engagement and enrolment among coworkers are seen essential [6]. Others have also confirmed the importance of CSs to embark upon collaborative activities in order to ensure highly productive working environment, considering the opportunities made available by these spaces, such as social interaction, networking and knowledge sharing [27].

Some scholars in the field of urban studies have made an attempt to investigate the location patterns and effects of CSs on the urban environment [8]. Findings of their empirical study on 68 CSs located in Milan shows that their location patterns resemble the service industries in urban areas, and mainly the so-called 'creative clusters'. Moreover, this research sheds light on some of the urban effects of CSs, such as the participation of CWs to local initiatives, contribution to urban revitalization trends, and the micro-scale physical transformations. Regarding the potential impact of CSs on the local urban context, a very recent publication on mid-sized cities in Ontario [28] has shed light on the importance of innovative, collaborative and inclusive approaches of such workplaces to local economic development; since they provide affordable, well-resourced spaces for new organizations and businesses, yet also for freelance workers and local entrepreneurs.

Although the academic literature on CSs is expanding, further research and more detailed studies are still needed to explore the dynamics of CSs at the local level, and more specifically to understand their interaction and role in neighbourhood communities. This paper, hence, aims to fill the gap in the literature by focusing on these aspects concerning the insertion of CSs within the new made-in-Italy phenomenon: *Social Streets*, which is explored in the following sections.

2.2. From A Facebook Group to a Neighbourhood Community: The Phenomenon of Social Streets

Gaspar and Glaeser [29] argue two opposing effects of improvements in telecommunications technology on face-to face interactions: they may decrease and become electronically (via social network services for instance), or in contrary the contacts may increase thanks to the technology. So, it is true that people tend to interact more virtually and electronically and may need physical places to meet. SoSts are, therefore, a new and innovative answer that goes exactly in this direction: *"tame places, make them familiar"* (Marc Augé's preface for the report on SoSts in Milan:"Vicini e connessi" [30]). A SoSt is born from the desire of the residents of an anti-social street to seek and create participatory and collective-meeting points in their neighbourhood, i.e., places to meet and to know each other; to do things together and help one another.

In cities, people have always needed places to meet one another and to be able to recognize urban elements, such as squares, public places, parks, and roads. Yet, cities, often, end up in creating *ghetto* neighbourhoods (gated communities) where cars dominate; people are isolated in their apartments and public spaces are increasingly hostile and unused. In recent years, however, a new kind of public space, called the SoSt, was created from the bottom, by the residents themselves [31].

One can consider the SoSt as "new places", where the point of reference is the public space, here is the street and the spaces around it. Unknown people who live on an anonymous street begin to get to know and meet one another; collaborate to transform the neighbourhood into a social place that is rich in relationships. Social networks are the perfect platform to trigger these ties between unknown neighbours. Therefore, people may become familiar with others easily through overcoming the initial threshold of the face-to-face encounter with strangers; online knowledge and collaboration quickly transforms into a real community that lives and regenerates the neighbourhood.

The idea of "Social Street" in Italy originates from the experience of the Facebook group "Residents in Via Fondazza-Bologna", born, in September 2013, from the observation of the general impoverishment of social relationships, which causes feelings of loneliness and loss of sense of belonging; urban degradation and lack of social control of the territory (See the website www.socialstreet.it). As a form of neighbourhood community, the SoSt aspires to promote good neighbourly practices; to socialize with the neighbours on their own way, and to establish links, share needs, exchange skills and knowledge; to carry out projects of common interest and gain all the benefits that derive from greater social interaction. SoSt may, therefore, allow people to socialize and to motivate virtuous circles of reciprocity and trust. The requisites to consider a SoSt is different, would be the spatial proximity [32]: the SoSt are served to spatially connect people, in limited portions of the district (the street or the neighbourhood); other main features are: social innovation, social inclusion and groundless.

The definition of SoSt is unique, but its characteristics may vary by: the number of participants, size of the neighbourhood, and the people's level of participation and commitment to the group. The first phase of launching a SoSt entails creating a neighbourhood based group on Facebook. This is the first step in which people may get in touch on the digital platform, asking for information and help from their online neighbours. The second step is the offline meeting, in which the neighbours decide to socialize even outside the virtual group page, to build links that are defined as "real". In the third phase (defined as "virtuous"), they can move from simple knowledge seeking to a real collaboration with common interests or utilities. In this phase, the neighbours collaborate for the sake of their area's common goods; for instance, arrangement of uncultivated flowerbeds, interventions on degraded areas or small redevelopment actions, etc.

The idea of the term "social street" was coined by the founder, joining the two key concepts: social network and place of real socialization (the street). The transition from the group of *via Fondazza* to the birth and diffusion of SoSts has necessitated the creation of a website to communicate, collect and disseminate experiences and good practices of the SoSt (see http://www.socialstreet.it/).

3. Empirical Insights

3.1. Exploring Coworking Spaces in Italy

Within the FARB research project (entitled "New working spaces. Promises of innovations, effects on the economic and urban context", which has been funded by Department of Architecture and Urban Studies (DAStU)—Politecnico di Milano) exploring new workplaces—coworking spaces and makers spaces—in Italy, the CSs located in Italy have been identified and mapped: total number of 549 CSs are recorded, of which about 51% are located in the Italian metropolitan cities, with Milan (97), Rome (46), Turin (18), and Florence (16) hosting about half of them (Figure 2).

Figure 2. The location of CS in Italy at the beginning of 2018. Source [7].

Besides, an on-line questionnaire has been sent to the coworkers (via the coworking managers). By July 2017, 236 coworkers have answered, from 137 CSs located in 19 Italian cities: 44% female and 56% male; 52% belong to the age group 36–50, followed by coworkers aged between 25 to 35 (38%), over 51 (9%), and those between aged 19–24 (1%).

As mentioned beforehand, the city of Milan hosts the majority of CS (97), which are agglomerated into five areas (Figure 3). The main location determinants of CS in urban areas, as already discussed by Mariotti et al. [8]:

(1) the high density of business activities, which is a proxy for urbanization and localization economies, as well as market size;
(2) the proximity to universities and research centres, which is a proxy for the availability of skilled labour force and business opportunities;
(3) the presence of a good local public transport network, which is a proxy for the level of accessibility.

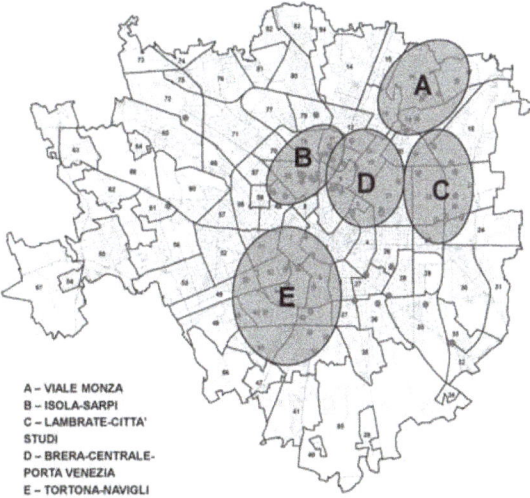

Figure 3. The agglomeration of CS in Milan. Source [8] (p. 10).

3.2. The Growing Number of Social Streets in Italy

From the studies, it was estimated that in the last quarter of 2013, just after the launch of the first SoSt, the total number rose to 140, and then up to 454 in January 2017 [30]. From the studies carried out by the SoSt observatory, the largest number is located in North-West 143 (34%) and North-East 133 (32%), we find 78 (19%) in the Centre, 36 (8%) in the South and Islands 30 (7%) [30]. Currently, in Italy there are a total number of 100,000 SoSt members (streeters), of which about 50% are residing in Milan.

This phenomenon is also emerging outside national borders: in January 2018 the SoSt observatory surveyed SoSts in Warsaw, Trondheim, Nelson Glenduan, Madison, Amsterdam, Lisbon, Montreal and Agudos [30]. In some cases, the SoSts were established from people visiting Italy who participated in one of them and then repeated this experience in their country.

The difference in numbers between the North and South can be associated with the technological development, and social innovation propensity in the northern areas. Regarding the number of SoSt, Lombardy leads with 112, immediately followed by Emilia Romagna with 100, then Lazio with 47 (Figure 4). Certainly because these are the regions that host the most important cities; in fact in Milan there are 77 SoSt, followed by Bologna with 67 and Rome with 34.

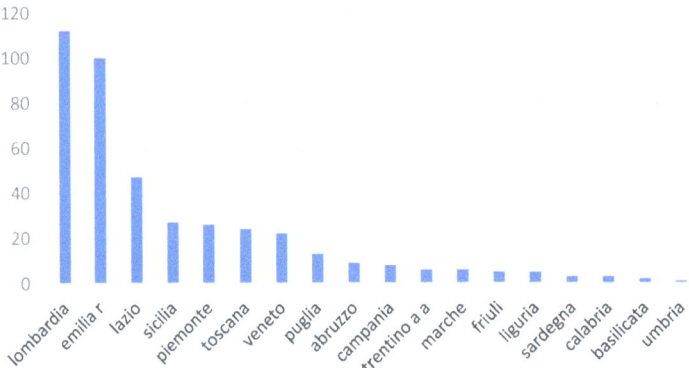

Figure 4. The location of Social Streets in the Italian provinces. Source: authors' elaboration from the reference [30].

Between January 2017 and January 2018, some cities have experienced a positive trend (Milan, Bologna and Rome), others have remained stable, while some have even closed their SoSt. Milan remains in the lead also for the number of followers in the Facebook page, about 50,000; once again followed by Bologna with 13,000 members. Yet, not always the number of SoSt corresponds to the number of streeters. For example, Novara and Brescia both have two SoSts, but the first has 5 members, while the second has almost 1000.

Milan is the capital of northern Italy, and the financial and economic core of the country. Many people have chosen to settle in this city, and among them there are people who do not appreciate the coldness of social relationships. But if you get to know your neighbours, and you could rely on them for little or important things, this could also improve your quality of life.

Milan is, hence, the right city for the expansion of this phenomenon, as it has always been characterized by innovation, creativity and development [33]. Through the expansion of the phenomenon, in the city there has been a growth boom in 2014, with the opening of 39 SoSt. As for other cities of the province, there are a total number of 10 SoSt. Indeed the numbers are significantly lower than Milan, but still significant.

In January 2018, 1760 members are registered in the SoSt groups, and some of them have confirmed as points of reference for the district, while we must remember that not all of them are active in the same way; not all are active both online and offline; senior citizens are not always the most active while count as the highest number of subscribers to Facebook groups.

Among the social networks in Milan, the one with the highest number of people registered is "San Gottardo-Meda-Montegani" with 7550 members, followed by Nolo Social District which, despite being the youngest, already has 5579 members. The spatial distribution within the city is not homogeneous: the SoSt have no administrative boundaries, they are fluid groups that by definition connect the neighbours of a street and their surroundings and are linked to the more social characteristics of some areas rather than others; such as the presence of parks or meeting places (namely Darsena, Navigli and Duomo).

3.3. The Effects of CSs on the Local Context and Collaboration with SoSts

As concerns the effects of CS on the urban environment and the neighbourhood, the answers of the 236 coworkers emphasise the agreements with local services as the most significant impact on the surrounding neighbourhoods, which can contribute, directly or indirectly to a degree of urban regeneration (see also [34]). Moreover, other activities which may show a potential higher impact on the neighbourhood are: organizing charity events, participating at a SoSt and belonging to an Ethical Purchasing Group (Gruppo di Acquisto Solidale—GAS) (Figure 5). These activities reveal the importance of CS as social and cultural hubs, in some cases with specific welfare-related activities such as childcare [33].

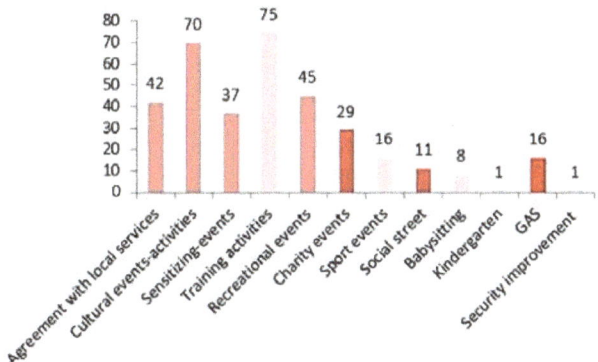

Figure 5. Activities OFFERED by the CSs. Source: [33].

3.4. The Case of "Lambrate-Milano-Social Street"

Out of a total number of 97 CSs in Milan, 19 are located in areas of SoSt that give rise to initiatives of different types within the district (other than to their coworkers). An example is provided by the case of Lambrate Social Street in Milan, which will be discussed in the next section.

In the last twenty years, the Lambrate neighbourhood, located in the Eastern part of the city, has experienced an urban regeneration process partly driven by: design, art, new spaces for work (such as CSs) open air at the markets, music and the desire of its inhabitants to live in a "new" neighbourhood. Since 2010, Lambrate hosts events of the Fuorisalone related to the Salone del Mobile (Milan Design Week). In recent years, a virtuous collaboration between coworkers, inhabitants and entrepreneurs of the district has been consolidated, which is progressively leading the area towards a process of urban regeneration "from below".

In 2015, with a few members on the Facebook page (all being neighbours), the SoSt Residents in Lambrate—Milan was formed. It has grown exponentially over the years, especially at the first auto events organized in Piazza Rimembranze, the main square of the district, a roundabout that was poorly used as a parking space and surrounded by car traffic. The benches were often occupied by families of nomads and homeless people, being deserted by the inhabitants of the neighbourhood as an unsafe place. The square's liveability issues was strongly felt by the residents; one of the main demands that emerged during the first meeting was, indeed, that of giving back life to the square.

Therefore, the idea of creating a shared garden was born, with the help of many residents who came on a Saturday morning in the square with plants, flowers, boxes, brooms and black bags to clean up. The children painted the boxes, prepared and spread seeds bombs. With the help of some creative designers and architects in Lambrate, the neighbours have built a beautiful garden in the square. Within a few months, the shared garden has become an important place for evening aperitives, to get to gather and communicate with one another.

These series of events has given a lot of visibility to the SoSt, the number of members has surged. Even other associations in the area have contacted them to make a network. Today the ViviLambrate Group—which was founded in October 2014 in a spontaneous and self-organized form, by a set of organizations and associations based in the Municipality 3, networked with the aim of promoting cultural and social initiatives to revitalize the Lambrate district—is active; it groups together various associations in the area, including the SoSt, and organizes once a month the Saturday of Lambrate, with activities and initiatives to repopulate and revive the square. The SoSt has also participated in several Saturdays of Lambrate with the counter of used clothes, a very successful initiative and high level of participation.

The Group promotes the redevelopment of the public and private spaces of the area, from the historical districts, up to the former industrial zones that constitute a great heritage yet little appreciated not only by the Lambrate citizens, but also by the Milanese. ViviLambrate's approach is to activate the human, creative and productive resources of the district and to promote citizen participation, in collaboration with the Municipality 3 and the support of the Institutions.

ViviLambrate is formed by 11 different organizations, which aggregates several thousand citizens of the area, yet also firms and private social actors active in different cultural, artistic and social fields, informal groups of citizens, start-ups, CSs, galleries of art and freelancers. From this network of experiences and the voluntary work of many citizens, the initiatives "There is life in the square! and "The Saturdays of Lambrate", enlivens the streets of the neighbourhood every month, with particular attention to the elderly and children, and strong creative and supportive spirit.

These have undoubtedly generated interest and convinced architects and creative designers to settle even temporarily in the district using the existing coworking spaces. As mentioned beforehand, this is establishing a virtuous collaboration between coworkers, inhabitants and traders of the district that is progressively taking the area to a real urban regeneration "from below" (Figure 6).

Figure 6. Activities offered by the CSs. Source: Lisa Astolfi (co-author).

4. Conclusions

While places and modes of work are becoming increasingly collective and collaborative, citizens (residents and city users) increasingly express the need for new social spaces and places to recognize themselves: *places to tame and make familiar*. In the parts of the city in which these two phenomena occur simultaneously, spontaneous processes of shared urban regeneration, from below, can be triggered. This process, apparently longer and more tiring than a project with a top-down approach, offers higher guarantees of success over time as it directly involves all the social and economic forces (without discrimination) of the interested area in all of its phases of conception and realization.

Both the two phenomena of CSs and SoSts are served as important 'third places' [15]; the former being an alternative workplace and the latter a place for social gathering where broader, more creative interaction in a free non-privatized environment is encouraged. With the main aim to understand the interaction between these coworkers and streeters, the present paper has discussed the first outcomes of a research study on the relationship between new workplaces, such as CSs, and SoSts. As stated previously, in Milan 19 CSs out of 97 are located in areas of SoSts and this gives rise to initiatives located in the district (other than to their coworkers) of which the presented case of Lambrate-Milano-Social Street is just one example of a much wider phenomenon.

The paper has, therefore, put in evidence how the new workplaces, which emphasise the sense of community, can foster the development of collaboration with SoSts and subsequently contribute to the improvement of urban spaces and eventually urban regeneration. Therefore, tailored policies may be designed to foster the growth of CSs, especially considering depressed areas.

Author Contributions: All four authors have equally contributed to the design and implementation of the research. More specifically, the introduction, Sections 2, 3.1 and 3.3 have been written by I.M. and M.A.; Sections 3.2, 3.4 and 4 have been mostly developed and written by L.A. and A.C.

Funding: The project has been funded by FARB (2016) research project "New working spaces. Promises of innovations, effects on the economic and urban context" at Department of Architecture and Urban Studies (DAStU)—Politecnico di Milano, Coordinator: Ilaria Mariotti; Mina Akhavan was part of the research team.

Conflicts of Interest: The authors declare no conflict of interest.

References

1. Durante, G.; Turvani, M. Coworking, the Sharing Economy, and the City: Which Role for the "Coworking Entrepreneur"? *Urban Sci.* **2018**, *2*, 83. [CrossRef]
2. Spinuzzi, C. Working Alone Together Coworking as Emergent Collaborative Activity. *J. Bus. Tech. Commun.* **2012**, *26*, 399–441. [CrossRef]
3. Moriset, B. Building new places of the creative economy. The rise of coworking spaces. In Proceedings of the 2nd Geography of Innovation International Conference, Utrecht, The Netherlands, 23–25 January 2014.
4. Gandini, A. The Rise of Coworking Spaces: A Literature Review. *Ephemer. Theory Politics Organ.* **2015**, *15*, 193–205.
5. Parrino, L. Coworking: Assessing the role of proximity in knowledge exchange. *Knowl. Manag. Res. Pract.* **2015**, *13*, 261–271. [CrossRef]
6. Mariotti, I.; Akhavan, M. The Effects of Coworking Spaces on Local Communities in the Italian Context. *Territorio* **2018**, accepted for publication.
7. Mariotti, I.; Akhavan, M. The Location of Coworking Spaces in Urban vs. Peripheral Areas. **2018**, under review.
8. Mariotti, I.; Pacchi, C.; Di Vita, S. Coworking Spaces in Milan: ICTs, Proximity, and Urban Effects. *J. Urban Technol.* **2017**, *24*. [CrossRef]
9. Joroff, M.L. Workplace Mind Shifts. *J. Corp. Real Estate* **2002**, *4*, 266–274. [CrossRef]
10. Singh, P.; Bhandarkar, A.; Rai, S. *Millennials and the Workplace: Challenges for Architecting the Organizations of Tomorrow*; Sage: New Delhi, India, 2012.
11. Golden, T.D.; Veiga, J.F.; Dino, R.N. The impact of professional isolation on teleworker job performance and turnover intentions: Does time spent teleworking, interacting face-to-face, or having access to communication-enhancing technology matter? *J. Appl. Psychol.* **2008**, *93*, 1412–1421. [CrossRef]
12. Cooper, C.D.; Kurland, N.B. Telecommuting, professional isolation, and employee development in public and private organizations. *J. Organ. Behav.* **2002**, *23*, 511–532. [CrossRef]
13. Moriset, B.; Malecki, E.J. Organization versus space: The paradoxical geographies of the digital economy. *Geogr. Compass* **2009**, *3*, 256–274. [CrossRef]
14. Fonner, K.L.; Stache, L.C. All in a day's work, at home: Teleworkers' management of micro role transitions and the work–home boundary. *New Technol. Work Employ.* **2012**, *27*, 242–257. [CrossRef]
15. Oldenburg, R. *The Great Good Place: Cafes, Coffee Shops, Bookstores, Bars, Hair Salons, and Other Hangouts at the Heart of a Community*; Da Capo Press: Cambridge, MA, USA, 1989; Available online: https://books.google.it/books?id=o4ZFCgAAQBAJ (accessed on 16 December 2018).

16. Martins, J. The Extended Workplace in a Creative Cluster: Exploring Space(s) of Digital Work in Silicon Roundabout. *J. Urban Des.* **2015**, *20*, 125–145. [CrossRef]
17. Di Marino, M.; Lapintie, K. Emerging Workplaces in Post-Functionalist Cities. *J. Urban Technol.* **2017**, *24*, 5–25. [CrossRef]
18. Waters-Lynch, J.; Potts, J.; Butcher, T.; Dodson, J.; Hurley, J. Coworking: A Transdisciplinary Overview. 2016. Available online: https://ssrn.com/abstract=2712217 or http://dx.doi.org/10.2139/ssrn.2712217 (accessed on 16 December 2018).
19. Bilandzic, M. Connected learning in the library as a product of hacking, making, social diversity and messiness. *Interact. Learn. Environ.* **2016**, *24*, 158–177. [CrossRef]
20. Capdevila, I. Coworkers, Makers, and Fabbers Global, Local and Internal Dynamics of Innovation in Localized Communities in Barcelona. Ph.D. Thesis, HEC Montréal École affiliée à l'Université de Montréal, Montreal, QC, Canada, 2014.
21. Capdevila, I. Different Entrepreneurial Approaches in Localized Spaces of Collaborative Innovation. 2014. Available online: https://ssrn.com/abstract=2533448 (accessed on 16 December 2018).
22. Fuzi, A.; Clifton, N.; Loudon, G. New in-house organizational spaces that support creativity and innovation: The co-working space. In Proceedings of the R & D Management Conference, Stuttgart, Germany, 3–6 June 2014.
23. Capdevila, I. Knowledge Dynamics in Localized Communities: Coworking Spaces as Microclusters. Available online: https://ssrn.com/abstract=2414121 (accessed on 9 December 2013).
24. Davies, A.; Tollervey, K. *The Style of Coworking: Contemporary Shared Workspaces*; Prestel Verlag: Munich, Germany, 2013.
25. Merkel, J. Coworking in the city. *Ephemer. Theory Politics Organ.* **2015**, *15*, 121–139.
26. Ibert, O. Relational distance: Sociocultural and time–spatial tensions in innovation practices. *Environ. Plan. A* **2010**, *42*, 187. [CrossRef]
27. Bueno, S.; Rodríguez-Baltanás, G.; Gallego, M.D. Coworking spaces: A new way of achieving productivity. *J. Facil. Manag.* **2018**. [CrossRef]
28. Jamal, A. Coworking spaces in mid-sized cities: A partner in downtown economic development. *Environ. Plan. A* **2018**, *50*, 773–788. [CrossRef]
29. Gaspar, J.; Glaeser, E.L. Information Technology and the Future of Cities. *Urb. Econ.* **1998**, *43*, 136–156. [CrossRef]
30. Pasqualini, C. *Vicini e Connessi. Rapporto Sulle Social Street a Milano*; Fondazione Feltrinelli: Milan, Italia, 2018.
31. Delpini, M. *Per un'arte del buon Vicinato*; Casa editrice ambrosiana: Milano, Italia, 2018.
32. Boschma, R. Role of Proximity in Interaction and Performance: Conceptual and Empirical Challenges. *Reg. Stud.* **2005**, *39*, 41–45. [CrossRef]
33. Mariotti, I.; Pacchi, C. Coworking spaces and urban effects in Italy. In Proceedings of the Urban Studies Foundation Seminar Series, EKKE, Athens, Greece, 8–9 February 2018.
34. Mariotti, I. The attractiveness of Milan and the spatial patterns of international firms. In *Milan: Productions, Spatial Patterns and Urban Change*; Armondi, S., Di Vita, S., Eds.; Routledge: London, UK; New York, NY, USA, 2018; pp. 48–59.

© 2018 by the authors. Licensee MDPI, Basel, Switzerland. This article is an open access article distributed under the terms and conditions of the Creative Commons Attribution (CC BY) license (http://creativecommons.org/licenses/by/4.0/).

Article

A Framework for Assessing Democratic Qualities in Collaborative Economy Platforms: Analysis of 10 Cases in Barcelona

Mayo Fuster Morell [1] and Ricard Espelt [2,*]

[1] Berkman Klein Center for Internet and Society, Harvard University, Cambridge, MA 02138, USA; mayo.fuster@eui.eu
[2] Internet Interdisciplinary Institute, Open University of Catalonia, 08289 Barcelona, Spain
* Correspondence: ricardespelt@uoc.edu; Tel.: +34-667-515-503

Received: 2 June 2018; Accepted: 21 July 2018; Published: 25 July 2018

Abstract: The term "collaborative economy" or "collaborative economy platforms" refers to exchange, sharing, and collaboration in the consumption and production of capital and labor among distributed groups, supported by a digital platform. Collaborative economies' use is growing rapidly and exponentially, creating high expectations of sustainability and their potential to contribute to the democratization of the economy. However, collaborative economy platforms lack a holistic framework to assess their sustainability and pro-democratization qualities. In addition, there is confusion about platforms which present themselves as collaborative when they actually are not, and similar uncertainties and ambiguities are associated with diverse models. To address this confusion, this article provides a framework for assessing the pro-democratic qualities of collaborative economy initiatives. It was applied to 10 cases in the context of the city of Barcelona. The methods used in this study include mapping and typifying 10 collaborative economy cases in the city, structured and in-depth interviews, and a co-creation session. The results indicate the presence of several modalities for favoring democratic values in a collaborative economy.

Keywords: collaborative economy; platform cooperativism; democratic quality

1. Introduction

The term "collaborative economy" or "collaborative economy platforms" refers to exchange, sharing, and collaboration in the consumption and production of capital and labor among distributed groups, supported by a digital platform. The use of collaborative economies is growing rapidly and exponentially, bringing high expectations of sustainability for its potential to contribute to the democratization of the economy. However, collaborative economy platforms lack a holistic framework for assessing these sustainability and pro-democratization qualities. In addition, there is confusion about platforms that present themselves as collaborative when they actually are not, and similar uncertainties and ambiguities are associated with diverse models [1].

The disruptive impact of the best-known economy platform model, that of extractionist "unicorn" corporation (a privately held startup company valued at over $1 billion) platforms such as Uber and Airbnb, has provoked huge controversy [2]. Successful "alternative" and truly collaborative models exist, such as open commons, platform cooperativism, and decentralized organizations based on social economy and open knowledge, but these have received limited research attention.

First, this article reviews collaborative economy conceptualization and previous attempts to classify collaborative economies to provide a framework of pro-democratic qualities. Then, we apply the resulting methodology in 10 relevant cases located in the city of Barcelona. At that time, we show the results and, finally, present the conclusions and discussion.

1.1. Collaborative Economy

The term collaborative economy or collaborative platforms economy (which can only be considered collaborative and commons-oriented under a particular set of conditions) refers to the exchange (matching supply and demand), sharing and collaborating in the consumption, and production of capital and labor among distributed groups supported by a digital platform [3]. It is growing rapidly and exponentially, and has become a top priority for governments around the globe (i.e., European Commission, 2016 [4]). However, the collaborative economy suffers from important challenges. We would like to highlight and address two of them: (1) The platform collaborative economy is creating high sustainability expectations for its potential to contribute to a sustainable development of society [5–9], and for its potential to contribute to the democratization of economy [10]. However, the platform collaborative economy lacks a holistic framework to assess these sustainability and pro-democratization qualities. Furthermore, the sustainable design of platform has considered questions of technological and economic aspects, but has not integrated other sustainability relevant questions, such as the environmental impact, gender and inclusion, or its policy implications, lacking a proper multidisciplinary perspective of the platform economy; (2) There is a confusion about the platforms which present themselves as collaborative while actually they are not, and similar uncertainties and ambiguities are associated with diverse models. The disruptive impact of the best known platform economy model, that of Unicorn extractionist corporation platforms such as Uber and Airbnb, is provoking huge controversy [2]. Successful "alternative" and truly collaborative models exist, such as open commons, platform cooperativism and decentralized organizations based on a social economy and open knowledge, with examples such as Fairmondo. Nonetheless, these have received neither policy nor research attention. Additionally, there is a lack of a classification system that helps to establish the difference.

1.2. Previous Attempts to Classify Models of Collaborative Economy

There have been previous attempts to classify collaborative economies. The Spanish Association of the Digital Economy (Adigital) carried out a study, "Collaborative models are on demand in digital platforms" [11], to distinguish among the activities of: (1) Collaborative Economy: a digital platform serving as an intermediary between equals, either between organizations or individuals, with or without economic consideration; (2) Economy on Demand: a digital platform serving as an intermediary between a professional and a user; and (3) Service Economy: a digital platform that, without disintermediation, connects users with goods for their temporary use, adapting to the effective use time required by users and making the spatial location more flexible.

If we focus on the first group, we see that it includes projects with such highly disparate approaches as AirBnB (a vacation rental platform owned by a multinational) and Goteo (a crowdfunding platform based on commons principles owned by a foundation). In fact, the interface or platform design both conditions and predefines the social relations—related, for example, to interaction mechanisms, regulation, profile information, or promotion—among users [12,13].

Netnographic investigation of 55 collaborative consumption platforms in The Triple Impact Assessment of P2P Collaborative Consumption in Europe project [14] defined three types of collaborative consumption platforms: (1) Network Oriented Platforms (e.g., Airbnb, Blablacar, TimeRepublick, or Eatwith), where users have many forms of communication in order to get digital reputation and show confidence to engage other users; (2) Transaction Oriented Platforms (Vibbo or Nolotiro), with fewer communication and interaction tools, focused on convenience and more connected to the traditional consumer and provider roles; and (3) Community Oriented Platforms (WWOPP voluntaries network, La Colmena que dice sí or CiroSel), linked to a social or environmental mission and to a strong code of conduct. These platforms develop some collective rules beyond self-management regulation based on the capacity of the individuals to manage their confidence networks. Gordo et al. [15] determined the relevance of the transformation of the consumer into an entrepreneur or the new role of prosumer. In the end, in some platforms, users provide knowledge, properties, or services while intermediaries are those who really earn money [8]. At the same time, netnographic research highlights the necessity to precisely review how each platform initiative works and the platform's social, economic, and environmental impacts [15,16].

In this context, where a critical and holistic review of digital platforms that promote the collaborative economy is required, a new key concept emerges: "platform cooperativism". According to Scholz [17], a digital platform must be based on collective ownership, decent payment and security of income for its workers, the transparency and portability of the data created, appreciation and recognition of the value generated by the platform's activity, collective decision-making, a protective legal framework, transferable protection of workers and the coverage of social benefits, protection against arbitrary conduct in the rating system, rejection of excessive supervision in the workplace, and, finally, the right of the workers to disconnect. As stated by Scholz, on the one hand, the platforms must be shaped around the values of cooperativism. On the other hand, digital tools must amplify the scalability and the social and economic impact of cooperative organizations. At the same time, Fuster Morell [10] indicated that the very construction of technology platforms is not a minor issue, and that cooperative platforms should adopt open software and licenses. In short, creating a self-managed governance that allows the articulation of community development around the digital commons [18] has to be approached as "open cooperativism" [19], an antithesis of the unicorn and corporate platforms.

There have been previous attempts to establish delimitations in collaborative production or commons-based peer production (CBPP) [20]. This is the case of the four freedoms of free software. The four freedoms are used in relation to whether a particular software program qualifies as "free" software. A program is free software if it adequately gives users all four freedoms. Although the four freedoms for software might resemble what we are trying to do here, CB relates to a collective process and delimitation criteria for the features of that process. By contrast, the definition of free software is individualistically driven and built based on individual freedoms, not the features of the process as a whole.

From our point of view, it is necessary to consider the complexity of the classification of collaborative economy platforms, and specific analyses are required to distinguish models. For example, during the last three years, a new type of agrofood consumer platform was spreading its activity in Barcelona: La Colmena que dice sí. Despite using an approach similar to that of cooperatives to engage potential members (disintermediation between local producers and consumers), the organization's values were far from the values of social and economic solidarity [21]. Departing from this reflection, in this paper, we provide a framework to characterize models of collaborative economy and visualize their qualities.

In this article, we propose a framework for the democratic qualities of collaborative economy platforms. The framework considers the dimensions of governance design, economical strategy, technological base, knowledge policies, and social responsibility regarding externalization impact of the platforms. The democratic balance is an analytical tool that helps to visualize the democratic qualities of collaborative economy initiatives, differentiate models, provide insight into the sustainability of their design, and inform technological development (see Figure 1).

Figure 1. Procommons collaborative economy analytical star framework.

1.3. A Framework of Democratic Qualities of Collaborative Economy Platforms

The democratic qualities of the collaborative economy are articulated around three main dimensions, with in six subdivisions:

1. Governance and Economic: We believe that these two sub-dimensions are interconnected. Thus, the way that the project or platform is governed is connected to the underlying economic model.

1.a. Governance: This aspect regards democratic enterprises and involving the community generated value in the platform governance. This aspect also regards the decision-making model of the organization, and mechanisms and political rules of participation in the digital platform.

1.b. Economic model: This aspect regards whether the project's financing model is based on private capital, ethical finance, or a distributed fund (crowdfunding or match-funding), the business models, mechanisms of economic transparency, how far profitability is driven in the whole plan, distribution of value generated, and equity payment and labor rights. This aspect regards ensuring equitable and timely remuneration, and access to benefits and rights for workers (maximization of income, salary predictability, safe income, protection against arbitrary actions, rejection of excessive vigilance at the workplace, and the right to disconnect).

2. Knowledge and Technological policies: In the same sense, knowledge and technological policies are interconnected. Thus, the adoption of certain technological tools or licenses is going to impact the way the platform promotes knowledge.

2.a. Knowledge policy: Regards the property type, as established by the license used (free licenses or proprietary licenses) for the content and knowledge generated, type of data (open or not), the ability to download data (and in which formats), and the promotion of the transparency of algorithms, programs, and data. This aspect regards privacy awareness, the protection of property including personal data, and preventing abuse and the collection or sharing of data without consent. This aspect also regards guaranteeing the portability of data and reputation.

2.b. Technological policy: This aspect regards the mode of property and freedom associated with type of software used and its license (free or proprietary) and the model of technology architecture: distributed (using blockchain, for example) or centralized (software as a service).

3. Social responsibility and impact. These dimensions relate to any source of awareness and responsibility regarding the externalities and negative impacts, such as social exclusion and social inequalities, the inclusion of gender, regarding the equal access to the platform of people with all kinds of income and circumstances in an equitable and impartial way (without discrimination). This aspect regards compliance with health and safety standards that protect the public, and the environmental impact (promoting sustainable practices that reduce emissions and waste, taking into account the rebound effect they can generate and the most efficient use of resources, the origin and production

conditions of the goods and services they offer, minimizing resource use, and recycling capacity), and the impact in the policy arena, and the preservation of the right to the city of its inhabitants and the common good of the city. This aspect also regards the protection of the general interest, public space, and basic human rights such as access to housing.

2. Materials and Methods

The methodology, aimed at testing the application of the above six democratic qualities, was based on an in-depth 10 case study comparison. Data collection was based on digital ethnography (to collect indicators for the cases and get familiar with them), co-creation sessions with the cases, and an interview with each of the cases. Data were collected in May 2017. Data analysis combined qualitative and visual analysis of data from co-creation sessions and interviews.

2.1. Sample

The empirical work departs from a previous mapping of 1000 cases of Collaborative Economy in Barcelona, based on the P2P Value directory on collaborative economy. From these resources, we selected 10 based on the following criteria:

1. Projects with activity in Barcelona.
2. Projects based on collaborative production.
3. Projects with a significant level of activity, rather than in a very preliminary stage.
4. Projects with a social orientation, meaning closer to the cooperative platform than to the unicorn platform scope.
5. We selected the cases to ensure diversity, and based on being significantly relevant.

The cases are El Recetario, SmartIB, Goteo, Katuma, Bdtonline, XOBB, FreeSound, Sentilo, eReuse, and Pam a Pam. A description of each is provided in Section 3.

2.2. Indicators Criteria

For each dimension, we assessed two variables with three grades of accomplishment.

2.3. Analytical Methods

We performed a previous web observation to collect more information about the selected platforms, a co-creation session (5 May 2017), and an interview of the 10 cases, following the case study methodology [22]. Departing from our 10 cases chosen, we designed a co-creation session divided into three steps with three main objectives. In the first part, the participants indicated their evolution in the form of a graph, highlighted milestones, and projected their future evolution. In the second part, each platform actively shared how their approach to each point of the commons star diagram (Figure 1: economic model, social responsibility, knowledge and technological policy, and governance model). Finally, all participants identified the challenges of a collaborative procommon economy in terms of specific needs of the sector, technological demands, and public policy recommendations.

3. Results: Analytical Framework for the Democratic Qualities of 10 Cases of Collaborative Economy in Barcelona

In this section, we present the analytical framework of the democratic qualities of collaborative economy (Figure 1) applied to 10 cases that we analyzed based on each collaborative economy's performance of the star of commons qualities (El Recetario, SMart IB, Goteo, Katuma, Bdtonline, FreeSound, XOBB, eReuse, Sentilo, and Pam a Pam). See Table 1 for a comparison of the cases on their performance of each of the qualities.

Table 1. Indicators of procommons collaborative economy assessment.

Dimension	Indicator	Fulfillment	Partial Fulfillment	Unfulfillment
GOV	Type of organization	Procommon organization (public administration)	Democratic type of governance (foundation, association, cooperative)	Private company
	Open participation	Governance is based on open participation	Some participation tools are provided	No participation tools are provided
ECON	Goal	Non-profit	Middle profit	Profit
	Transparency	Any member of organization can access to the economic information	Some economic information is accessible to the community	No economic information is provided
TECH	Free and open-source software (FOSS)	All tech tools are based on FOSS	Some of tech tools are based on FOSS	No tech tool is based on FOSS
	Decentralized	Tech architecture is fully decentralized	Tech architecture is partially decentralized	Tech architecture is centralized
KNOWL	Copyleft	Content licenses are copyleft	Part of the contents are open access	All rights of contents are reserved
	Open data	All data are downloadable	Some data are downloadable	No data are downloadable
SOC	Inclusion	Project has a relevant role in inclusion	Project has some inclusion policies	No policy or action about inclusion
	Green	Project has a relevant role in environment	Project has some environment policies	No policy or action about environment

3.1. The Democratic Qualities of 10 Cases of Collaborative Economies in Barcelona

Analysis of the cases regarding the commons balance follows.

3.1.1. El Recetario

A collaborative platform, created in 2007, focused on research, experimentation, and reuse of waste for the construction of furniture and accessories, where the community of creators (700) share what they do and how they do it (through recipes, 450), learning from it and collaborating with others.

- Governance: Voluntary open participation.
- Economic model: Participated in a Universidad Internacional de Andalucia (UNIA) match-funding Goteo campaign (2015), which allows them to improve the project. However, a sustainable economic model is not yet defined.
- Technological policy: The technological platform is developed in Wordpress and, despite being planned, the whole platform code is not yet open.
- Knowledge policy: At the same time, the content is under a Creative Commons license (BY-SA. 4.0 copyleft license).
- Social responsibility: El Recetario is in the transition of becoming a consumer/producer cooperative platform.

3.1.2. SMart IB

SMart is an abbreviation for the French phrase, "Societé Mutuelle pour Artististes". SMart is a non-profit organization that was launched in Belgium in 1994 under the name of SMartBe. Through the ESempleo Program, founded by European sources and managed by CEPES Andalucía, SMartBe came into contact in 2011 with a cooperative business group from Andalucía that brought together the social cooperatives AURA ETT, ACTÚA SERVICIOS, and A2A Formación, among others. Finally, the new Law 14/2011 of Andalusian Cooperative Societies introduced advanced societal models of social innovation, creating a legal environment in which SMart Ibérica could begin to operate in Spain in May 2013. Currently, the Spanish cooperative receives the economic support of the Belgian cooperative. The project has expanded well, with 3000 members in Spain and 800 in Catalonia.

- Governance: A governing board makes the decisions of the cooperative, and the users are invited once or twice a year to hold an assembly.
- Governance: Voluntary open participation.
- Economic model: Each member pays a 150 € initial share capital contribution and 7.5% services commission. With this capital, the organization pays members' bills in advance.
- Technological policy: There is no technological platform running yet.
- Knowledge policy: The knowledge generated is not open.
- Social responsibility: The project promotes cultural and artistic activity.

3.1.3. Goteo

Goteo is a crowd/match-funding platform constituted as a foundation. The project started through a collaborative founding investigation in 2010, and the first version of the platform launched in 2011. Currently, Goteo has more than 90,000 users, raising 4 million Euros.

- Governance: As a foundation, the decision-making process is carried by a small group of people.
- Economic model: Users pay a 4% commission, but the promoters intend to arrive at 0%.
- Technological policy: Software is subject to a copyleft license (AGPL).
- Knowledge policy: Some platform data are freely downloadable.
- Social responsibility: In terms of social impact, all projects which participate in campaigns must define the social responsibility of their actions.

3.1.4. Katuma

Katuma is an Agro-food consumption platform based on commons collaborative economy values. The project was launched in 2017 and was developed by Coopdevs, a non-profit association focused on free and open software to promote social and solidarity economy projects.

- Governance: A membership cooperative governance is planned.
- Economic model: The intention is to found the platform with membership fees.
- Technological policy: The platform is developed with open software.
- Knowledge policy: The contents are under a Creative Commons (BY NC) license.
- Social responsibility: The project focuses on connecting producers and consumers in terms of social justice.

3.1.5. Bdtonline

Bdtonline is a platform of a time banking association, Associació pel Desenvolupament dels Bancs del Temps (ADBdT), which uses TimeOverFlow software, also created by Coopdevs. The association and software were developed and raised in 2012. Currently, 47 organizations use this platform with 5800 users. One of the main goals of the organization is its usability independently of the characterization of the organization.

- Governance: Annual assembly, they use Loomio groups as a framework of members' participation.
- Economic model: All economic information is published on the website. The project is supported by membership fees and a small number of monthly voluntary donations, which are not enough to invest in improving the project, this being just the developer's task.
- Technological policy: Public domain license.
- Knowledge policy: Wiki space under public domain license.
- Social responsibility: Large number of organizations and users.

3.1.6. FreeSound

The project, started in 2005, is promoted by Pompeu Fabra University and has a research group with the objective of gathering free content for educational purposes and research. It was a success, winning prizes from the City Council (2005) and Google (2009). Currently, the platform, which is hosted in a central server, has more than six million registered users and over 400,000 registered sounds.

- Governance: Open forum participation moderated by research members.
- Economic model: Growth has been deliberately slow to avoid any financial problems, which could force it to close. The majority of limited economic sources are from research. Promoters are studying new ways of funding based on different types of users or a Wikimedia donations model.
- Technological policy: Open source platform.
- Knowledge policy: Creative Commons license (CC BY) and data are open.
- Social responsibility: Most creators or producers use FreeSound to find sound sources.

3.1.7. XOBB

The project, constituted as a cooperative, is the result of matching two research groups from different disciplines, sociology and technology, within Universitat Autonoma de Barcelona (UAB). After the rejection of the national blind association, ONCE, the promoters, with the support of other associations for the visually impaired, got resources from a Barcelona City Council grant to finance the first prototype in Creu Coberta Street. Beacons allow blind people to find information about establishments (e.g., products, offers, and open hours).

- Governance: Periodic assembly meeting.
- Economic model: Everybody could use it for free, but if somebody gets economic profit from the network they must pay for it.
- Technological policy: The project, based on a replicable open digital infrastructure, is just starting.
- Knowledge policy: Open data.
- Social responsibility: The main objective of the project is based on inclusion.

3.1.8. eReuse

Computers today are just recycled, not reused. eReuse develops open-data and open-source tools and services to reduce the costs of refurbishing and reusing computers. It was created in 2015 by Pangea, an independent non-profit association, with 15 community organizations. eReuse launched a tool to trace the origin of reused material and see if it is recycled at the end of its life.

- Governance: The decision-making process of participation focuses on local sovereignty and global federation.
- Economic model: The possibility of agreement with Abacus, in 2017, has allowed the project to get a new dimension by introducing machine cooperative to the recycling circuit. In that sense, there are good prospects for paid services growth (e.g., equipment redistribution, devices appraisal, or reporting information).
- Technological policy: Based on decentralized open-source software.
- Knowledge policy: Open data.
- Social responsibility: The project is based on reuse to decrease unnecessary production impact.

3.1.9. Sentilo

Sentilo is a platform to collect data from sensors. It was formed by the Barcelona City Council in 2012 in the framework of the Internet of Things. The proposal was based on the scenario of exponential sensors growth, when a space would be needed with structured information on each sensor system. Ten other cities, such as Terrassa, have subsequently implemented it.

- Governance: The organization works as a foundation and the participation model is open.
- Economic model: Some of the proceedings are published on the website.
- Technological policy: FOSS (LGPL3).
- Knowledge policy: Open data.
- Social responsibility: One of the project's objectives is to avoid duplicate networks.

3.1.10. Pam a Pam

The platform, born in 2012, is a project by Setem and XES (two organizations linked to SSE) to promote responsible consumption. A community of volunteers maps the initiatives through a qualitative questionnaire. Currently, the project is in a renewal phase with a revitalization plan to face the difficulty of maintaining territorial community mobilization. At the same time, the promoters want to get a self-managed sustainability funding model, apart from subsidies, and legal independence from Setem.

- Governance: Periodic members' assemblies and open participation.
- Economic model: A grant from Barcelona City Council, proposed by Setem, allowed the initial founding. In 2014, a European grant permitted the incorporation of territorial facilitators and launched a new website that was more systematic and elaborate.
- Technological policy: FOSS.
- Knowledge policy: Open data on demand. The new website will allow it to be downloaded.
- Social responsibility: The whole project is linked to the social and solidarity economy.

3.2. Curve of Growth and Evolutionary Stages of the Cases

The curve of growth shown in Figure 2 represents the stages of evolution and growth of an organization, with an initial kick-off, deep growth, maturation with stabilization, and the renewal or gradient phase. At the co-creation session, each of the 10 cases positioned themselves on the curve. The cases positioned themselves in various stages on this curve of growth. The majority of them, however, located themselves in a positive stage of their activity.

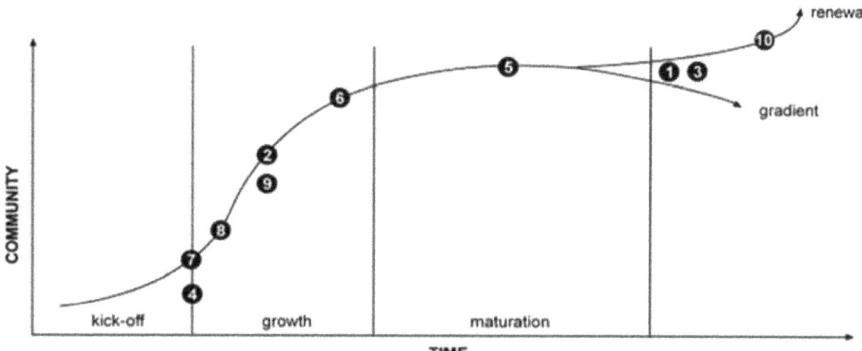

Figure 2. Summary of project stage evolution: (1) El Recetario; (2) SmartIB; (3) Goteo; (4) Katuma; (5) Bdtonline; (6) XOBB; (7) FreeSound; (8) eReuse; (9) Sentilo; (10) Pam a Pam.

3.3. Case Comparison Analysis

According to the results (Table 2: case comparison between the cases of the commons balance), none of the cases fulfill 100% of the five qualities. However, the majority of them accomplish aspects of the commons star collaborative economy review at a good level. Cases 3 (Goteo), 8 (eReuse), and especially 10 (Pam a Pam) achieve in a holistic approach achieving the majority of commons criteria. Two of these projects (Goteo and Pam a Pam) are in a post-maturation evolutionary stage. The qualities linked to the non-profit economic dimension and open participation in governance are the ones more cases fulfill, while technological decentralization, open data, and inclusion indicators (in these order) are the areas less fulfilled by the cases. The governance and economic model get the best evaluation, but open participation and non-profit organization have better valuation than cooperative governance and transparency, respectively. Overall, Case 2 (SmartIB), which is in the early platform development stage, has accomplished the fewest criteria.

Table 2. Case comparison between the cases of the commons balance. Green: fulfilment, Orange: Partial fulfilment; Red: unfulfillment. Cases: (1) El Recetario; (2) SmartIB; (3) Goteo; (4) Katuma; (5) Bdtonline; (6) XOBB; (7) FreeSound; (8) eReuse; (9) Sentilo; (10) Pam a Pam.

Dimensions	Sub-Dimensions	1	2	3	4	5	6	7	8	9	10
GOV	Type of organization	G	G	G	G	G	R	G	G	G	G
	Open participation	G	O	G	G	G	G	G	G	G	G
ECON	Goal	G	G	G	G	G	G	G	G	G	G
	Transparency	G	O	G	G	O	R	G	R	O	G
TECH	FOSS	G	R	G	G	G	G	G	G	G	G
	Decentralized	R	R	R	R	R	R	O	R	R	R
KNOWL	Copyleft	G	R	G	G	G	G	G	G	G	G
	Open data	R	R	G	O	R	R	G	G	G	O
SOC	Inclusion	G	O	G	O	O	O	R	O	R	G
	Green	G	G	G	G	G	G	G	G	G	G

4. Discussion

According to the application of the framework to the sample of 10 cases, we observe that there is no case which fulfills all of the dimensions, but several modalities of being pro-democratic as a digital platform.

Regarding business models, the majority of the 10 cases studied depart from a grant or public funding model and instead have a grassroots character. Four of the projects were connected to H2020 European funds. The main problem of this model is project maintenance when the economic support ends. Only one of the 10 cases mentioned here was awarded and used the services for entrepreneurship of Barcelona Activa, the Barcelona agency of development.

Regarding governance, several of the cases had the intention to get another legal constitution at the time of the study. The current legal formulas for economic association do not adapt well to commons collaborative economy activity. Several of these cases were provided by institutions, whether universities, such as FreeSound and eReuse with the UPF, or public administrations, as in the case of Sentilo being supported by the Barcelona City Council. Those that were legally constituted did so through an association (the simplest formula bureaucratically), a foundation, or a cooperative. In this sense, some associations (Bdtonline and Katuma, for example) manifested in the interviews the intention to become cooperatives. Others were already in the process of doing so (such as XOBB). We also observed other cases of collaborative economy platforms (such as femProcomuns) that were constituted as cooperatives but were not analyzed in this initial study. If the legal cooperative formula spreads among collaborative economy platform projects, as this investigation has found, we can expect new bonds in the growth of cooperatives [23] and the expansion of the social solidarity economy movement in the city of Barcelona [24].

Regarding technological policies, the majority of cases considered FOSS. At the same time, almost all of them centralized their architecture. In the same sense, with regard to knowledge policies, open licenses were more often extended than open data.

Accomplishment of social responsibility criteria in the cases analyzed was not regular. Some cases were highly connected to environmental uses (such as eReuse or Katuma) while other favored social inclusion (such as XOBB). If we assess the 10 cases together, both subdimensions—green and inclusion—were half fulfilled.

Our analysis reflects another relevant issue to consider for future research into the ecosystem dimension of the cases. Collaborative economy has an important presence in Barcelona. More than 1000 cases have been identified as commons collaborative economies (see directori.p2pvalue.eu) [18]. The model is also very adaptable. A total of 33 areas of activity (with a broad range: culture, leisure, shopping, etc.) where the model is present in Barcelona have been identified [10]. Barcelona's collaborative economy has an important ecosystem dimension. This phenomenon links with the high number of social innovation practices that have a great tradition in the city [25] and shows the role of citizens in its transformation [26]. This is the case of the collaborative economy platform Katuma (one of the studied cases), for example, which is a potential tool to scale the activity of agroecology cooperatives that have been in Barcelona for over three decades [27].

The 10 cases analyzed showed different levels of connection with the Social and Solidarity Economy (SSE) and Digital Commons framework, network, and values. On the one hand, Goteo was the strongest project in the Digital Commons area. On the other hand, Pam a Pam was the most mature project with the SSE framework in terms of digital platform.

Despite the strong ecosystem, the majority of initiatives start but remain at initial stages, as a fabric of ideas and training, or kick off and grow to a certain level of satisfactory activity. Frequently, there is neither the expectation nor the intention to scale largely. The 10 cases in our sample positioned themselves at a developmental or mature position in the curve of growth, even if they were not considered "mainstream" or established with the big public. This is consistent with the results of the P2P Value investigation over a sample of 300, which pointed to a normal distribution of "success" (many medium cases), instead of a power law distribution with few very successful and the majority unsuccessful [28].

To sum up, our investigation shows that, beyond the controversial and unethical unicorn economy platforms, an alternative model of collaborative economy exists based on democratic qualities of procommon. The nature of these procommon alternatives is connected to the development of the platforms based on the principles of cooperativism. Nevertheless, the main challenge of these procommon collaborative economy projects is their scalability and sustainability.

Regarding future research, even if this study has allowed testing a framework to evaluate the qualities of sustainability and pro-democratization collaborative economy platforms, we consider it necessary to conduct a new investigation. It would, on the one hand, contemplate a broader sample of cases and, on the other hand, cosnider platform projects with different characterizations, from unicorn platforms to procommon platforms, passing through hybrid projects. This new research should provide a broader view of the key aspects of each of the approaches and the pathways of connection and learning between them.

Author Contributions: M.F.M. and R.E. contributed to the design and implementation of the research, to the analysis of the results and to the writing of the manuscript.

Funding: This research is part of the work carried out by the Dimmons research group in the framework of DECODE project (funded by the European Union's Horizon 2020 Programme, under grant agreement number 732546).

Conflicts of Interest: The authors declare no conflict of interest.

References

1. Fuster Morell, M. The unethics of sharing: Wikiwashing. *Int. Rev. Inf. Ethics* **2011**, *15*, 9–16.
2. Codagnone, C.; Biagi, F.; Abadie, F. *The Passions and the Interests: Unpacking the 'Sharing Economy'*; JRC Science for Policy Report; Institute for Prospective Technological Studies: IPTS, Seville, Spain, 2016.

3. Fuster Morell, M.; Carballa Smichowski, B.; Smorto, G.; Espelt, R.; Imperatore, P.; Rebordosa, M.; Rocas, M.; Rodríguez, N.; Senabre, E.; Ciurcina, M. *Multidisciplinary Framework on Commons Collaborative Economy*; H2020–ICT-2016-1; DECODE: Barcelona, Spain, 2017.
4. European Commission. *Communication from the Commission to the European Parliament, the Council, The European Economic and Social Committee and The Committee of the Regions*; A European Agenda for the Collaborative Economy; 2.6.2016 COM(2016) 356 Final; European Commission: Brussels, Belgium, 2016.
5. Algar, R. Collaborative Consumption. *Leis. Rep.* **2007**, *4*, 16–17.
6. Botsman, R.; Rogers, R. *What's Mine Is Yours: How Collaborative Consumption Is Changing the Way We Live*; Harper Business: New York, NY, USA, 2010.
7. Cohen, B.; Kietzmann, J. Ride On! Mobility Business Models for the Sharing Economy. *Organ. Environ.* **2014**, *27*, 279. [CrossRef]
8. Heinrichs, H. Sharing economy: A potential new pathway to sustainability. *GAIA* **2013**, *22*, 228–231. [CrossRef]
9. Palos-Sanchez, P.; Correia, M.B. O impacto da economia colaborativa medido através de termos de pesquisa na internet: Estudo de caso Blablacar. *Rev. Tur. Desenvolv.* **2018**, *1*, 1341–1354.
10. Fuster Morell, M. Cooperativismo de plataforma: Remover la economía colaborativa para un futuro sostenible. In *Nexe.com, Quaderns d'Autogestió i Economia Cooperativa*; Federació de Cooperatives de Treball de Catalunya: Barcelona, Spain, 2016.
11. Adigital. Los Modelos Colaborativos en Plataformas Digitales. 2017. Available online: https://www.adigital.org/informes-estudios/los-modelos-colaborativos-demanda-plataformas-digitales/ (accessed on 1 June 2017).
12. De Rivera, J.; López Gordo, Á.; Cassidy, P.; Apesteguía, A. A netnographic study of P2P collaborative consumption platforms' user interface and design. *Environ. Innov. Soc. Transit.* **2017**, *23*, 11–27. [CrossRef]
13. Finkel, L.; Gordo López, Á. Investigating Digital Social Networks: A Methodological Approach for Identifying Women Inclusion in Commercial Branding. In *World Social Science Forum. Social Transformations and the Digital Age*; International Social Science Council: Montreal, Canada, 2013.
14. Gordo, A.; De Rivera, J. The triple impact assessment of P2P collaborative consumption in Europe. In *Research Report, with the Collaboration of María Avizanda (Desk Research & Delphi Study Research Assistant)*; Cibersomosaguas Universidad Complutense: Madrid, Spain, 2015.
15. Gordo López, A.; De Rivera, J.; Apesteguía, A. Facing the Challenge of Collaborative Consumption in Europe: A Time for Independent Metrics. In Proceedings of the Second International Workshop on the Sharing Economy (#IWSE) @ESCP Europe, Paris Campus, Paris, France, 28–29 January 2016.
16. Hernández Bataller, B. *Consumo Colaborativo o Participativo: Un Modelo de Sostenibilidad Para el Siglo XXI*; Dictamen de Iniciativa, 21 January 2014; European Economic and Social Committee: Brussels, Belgium, 2014.
17. Scholz, T. *Platform Cooperativism. Challenging the Corporate Sharing Economy*; Rosa Luxemburg Stiftung: Berlin, Germany, 2016.
18. Fuster Morell, M.; Salcedo, J.; Berlinguer, M. Debate about the Concept of Value in Commons-Based Peer Production. In Proceedings of the International Conference on Internet Science (INSCI 2016), Florence, Italy, 12–14 September 2016. Lecture Notes in Computer Science Series (LNCS) 9934.
19. Bauwens, M. Cooperativismo Abierto Para la era del P2P. Guerrilla Translation. 3 July 2014. Available online: http://www.guerrillatranslation.es/2014/07/03/cooperativismo-abierto-para-la-era-p2p/ (accessed on 1 April 2017).
20. Benkler, Y. *The Wealth of Networks: How Social Production Transforms Markets and Freedom*; Yale University Press: New Haven, CT, USA, 2006.
21. Espelt, R.; Peña-López, I.; Vega, N. Plataformas digitales: Grupos y cooperativas de consumo versus La Colmena que dice sí, el caso de Barcelona. In *La Economía Colaborativa en la era Del Capitalismo Digital. Revista de Estudios para el Desarrollo Social de la Comunicación (Redes.com)*; Grupo Interdisciplinario de Estudios en Comunicación, Política y Cambio Social: Sevilla, Spain, 2017.
22. Tellis, W.M. Application of a case study methodology. *Qual. Rep.* **1997**, *3*, 1–19.
23. Roelants, B.; Hyungsik, E.; Terrasi, E. *Cooperatives and Employment: A Global Report*; CICOPA/Desjardin: Quebec City, QC, Canada, 2014.
24. Fernández, A.; Miró, I. *L'Economia Social i Solidària a Barcelona*; La ciutat invisible: Barcelona, Spain, 1997.

25. Blanco, I.; Cruz, H.; Martínez, R. *Barris Desafavorits Davant la Crisi: Segregació Urbana, Innovació Social i Capacitat Cívica*; Universitat Autònoma de Barcelona, Recercaixa: Bellaterra, Spain, 2015; Available online: https://barrisicrisi.wordpress.com (accessed on 15 January 2018).
26. Nel·lo, O. *La Ciudad en Movimiento: Crisis Social y Respuesta Ciudadana*; Díaz&Pons: Madrid, Spain, 2015.
27. Espelt, R.; Peña-López, I.; Losantos, P.; Rodríguez, E.; Martín, T.; Pons, F. Mapping agro-food consumption groups in the city of Barcelona. In Proceedings of the XXVI ESRS Congress, Aberdeen, Scotland, 18–21 August 2015; Kohe, M., Koutsouris, A., Larsen, R.B., Maye, D., Noe, E., Oedl-Wieser, T., Philip, L., Pospěch, P., Rasch, E.D., Rivera, M.J., et al., Eds.; The James Hutton Institute: Aberdeen, Scotland, 2015.
28. Fuster Morell, M. Towards a theory of value of platform cooperativism. In *Ours to Hack and to Own. The Rise of Platform Cooperativism. A New Vision for the Future of Work and a Fairer Internet*; Scholz, T., Schneider, N., Eds.; OR Books: New York, NY, USA, 2017; Available online: http://www.orbooks.com/catalog/ours-to-hack-and-to-own/ (accessed on 24 February 2018).

© 2018 by the authors. Licensee MDPI, Basel, Switzerland. This article is an open access article distributed under the terms and conditions of the Creative Commons Attribution (CC BY) license (http://creativecommons.org/licenses/by/4.0/).

Article

Engaging the Senses: The Potential of Emotional Data for Participation in Urban Planning

Afif Fathullah and Katharine S. Willis *

School of Art, Design and Architecture (Faculty of Arts & Humanities), Roland Levinsky Building, Drake Circus, Plymouth, Devon PL4 8AA, UK; afif.fathullah@students.plymouth.ac.uk
* Correspondence: katharine.willis@plymouth.ac.uk; Tel.: +44-1752-585191

Received: 3 July 2018; Accepted: 11 September 2018; Published: 21 September 2018

Abstract: This paper presents an exploratory study on the potential for sharing urban data; one where citizens create their own data and use it to understand and influence urban planning decisions. The aim of the study is to explore new models of participation through the sharing of emotional data and focuses on the relationship between the physical space and emotions through identifying the links between stress levels and specific features of the urban environment. It addresses the problem in urban planning that, while people's emotional connection with the physical urban setting is often valued, it is rarely recognised or used as a source of data to understand future decision making. The method involved participants using a (GSR) device linked to location data to measure participant's emotional responses along a walking route in a city centre environment. Results show correlations between characteristics of the urban environment and stress levels, as well as how specific features of the city spaces create stress 'peaks'. In the discussion we review how the data obtained could contribute to citizens creating their own information layer—an emotional layer—that could inform a shared approach to participation in urban planning decision-making. The future implications of the application of this method as an approach to public participation in urban planning are also considered.

Keywords: emotions; participation; digital participation; physiological sensors; galvanic skin response; GSR; stress levels; emotional layer; urban

---

1. Introduction—Sharing Cities

A sharing cities approach focuses on bring local people together through shared activities and cooperation for the benefit of the city and includes initiatives such as carsharing, community currencies, cohousing, hackerspaces, timebanks and tool or kitchen libraries. These new forms of sharing, enabled by technological devices and platforms [1] work by enabling citizens to create, adapt and exploit data [2] and can create new ways in which citizens participate in the governance of the city. For example, civic apps, developed by citizens, civic organisations and commercial companies [3] have become widespread and typically create some form of two-way interaction where citizens contribute to commenting on or providing data on public services usually offered by the city such as crime prevention, rubbish collection, public transportation and pollution reduction. Mclaren and Agymen present as new model for collaboration and sharing around the city where "the same measures that enable sharing online, also–if civil liberties are properly protected–enable collective politics online. We see the increasingly blurred nexus between urban- and cyberspace enabling transformation–this time in the political domain. These spaces are fundamentally important for forms of participation invented and controlled by the people" [4]. This takes a model of participation, or sharing data that is termed 'co-production' whereby 'citizens perform the role of partner rather than customer in the delivery of public services' [5]. The challenge is how to enable citizens who are non-experts to gather, analyse and share data in a way that can meaningfully contribute to urban planning processes. The aim of this paper is to look at the potential of emotional data for enabling participation in urban planning, that contributes towards a shared cities approach. The objective of this approach to propose that a sharing emotional data can enable better insights of the city and its inhabitants which could lead to a citizen-centred approach in urban planning processes.

In this paper, we take the approach that sharing practices present an alternative model of participation in city decision-making. Conventional citizen participation methods in city planning are typically linear and include referenda, public hearings, public surveys, charettes, public advisory committees or focus groups which often require the participants to be physical present at particular time and place (see Figure 1). The qualitative nature of data gathering and sharing means that citizens that have input into such consultations typically participate through methods such as completing surveys and contributing verbal comments, which are qualitative in nature and require further analysis to be used effectively. These forms of data are not easily translatable into the types and format of data and outcomes that are used by urban planners; such as urban plans, maps and GIS data. In addition factors such as the time required of citizens to participate often results in apathy among citizens [6], so that actual participation rarely represents a majority of inhabitants or involves the full range of stakeholders [7].

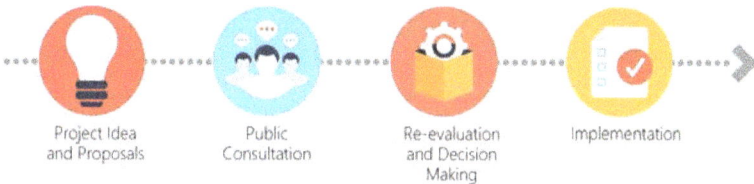

Figure 1. Current model of participation in Urban Planning process.

Digital technologies can address some of the issues of participation in the urban planning process by enabling a more accessible system for the public to shape their neighbourhood's future [8]. Munster et al. outline potential advantages of digital participation which include the use of wider pool of knowledge through broader audience and participants, which creates an interactive and communication-oriented planning process [9]. They can lower barriers for participation, involve a wider range of participants, and by enabling people to discuss urban design proposals in place can foster interest in public participation [9]. This offers new perspectives for designers and planners to "transforming planning work into an iterative, agile work process, in contrast to sequential and linear workflows that have shaped urban design practice in the past" [9]. Crivellaro et al. [10] have looked at how local people use data sharing through Facebook to mobilise around a local social movement. They recognised the importance of forming a like-minded community, but also acknowledged the struggle of the group to translate their emotions to the authority and decision makers. Hasler et al. [11] in another research found that the multiplication and diversity of contributions by citizens through digital participation increases complexity which means that prioritising relevant data can be problematic. This illustrates how data sharing can facilitate discussions that are planning-related, but turning them into actionable policies proven to be difficult. The research question this paper therefore seeks to explore is: Can sharing emotional data offer a method for participation in the urban planning process?

The paper presents a potential methodological contribution in terms of the incorporation of physiological sensing device and GPS tracking technologies for measure and analysing emotional data in urban environments. To do this, we first review the literature on the urban planning process, showing how the development of the discipline has sought to enable citizen participation. This is mapped against Arnstein's 'Ladder of Participation' to highlight how much of this participation typically does not enable citizens to control and act in the process, and is therefore the participation is often tokenistic. The potential of incorporating digital tools for participation is presented, and in particular, the value of incorporating emotional data as a way of capturing a more person- centric understanding of urban space. In the study described in the paper, a small number of participants used a galvanic skin response (GSR) linked to location data to record stress levels in a walk through an urban city centre space with different characteristics. The findings aim to explore whether this emotional data might have benefit for enabling new models of shared data in urban planning processes.

1.1. The Challenge of Participation in the Urban Planning Process

"Cities have the capability of providing something for everybody, only because, and only when, they are created by everybody" [12].

Many people now live in cities, but despite Jacob's plea above, very few participate in how they are created, designed and planned. Therefore, the contribution of this study addresses the following broader question: 'how to enable meaningful participation in the urban planning process'? To do this, the paper first provides some context on how urban planning evolved and the developing role of participation. The origins if urban planning in the western world in the early 20th Century, were heavily influenced by the rational-comprehensive approach where the planning sequence involves: a survey of the region, an analysis of the survey, and finally the development of the plan [13]. Hall [14] argued that Geddes "gave planning a logical structure" by developing the survey-analysis-plan sequence of planning. However, this method of planning has been criticised to be too top-down; seeing the planner as "the omniscient ruler, who should create new settlement forms without interference or question" [14] as well as being too reductionist as planners have to make assumptions and predictions which required them to have complete certainty [15]. This then caused the planners to proceed on the basis of simplifying the world around them which later led to a lot of failure of the predictions [15]. The failures of the rational-comprehensive approach in urban planning led it to being succeeded by synoptic planning approach in 1960s and Hall argued that this change represents a fundamental shift in the role of the planners and their relationship with the public. However, Faludi [15] argued that this early form of participation was still based on the assumption that the society is homogenous–implying the homogeneity of interest. This means that participation is only required to validate and uncritically legitimise the goals of planning and any objection to planning proposal tends to be stigmatised [15].

Even when public participation has become an integral part of current urban planning process, Innes and Booher [6] argued that they still "do not achieve genuine participation". This is because current form of public participation does not satisfy members of the public that they are being heard and often does not improve the decisions that agencies and public officials make and [6]. The scepticism posed by Innes and Booher [6] to the way that current participation is being practiced could be traced back to Arnstein's widely known 'Ladder of Participation' [16]. As she put it, "there is a critical difference between going through the empty ritual of participation and having the real power needed to affect the outcomes of the process" [16]. The fundamental point of these criticisms was that if urban planners seek public participation, it is necessary that there be a redistribution of power [16]. She regarded power in public participation as a ladder or a spectrum ranging from 'nonparticipation' through to 'degrees of citizen power' (see Figure 2), which correspond to the degree of power or control participants can exercise in the quest of shaping the outcome. The ladder outlines steps of public participation from manipulation (level 1), education (level 3), and consultation (level 4), through to sharing power through 'partnership' (level 6) and beyond.

Notably, Arnstein's framework regards consultation as 'tokenism' similar to the way Innes and Booher [6] viewed the level of public participation in current urban planning process. However, Painter [17] argued against Arnstein's analysis by stating that her ladder of participation model inaccurately apprehends power i.e., it confuses 'potential power' with 'actual power' [17]. While the official decision-making power may rest with institutional decision-makers in a consultation process, to regard the process as tokenistic disregards the fact that "if the exercise of influence [by participants] is effective, then this formal power is an empty shell" [17] (p. 23). He also argues that Arnstein's model often assume decision-making in planning occurs at a single point in the process. This ignores the fact that there is rarely an identifiable, or single, 'point of decision' in policy-making [17]. The primary value of this discussion is that it exposes that participation in planning can include the exercise of both formal and informal power. Hence, having power in decision-making processes is not the only way towards achieving genuine participation, as it could also be realised through ranges of other participatory activities—as long as the engagement with citizens contribute positively towards the outcome of a planning project.

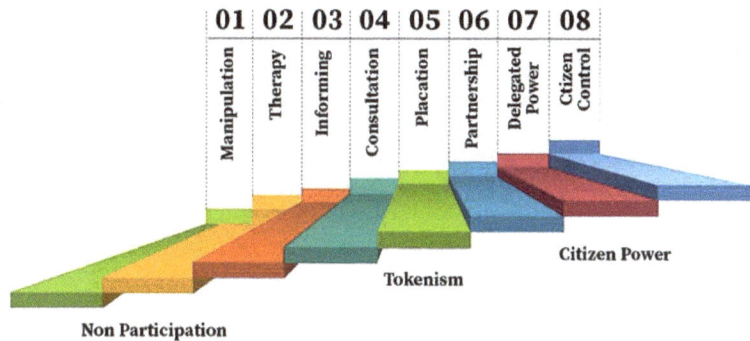

Figure 2. Arnstein's Ladder of Participation.

1.1.1. Emotions and Planning

This paper explores whether sharing emotional data about a particular city setting can be used to inform the urban planning process. Although the link between the built environment and human's emotional aspects in urban planning research has found a growing interest in recent years, it is still a rather new approach in the field [18]. Typically, in urban planning, planning is seen as an objective process, so emotion is not seen as qualities or analysis that can be meaningfully included in decision making [19]. They believe that urban planners should avoid allowing emotions to influence their analysis or recommendations and this is largely due to the fact that urban planners are taught to operate in a rational manner [19]. Despite the neglect of emotional aspects by many planning officials, there are also some urban planners who do recognise the importance of emotions within the field. For example, Lynch [20] recognises the emotional aspect through its link with emotions and mental maps while Ferreira [21] has urged that emotions should be presented as constructive drives with the power to positively inspire the planner to become a more competent professional. Porter et al. [22] on the other hand have claimed that attachments to community members improve the ability of planners to understand and work with residents while Gunder and Hillier [23] have interpreted planning issues through a Lacanian psychological model which acknowledge the entire process of becoming and being a planner is typically associated with strong emotional experiences. These authors have provided a meaningful theoretical discourse in terms of acknowledging the importance of emotions within urban planning. However, the majority of them have kept their focus on the planner side of the equation rather than on the users' side. Most of them recognise that planners should positively address emotions but very few have put the emphasis on citizens' emotional interactions with the urban environments itself. This should not be the case if we were to truly understand the relationship between emotions and urban spaces. According to Zeile et al. 'the long-term goal is to develop a new information layer for planners, in which a visualization of the measured spatial perception is possible. These visualizations allow conclusions about human behavior in an urban environment and enable a new citizen-centered perspective in planning processes' (Zeile, Resch, Exner, and Sagl, 2015). Hence, by linking it to public participations and the developments of digital tools, the next subsection will review some of the literature and studies around the spatial-emotional interactions of the city's users as its main focus to understand the significance of emotions in the urban planning field.

1.1.2. Digital Tools as Means for Measuring Emotions

Recent technological developments have allowed the incorporation of emotions in public participation within the planning field. It also allows current urban planners to increase their understanding of the relationship between citizens and urban spaces by measuring their emotions using newly developed digital tools. Most of the studies around this topic can largely be divided into three categories based on the tools they have used to extract emotional data either through: (1) social media, (2) mobile apps, or (3) physiological wearable devices. The similarities within all of these studies and perhaps the most important one for incorporating emotional experiences in spatial analysis is the capability to cross reference emotional data with accurate locational data i.e., the ability to geo-locate those data to a specific place within a city. For example, under the first category, Mislove et al. [24] extract the moods of people from different cities by mining information on social media, in this case, Twitter. This information however tends be at a low level of granularity; it is generally at a large spatial scale such as city, state or region and not collected at a detailed spatial level, such as a street or a city centre. Nevertheless, there is other recent research on mining emotional responses towards particular spaces from social media such as Tauscher and Neumann [25] who generated sentiment maps of tourist locations.

The Urban Emotion Research Lab developed a methodology for the extraction of contextual emotion information for decision support in spatial planning which enabled crowdsourcing physiological conditions (technical sensors measuring psycho-physiological parameters) and subjective emotions (human sensors contributing subjectively perceived emotions) [26–28]. Drawing on this work, Hauthal and Burghardt [29] and Aiello et al. [30] both extract location-based emotions from photo titles, descriptions, and tags from Panoramio and Flickr respectively to generate maps of specific streets within various cities with emotional attributes. Mody et al. designed a location-based social networking tool that enables users to share and store their emotional feelings about places 'WiMo' [31]. They found that it was possible to create a recognisable and useable framework for gathering users individual emotional responses in a shared map interface. Key to this was defining 'places' rather than distinct geographical locations as these elicited an emotional response. Meanwhile, Zeile et al. [32] has established a dedicated algorithm to source emotional expressions from Twitter before plotting them onto the map of downtown Boston, USA.

Some researchers have started to focus on developing mobile apps, to gather users' wellbeing and feelings and to relate them to the geographic reference of their occurrence. For example, Ettema and Smajic (2015) used smartphones to gather self-recorded experiences of students during a walk. They have then later found out that the level of happiness was the highest in areas where many activities were happening and where a lot of people were around (Ettema and Smajic, 2015). MacKerron and Mourato (2013) in their project "Mappiness" used an iPhone app to collect frequent reports of temporary happiness at random times. They found that participants are generally happier in green or natural environments than in urban environments (MacKerron and Mourato, 2013). Similarly, Klettner et al., (2013) designed mobile apps called EmoMap to collect people's emotional responses to space through mobile phones, as well as modelling, and visualizing these data. The findings indicate that environments varying according to the amount of vegetation and traffic are perceived differently, with highest positive ratings for the urban-green area, and lowest ratings in the heavy traffic urban area (Klettner et al., 2013).

While semantic analysis from social media data and citizen feedbacks from mobile apps offer subjective evaluations on emotional experience of participants, physiological emotional extraction technique using wearable devices propose the investigation of the more objective element of emotions. This is on the basis that physiological responses would provide useful indications of the users' current emotional states when they interact with the physical environment. Over the last ten years, some urban researchers have been investigating this relationship and Nold's [33] 'emotional cartography' is perhaps the most significant in laying a fundamental underpinning to explore the changes in physiology in the urban space. His 'BioMapping' project, undertaken between the years 2004 to 2009, was the first to integrate GPS data with biometric human sensor data and explore the idea of visualising cartographically referenced emotional data. In the fieldwork, he gathered the change of the skin conductance levels and skin temperature of participants wearing a galvanic skin response (GSR) device as they walked in several cities, which was then mapped based on their GPS locations to describe areas in terms of emotional arousal [33].

Similar work was done by Zeile et al. [34] who mapped the stress levels of cyclists in Cambridge, Massachusetts by measuring skin conductance levels during their ride using a GSR device. They also attached a video recording device to allow footages to be taken along the route in order to accurately understand what caused the physiological changes in their participants [34]. A dedicated smartphone app was then used to allow geo-tagged reporting of the experiment. Their findings include the detection of what caused negative arousal in cyclists and they found out that the triggers include dangerous intersections, physical obstacles, pedestrians crossing, cars passing close by and damaged road surface [34]. They also mapped the cycling route with all the moments of stress and triggers as well as some specific emotions based on the input from the participants and their rides.

The studies conducted by Nold [33] and Zeile et al. [32] all benefited from the use of the GSR device that offers physiological data collection of emotions of the participants. As the GSR device measures levels of emotional arousal through the change in skin conductance and resistance levels, these data can be easily quantified resulting in a more objective measure of emotions rather than just qualitative. This method is valuable since objective measurement of emotions has proven to be beneficial in terms of producing a more accurate representation of emotions. Hence, the next subsection will explore the mechanism operating the GSR device and its uses in measuring negative emotional arousal within the field. As mentioned previously, the work of Zeile and colleagues and Nold have undertaken key work [28,33,35] that has objectively investigated the relationship between emotions and physical environments using physiological responses methods. This work has laid important theoretical and methodological foundations for integrating the use of galvanic skin response (GSR) within urban spatial analysis and city planning, hence. In this paper, we draw on these methodological approaches and further investigate the link between and urban spaces to gain understanding of how features in the urban space can be mapped against emotional response and the corresponding potential for this in participatory urban planning.

1.1.3. Physiological Measures of Stress Levels Using a GSR Device

A range of physiological measures has been employed to assess emotions in research. As mentioned before, physiological responses of the sympathetic nervous system, especially changes in electrodermal activity (EDA), blood pressure, heart rate, and cortisol levels, are broadly used to reflect changes in emotional arousals [36]. However, because the change in blood pressure and heart rate are also influenced by physical activities, the EDA offers a more accurate measure of emotional arousal [36]. Boucsein have discussed EDA at length and regarded it as a common term for all electrical phenomena including active and passive electrical properties which occurs in the skin [37]. One of the most well-known EDA measures is the galvanic skin response (GSR) defined simply as 'a change in the ability of the skin to conduct electricity' [37]. GSR can be measured using a GSR device in which the fundamental physiological mechanism that operates the response is 'the subtle change in sweat secretion from eccrine sweat glands throughout the body which increased when there is a high level of emotional arousal [35]. This phenomenon is called emotional sweating and can be observed and measured most easily and accurately on hands and feet. As the secretion of sweat increases, skin surfaces become moistier, thus improving the conduction of an electric current [35]. This allows for the skin conductance and resistance level to increase or decrease, and this change is recorded by the GSR device.

The current state-of-the-art in physiological sensor data analysis research suggests that negative emotional arousal can be correctly distinguished through the analysing of the skin conductance level. According to leading researchers in the field, such as Kreibig [38] and Rodrigues et al. [39], skin conductivity increases (while its resistivity decreases) when a negative experience occurs as this negative arousal is an indicator for a stress event. Zeile et al. supported this argument as their study has found out that "[if] for instance a test person has the experience of anger or fear—a negative emotion—skin conductance (the difference between sweat production and absorption of the skin) increases" [32]. Dakker et al. found in studies that GSR can be used not just to detect emotions but also for change detection in emotions since 'emotional experiences trigger changes in autonomic arousal quite impressively'. This can be used to link levels of emotional arousal with stress [40]. Bakker et al. distinguish stress in patterns of sharp rising emotional arousal at the peak, prior to a slow return to a relaxed state (see Figure 3) as highlighted in grey in the adapted GSR data graph below.

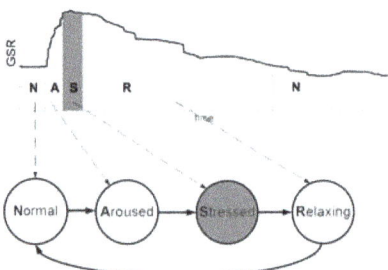

Figure 3. (Adapted from Bakker et al.)—'An example of acute stress pattern observed from GSR data and how it can be mapped to the symbolic (time-stamped) representation of person's stress' [40].

In this paper, we focus on change detection in emotions using a GSR device and through correlating with changes in the urban context aim to investigate whether this has potential for mapping emotional change to particular urban planning features and qualities.

2. Materials and Methods

In this study, individual participants were asked to walk through a specific route in the city, while linked up to a galvanic skin response (GSR) device attached to their fingers and a GPS tracker app (Figure 4) in a backpack which they carried. Stress levels were measured using the GSR device which operates by detecting the subtle change in sweat secretion from eccrine sweat glands. Prior to the walk the quality of the GSR signal was checked in the visualisation software and the data feed was tested with the participant to resolve any potential issues and visualize the impact of breathing, movements, and talking.

During the fieldwork, the GSR device was first fixed to participants' fingers and then connected to a laptop that runs an accompanying software called GSR Studio (Figure 5) that records changes detected by the GSR device and automatically plots a readable graph of skin resistance levels against time. GPS data was recorded at 1-min intervals during the walk, and the GSR data was then read in conjunction with features and characteristics of the urban setting to identify how this correlated with emotional arousal levels. In this study, the focus is on positive and negative emotional arousal.

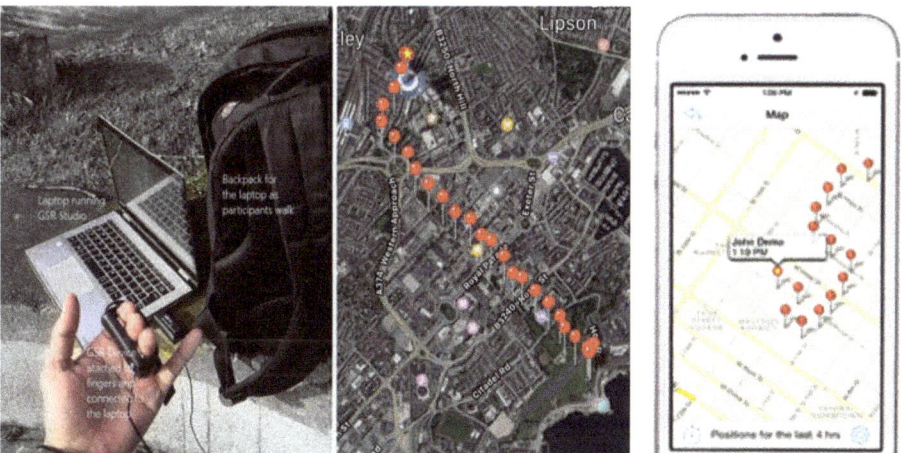

Figure 4. Experiment set-up consisting of a finger mounted GSR device, a laptop, and a backpack linked to a GPS Phone Tracker App that was used to track participant's location at 1-min intervals during the walk.

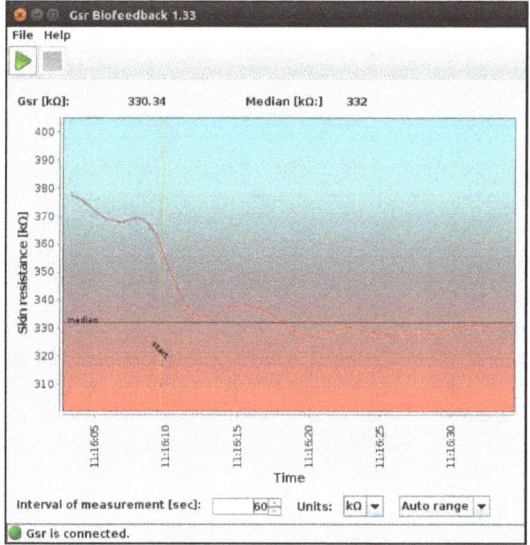

Figure 5. GSR Studio software plots data into graph in real time (photo from supplier).

The GSR device used in this study (https://www.happy-electronics.eu/biofeedback/products-en-2/skin-response-biofeedback/) was a low cost and low-tech piece of equipment (costing under €100), and required no specialist training prior to use.

2.1. Participants

A total of 9 participants, 3 males and 6 females, aged between 23–28 years old were recruited for the study. They were selected based on the criteria that they had lived in the city for between 1–3 years, so that they had some basic equivalence in terms of the background spatial knowledge of the setting. All of them were international students at the University of Plymouth. The participants were accompanied on the walk by a researcher, who followed the participant's' unobtrusively.

2.2. Setting

The route was chosen primarily because it covers three distinct areas in Plymouth City Centre. Participants were asked to walk from Plymouth Hoe, a popular recreational park in Plymouth, continuing their walk through Armada Way, a pedestrianized area, and ending at the North Road East (see Figure 6), a walk which took about twenty minutes in total. The urban spaces along the walk had different characteristics, ranging from the park at the beginning of the walk to a busy road at the end of the walk (see Table 1).

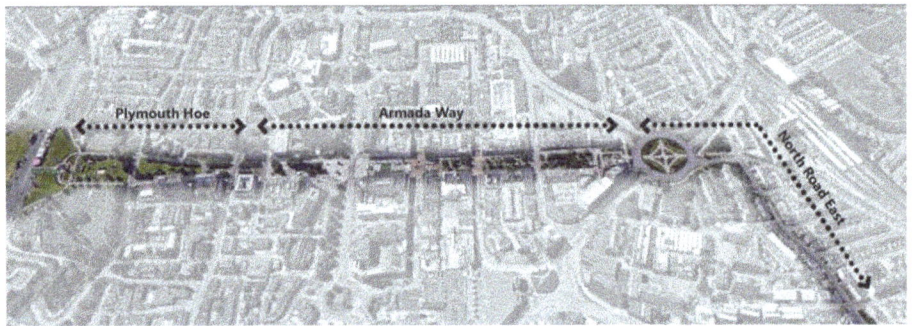

PLYMOUTH HOE　　　　　　　　ARMADA WAY　　　　　　　　NORTH ROAD EAST

Figure 6. Study Route—Participants start walking from Plymouth Hoe, through Armada Way and ends in North Road East.

Table 1. Names and types of key urban spaces along the walking route- ranging from green space on Plymouth Hoe to a busy road at North Read East.

Location on Walk	Name	Type of Space	Urban Characteristics
Start of the walk	Plymouth Hoe	Park	Fully pedestrianised greenspace with the least traffic
Mid-way through the walk	Armada Way	Urban pedestrianised	A mix of both pedestrianised area and traffic (with some green space and natural features)
End of the walk	North Road East	Urban road	Busy road with very limited natural features

The route chosen for this study consists of three distinct areas summarized in the table below (Table 1):

The route included several junctions with varying levels of car and pedestrian traffic summarized in the table below (see Figure 7 and Table 2): These had different characteristics, with some junctions being busy with high levels of traffic, some being pedestrianized and some being road junctions but relatively quiet.

Figure 7. Participant's walking route—main crossings or junctions along the route.

Table 2. Names and characteristics of road junctions along the walking route.

Name	Type of Space	Characteristics
Citadel Road	Busy road junction	Busy road with high levels of traffic
Royal Parade	Busy road, with busy pedestrian crossing	Busy road with high levels of traffic, including buses and taxis. Main pedestrian crossing of city centre with high pedestrian traffic
Mayflower Street	Road junction	Busy road
New George Street	Pedestrianised	Fully pedestrianised wide shopping avenue with high pedestrian traffic
Cornwall Street	Pedestrianised	Fully pedestrianised wide shopping avenue with high pedestrian traffic
Derry Avenue	Quiet road junction	Road with low levels of traffic

There were also twelve identified crossings and junctions along the walking route which require participants to cross to get the other side. One of them is in the Plymouth Hoe area, six in the Armada Way area and five in the North Road East area. The nature of the setting means, with the different types of spaces can be said to correlate with typical regional city centre environments in the UK.

2.3. Limitations of the Methods

There are several limitations in the methodology, which should be taken into account, and these are described below in order to demonstrate how these were allowed for in the results. In terms of the participant's there was a low number, and we did not test participants for their background spatial knowledge (although participants were selected based on spatial knowledge criteria). As a consequence, in our results the work is presented as exploratory in nature and the analysis is limited to qualitative outcomes. The second limitation of the study is the accuracy of the GSR equipment used in the study. A low cost GSR device was chosen for this study as it is aimed at demonstrating the possibility for the use of such equipment on a wider scale and by non-experts. Therefore the GSR results cannot be assumed to have the accuracy of data from products such as Movisens Edamove or Empatica E4 [37] (although Boucsein et al. do state that a finger GSR device, such as that used in this study can be more sensitive than a wrist-based device). According to Bakker et al. 'the reliable translation of physiological data gathered by using sensor technology into the "stress level rates" is only possible when additional sources of information are available' [40]. The results are presented comparatively showing the difference or similarities between participants rather than as discrete, and were mapped using the GPS data against the features of the physical context. The use of GPS locational data mapped against the GSR data means that it was possible to assess the relation between spatial context and emotional response data at a fairly fine grain level.

3. Results

3.1. General Change in Participants' Emotions

The results showed that eight out of nine participants started with higher skin resistance level (less sweaty fingers) and ended the walk with a lower skin resistance level (sweatier fingers) (see Figure 8). As higher skin resistance level equates to lower stress levels, the change pattern in the results indicates that almost all the participants had lower levels of emotional arousal at the beginning of the walk i.e., at Plymouth Hoe park compared to when they were walking along the North Road East at the end of the experiment. Only one participant (participant 06) ended the walk at about the same level as when they started it.

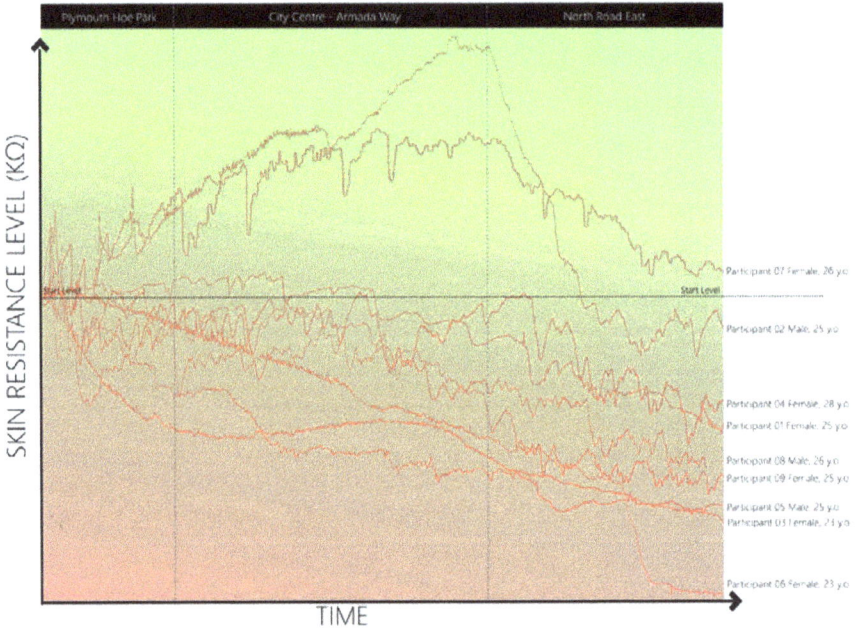

Figure 8. Results—Combined results of all participants showing a general trend of a higher skin resistance level at the start of the walk and lower skin resistance at the end.

It could also be observed that seven out of nine participant's recorded their highest level of skin resistance at the start of the walk in Plymouth Hoe than any other area of the walking route, and their skin resistance levels gradually decreased throughout the journey as they enter Armada Way and ended at the lowest level at the end of North Road East. If we see this pattern of emotional change as being linked to stress levels, then this result indicates that most participants find Plymouth Hoe park to be the least stressful area followed by Armada Way and then North Road East, where most participants find it to be most stressful. Two out of the nine participants (participant 02 and 06) on the other hand appeared to have their lowest stress levels when they were walking in the Armada Way. However, both of their apparent stress levels then changed dramatically as it steeply increased when they entered the North Road East area.

Further analysis on the participants' skin resistance levels can be made by drawing trend lines of their individual graphs for each area along the walking route. From the results it can be observed that the highest number of participants (5 out of 9 people) recorded an increasing level of skin resistance while walking through Plymouth Hoe. This suggests that most participants find Plymouth Hoe to be the least stressful place as their level of stress decreases as they walk through the park. Meanwhile, as participants walk through Armada Way, five participants experienced decreasing skin resistance compared to the number of people who experience increasing skin resistance levels (four participants). At North Road East, all of the nine participants recorded a decreasing skin resistance level. This further suggests that North Road East is the most stressful area compared to the other two areas as all of the participant's skin resistance levels decreased as they walked along the road.

The aggregate emotional arousal levels for all of the participants, where an average of the participants' data was visualised and projected onto the map of the city centre (see Figure 9), show a clear correlation between stress peaks and urban features.

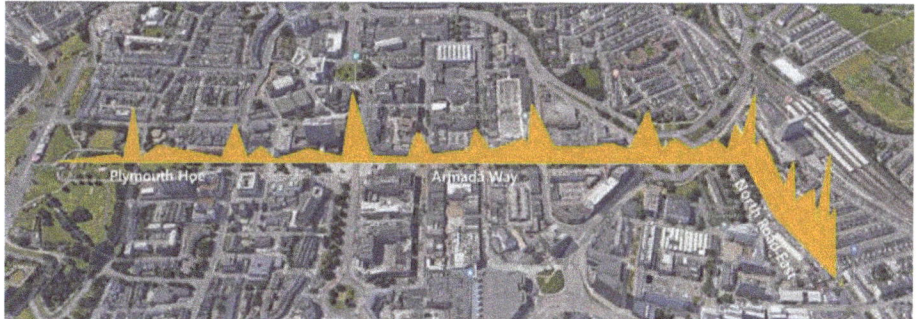

Figure 9. Average of all the participant's stress levels combined and visualised onto the map of Plymouth City Centre, showing the 'peaks' of negative emotional response at road crossings and junctions.

The participant's data showed 'peaks' (that correspond to Bakker's et al.'s findings [40]) that can be identified as sharp increases in stress levels whenever they encountered road junctions along the walk. In addition, the figure also shows that as participants walk from Plymouth Hoe to North Road East, their apparent stress level gradually increases, providing another an indication as to how different areas within the city affect the level of stress of their inhabitants.

3.2. Change in Stress Levels at Crossings and Junctions

Another clear finding from this study is the relationship road crossings and junctions have with the change in stress levels of the participants. A typical participant is shown in Figure 10 with the crossings and GSR data levels indicated. The overall results (see Figures 11–13) show that all of the crossings have at least three people experiencing a sudden drop in skin resistance level- or a stress 'peak'. Crossings at Citadel Road, Royal Parade, and Mayflower Street (see Figure 11) recorded the highest number of participants (i.e., all of the 6 participants) experiencing a sudden a stress 'peak'. Derry Avenue crossing and junctions at New George St. and Cornwall St., on the contrary, recorded the lowest number of participants (3 participants) that experienced the stress 'peak' (see Figure 12). The other 3 participants recorded generally unchanged stress levels when encountering these roads. Crossings at Citadel Road, Royal Parade and Mayflower St. are notably busier than junctions at New George St., Cornwall St., and Derry Ave. This resulted in more participants experiencing a sudden stress 'peak' at the former 3 crossings rather than at the latter 3. In fact, junctions at New George St. and Cornwall St. are at a fully pedestrianised area thus have no traffic presence.

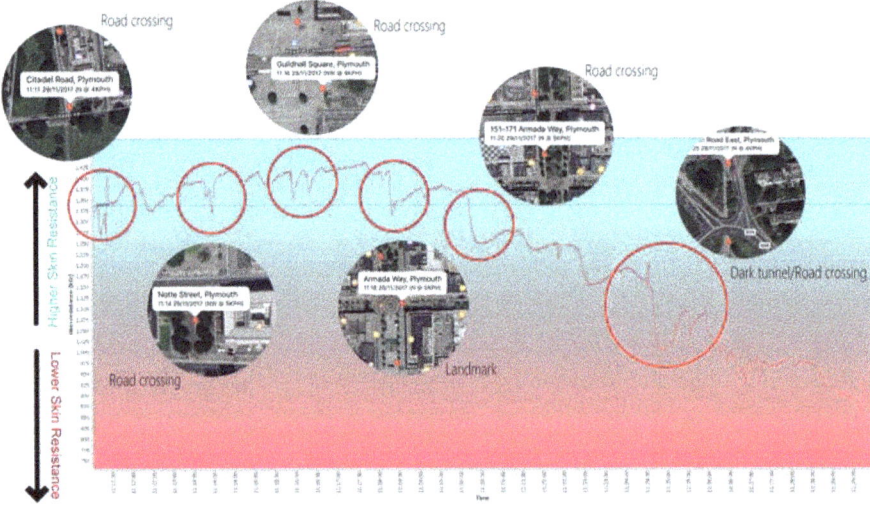

Figure 10. Typical participant's GSR data graph with crossings indicated and corresponding stress 'peaks' circled.

3.3. Relationship between Stress Levels and the Presence of Traffic and Natural Features

These different characteristics of each type of urban space encountered on the walk provides a clear variable which allows this paper to narrow down its research i.e., the relationship between emotions and physical environment can be studied in a more explicit manner. This means that the connection emotions have with specific urban features, in this case the presence of traffics and natural features, can be established more clearly. One observation that could be made from the findings is that area which was had the most 'green' space and natural features (Plymouth Hoe) created a generally less stressful environment for the participants. In contrast, areas with relatively less green space caused participants to feel less emotionally aroused. This observation is supported by many other previous studies such as MacKerron and Mourato's [41] "Mappiness" project and Klettner et al. [42] EmoMap project which have shown that green or natural environments have positive effects on emotions.

The results suggest that participants feel the least stressed at areas where the traffic levels were low and vice versa exhibited higher stress levels at busy roads. This can also explain the difference in number of participants experiencing stress 'peaks' at different junctions along the route. It was noted that Citadel Road, Royal Parade, and Mayflower Street junctions in particular have the most number of people experiencing the stress 'peaks' as they are significantly busier crossings than the others. Crossings at New George St., and Cornwall St. on the other hand have the least number of people experiencing sudden increase in stress levels because they are notably calmer and less busy in terms of traffic presence. In fact, junctions at New George St. and Cornwall St. are fully pedestrianised areas and thus the levels of traffic presence at these areas are actually zero. Previous studies, particularly, Klettner et al. [42] in their EmoMap project supported this claim as they have also found that participants give the lowest positive ratings (in terms of emotional response) when they are in an urban area with heavy traffic.

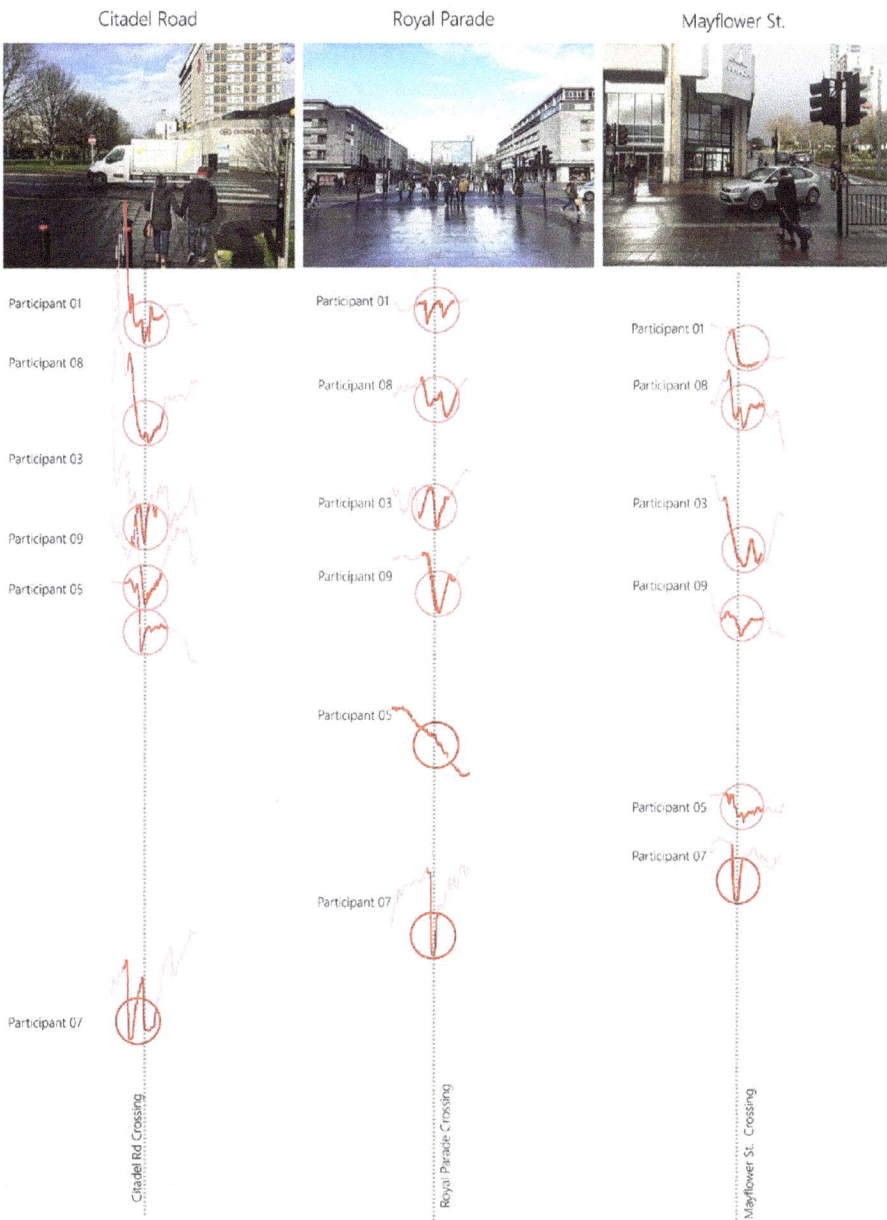

Figure 11. Crossings at Citadel Road, Royal Parade and Mayflower Street recorded the highest number of participants (all of the 6 participants) experiencing a stress 'peaks'.

Figure 12. Derry Ave. crossing and junctions at New George St. and Cornwall St. on the contrary, recorded the lowest number of participants (3 participants) that experience the stress 'peak'.

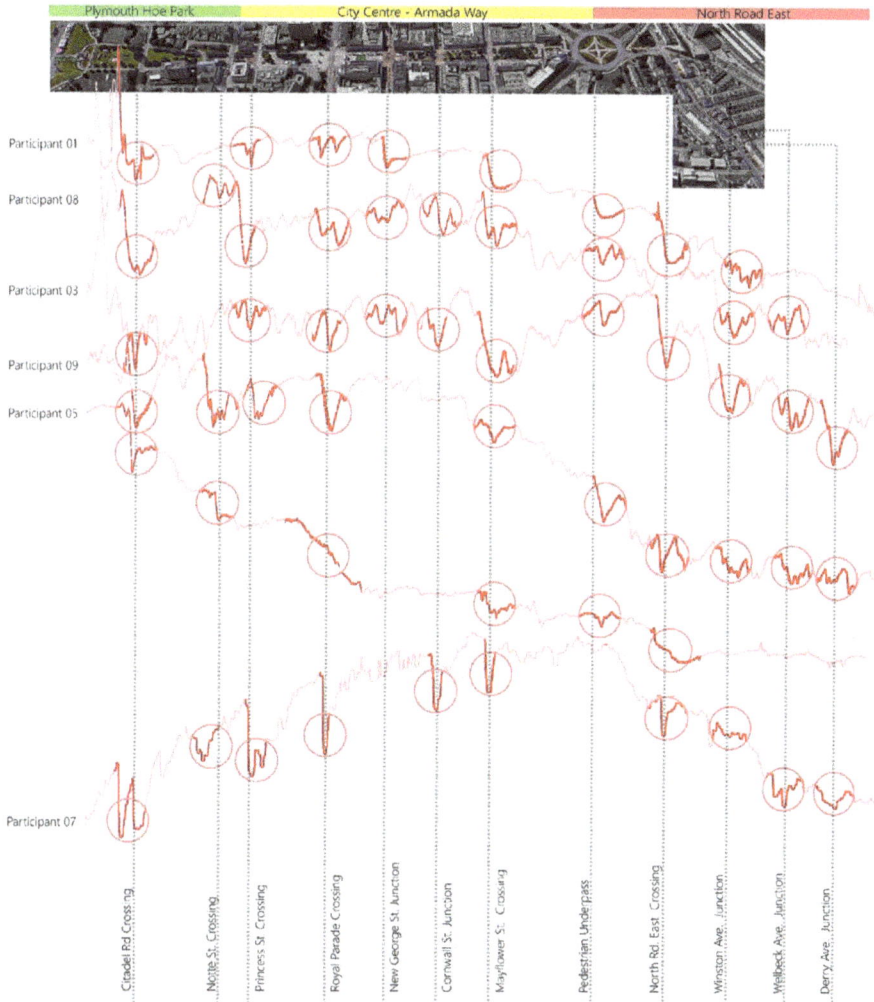

Figure 13. Overall results from all of the 6 participants with their graphs cross referenced with their GPS locational data. It could be noted that all of the crossings have at least 3 people experiencing a sudden drop in skin resistance level which equates to a stress 'peak'.

4. Discussion

As Nold and Zeile et al. have demonstrated [32,33] emotional data can offer a new layer of data and provide new dimensions for both urban planners and citizens to share understanding of the city they live in. This study identified two potential ways in which emotional data can be used; firstly, through the link between a change in emotions and distinct urban planning features and secondly through the change in process to people gathering their own quantitative emotional data over time and in situ.

4.1. Changes in Emotions and the Link with Urban Planning Features

The findings show clear links between emotional response and corresponding characteristics of urban spaces as follows:

- Areas with more green space and natural features result in creating a less stressful environment for the participants (e.g., Plymouth Hoe).
- Areas with higher levels of urban traffic (more cars) result in creating a more stressful environment for the participants (e.g., North Road East).
- Road crossings and junctions result in stress 'peaks' or sudden increase in stress level by the participants (e.g., Royal Parade).

The study identified a correlation between emotional stress 'peaks' and urban design features and characteristics that could be used as a quantitative input into urban planning discussions. While this study is small scale in terms of the number of participants, the nature of the findings does indicate that the method could be replicated with larger number of participants to increase the level of data and coverage. Shoval et al. [35] recognised that products of such analysis "lead to important insights into how people perceive and interact emotionally with the urban environment; it can therefore be of great use in an improved planning process" [35]. Zeile et al. have acknowledged that their results can be used "as a source of information to help improve bicycle traffic planning and to identify peaks in urban planning deficiencies" [34]. The current model of planning allows for consultation, but this is limited in terms of modes of participation and the information layer (see Figure 1 earlier in this paper). The gathering of emotional data and the subsequent understanding gained from this analysis would help create a readily available layer of shared data (Figure 14) directly inputting into the urban planning process.

Figure 14. Emotional Data Model of participation in Urban Planning process.

While this study was undertaken in an existing city space, there is also the potential to draw some more general conclusions that could inform urban design proposals. It could therefore provide better insights of the city and its inhabitants—enabling a new citizen-centered perspective in urban planning processes.

4.2. Physiological Data for Citizen-Centric Participatory Planning

A shared approach to participation in urban planning processes could involve the provision of a new information layer within urban planning analysis through the gathering of citizens' emotional data through physiological responses methods. Unlike traditional forms of urban planning participation such as public meetings, consultations and hearings, this study suggests that humans, as the users of a city, could share qualitative emotional data. Jacobs [12] pointed out an important change in urban planning procedures which includes bottom up processes of participation that proactively involve citizens in urban change. This study has explored the potential of using physiological sensor technology to directly, objectively and cheaply measure citizens' emotions. Scaled up, this approach would mean that a city could involve citizens in sharing emotional data that would regularly provide new emotional data near real-time and as a readily available information layer to the city council. The model used in this study was for citizens to gather their own data and share it with others in order to understand their experience of the city in a more quantitative manner. However, it should be recognized that there are recognized and valid issues around the ethics and nature of consent around crowdsourcing urban data. For instance Gabrys argues that 'enabling citizens to monitor their activities convert these citizens into unwitting gatherers and providers of data' that can be used for political or commercial purposes beyond that which citizens are aware of [43]. However, when used by the citizen for their own benefit Haklay asserts that 'the act of mapping itself can be an act of asserting presence, rights to be heard or expression of personal beliefs in the way that the world should evolve and operate' [44].

When reviewed against Arnstein's [16] 'Ladder of Participation', this method of using physiological device to gather citizens' emotional data would still fall under tokenism at either 'consultation' or 'placation' rung of the ladder. This is because participants of this study only provide emotional data input and do not have the actual power to influence how the data will be used in urban planning process. In the end, city planners still play a central role in planning decisions. However, the lack of 'citizen power' in this participatory method could be outweighed by the fact that using physiological sensing technology such as the GSR provides an accurate and objective data resource of citizens' emotions. It could also potentially be done at scale to create a large information database. During a traditional consultation process, citizens would subjectively express concerns about a planning project and the relevant authority would re-evaluate the project based on their feedback. In this citizen sensing participatory planning approach however, there is no need to wait until a planning project is established before actions or decisions could be made. In fact, the collection of emotional data can be continuous and ongoing and can be used at any time to inform any new planning projects. Therefore, for as long as the emotional data inputs from citizens influence the outcome of any planning decisions, even without any exercise of 'power', this form of participatory process could move beyond tokenism towards Arnstein's model of 'citizen power'.

5. Conclusions

A sharing cities approach can enable citizens to gather, share and analyse urban data which can give them an enhanced understanding and greater accessibility in city planning decisions [45]. This tends to relate to enabling citizens to gain access to self-generated sources of data, which enables a more informed understanding of issues in their urban environment. Digital participation using technologies such as physiological sensing devices, smartphones, and GPS technology present opportunities for a more effective and human-centred approach to participatory planning. This paper explored the potential of citizen's emotional data using digital tools such as the galvanic skin response (GSR) and GPS devices to objectively measure emotional response of people to a geo-located urban space. The study described in this paper extended the work of Nold (2009), Zeile et al. (2015) and Shoval et al., (2017) who found that emotional data mapped against high-resolution spatial analysis can have potential for informing urban planning decision making [35]. The potential of this method was discussed, and future directions for the research would be to replicate the study with larger numbers of participant's and to test a range of different urban settings. In particular, it would be valuable to test whether the findings around green space and busy roads creating different levels of emotional arousal could be replicated in different, but comparable cities. Furthermore, the link between road junctions and stress 'peaks' could have potential to be tested with a range of urban planning features. In terms of participatory methods, these could be used by citizens at both pre- and post implementation stage to quantitatively measure the actual response of people to an urban planning project.

The results prove that there is a significant relationship between humans and the physical environments and by objectively measuring and analysing the data, this method provides innovative opportunities for urban planners to understand how citizens relate and interact emotionally to the city's urban environment. The data gathered through this approach could add a new dimension in the form of a new additional layer of information in urban planning analysis to assist urban planners in decision-making processes. This has implications for urban planning policy in terms of how they could better incorporate participatory data into their practice, and how citizens could be empowered to share their emotional experiences of the city.

Author Contributions: A.F. and K.S.W. developed the topic, methods and analytical framework; A.F. supervised students and conducted the field investigations and analyzed the data; A.F. and K.S.W. wrote the paper.

Funding: This research received no external funding

Acknowledgments: Thank you to the support of the School of Architecture, Design and Environment at Plymouth University, UK.

Conflicts of Interest: The authors declare no conflicts of interest.

References

1. Willis, K.S.; Aurigi, A. *Digital and Smart Cities*; Routledge: London, UK, 2017.
2. Cowley, J.E. Planning in the age of facebook: The role of social networking in planning processes. *GeoJournal* **2010**, *75*, 407–420. [CrossRef]
3. Desouza, K.C.; Bhagwatwar, A. Citizen apps to solve complex urban problems. *J. Urban Technol.* **2012**, *19*, 107–136. [CrossRef]
4. Mclaren, D.; Agyeman, J. *Sharing Cities: A Case for Truly Smart and Sustainable Cities*; MIT Press: Cambridge, MA, USA, 2015.
5. Linders, D. From e-government to we-government: Defining a typology for citizen coproduction in the age of social media. *Gov. Inf. Q.* **2012**, *29*, 446–454. [CrossRef]
6. Innes, J.E.; Booher, D.E. Reframing public participation: Strategies for the 21st century. *Plan. Theory Pract.* **2004**, *5*, 419–436. [CrossRef]
7. Renn, O.; Webler, T.; Rakel, H.; Dienel, P.; Johnson, B. Public participation in decision making: A three-step procedure. *Policy Sci.* **1993**, *26*, 189–214. [CrossRef]
8. Wilson, A.; Tewdwr-Jones, M.; Comber, R. Urban planning, public participation and digital technology: App development as a method of generating citizen involvement in local planning processes. *Environ. Plan. B Urban Anal. City Sci.* **2017**. [CrossRef]
9. Münster, S.; Georgia, C.; Heijneb, K.; Klamerta, K.; Noennig, J.R.; Pump, M.; Stelzle, B.; Meer, H.V.D. How to involve inhabitants in urban design planning by using digital tools? An overview on a state of the art, key challenges and promising approaches. *Procedia Comput. Sci.* **2017**, *112*, 2391–2405. [CrossRef]
10. Crivellaro, C.; Comber, R.; Bowers, J. A Pool of Dreams: Facebook, Politics and the Emergence of a Social Movement. In Proceedings of the 32nd annual ACM conference (CHI '14), Toronto, ON, Canada, 26 April–1 May 2014; ACM Press: New York, NY, USA, 2014; pp. 3573–3582.
11. Hasler, S.; Chenal, J.; Soutter, M. Digital tools as a means to foster inclusive, data-informed urban planning. *Civ. Eng. Arch.* **2017**, *5*, 230–239. [CrossRef]
12. Jacobs, J. *The Death and Life of American Cities*; Random House: New York, NY, USA, 2002.
13. Lane, M. Public participation in planning: An intellectual history. *Aust. Geogr.* **2005**, *36*, 283–299. [CrossRef]
14. Hall, P. *Urban and Regional Planning*, 3rd ed.; Routledge: London, UK, 1992.
15. Faludi, A. *Planning Theory*; Pergamon: New York, NY, USA, 1973.
16. Arnstein, S. A ladder of citizen participation. *J. Am. Plan. Assoc.* **1969**, *35*, 216–224. [CrossRef]
17. Painter, M. Participation and power. In *Citizen Participation in Government*; Munro-Clarke, M., Ed.; Hale & Ironmonger: Sydney, Australia, 1992.
18. Raslan, R.; Al-hagla, K.; Bakr, A. Integration of Emotional Behavioural layer "emobel" in city planning. In Proceedings of the REAL CORP 2014—PLAN IT SMART! Clever Solutions for Smart Cities: 19th International Conference on Urban Planning, Regional Development and Information Society, Vienna, Austria, 21–23 May 2014; pp. 309–317.
19. Baum, H. Planning with half a mind: Why planners resist emotion. *Plan. Theory Pract.* **2015**, *16*, 498–516. [CrossRef]
20. Lynch, K. *The Image of the City*; MIT Press: Cambridge, MA, USA, 1967.
21. Ferreira, A. Emotions in planning practice: A critical review and a suggestion for future developments based on mindfulness. *Town Plan. Rev.* **2013**, *84*, 703–719. [CrossRef]

22. Porter, L.; Sandercock, L.; Umemoto, K.; Bates, L.; Zapata, M.A.; Kondo, M.C.; Zitcer, A.; Lake, R.W.; Fonza, A.; Sletto, B.; et al. What's love got to do with it? Illuminations on loving attachment in planning. *Plan. Theory Pract.* **2012**, *13*, 593–627. [CrossRef]
23. Gunder, M.; Hillier, J. *Planning in Ten Words or Less*; Ashgate: Farnham, UK, 2009.
24. Mislove, A.; Lehmann, S.; Ahn, Y.Y.; Onnela, J.P.; Rosenquist, J.N. Pulse of the nation: US mood throughout the day inferred from twitter. *Rumpus*, 7 March 2010.
25. Tauscher, S.; Neumann, K. Combining web map services and opinion mining to generate sentiment maps of touristic locations. In *Service Oriented Mapping*; Jobst, M., Ed.; JobstMedia Management Verlag Wien: Wien, Germany, 2012; pp. 277–286.
26. Resch, B.; Summa, A.; Sagl, G.; Zeile, P.; Exner, J.-P. Urban emotions—Geo-semantic emotion extraction from technical sensors, human sensors and crowdsourced data. In *Progress in Location-Based Services*; Gartner, G., Huang, H., Eds.; Springer International Publishing: Berlin/Heidelberg, Germany, 2015; pp. 199–212.
27. Resch, B.; Sudmanns, M.; Sagl, G.; Summe, A.; Zeile, P.; Exner, J.E. Crowdsourcing physiological conditions and subjective emotions by coupling technical and human mobile sensors. *J. Geogr. Inf. Sci.* **2015**, 514–524. [CrossRef]
28. Resch, B.; Summa, A.; Zeile, P.; Strube, M. Citizen-centric urban planning through extracting emotion information from twitter in an interdisciplinary space-time-linguistics algorithm. *Urban Plan.* **2016**, *1*, 114–127. [CrossRef]
29. Hauthal, E.; Burghardt, D. Extraction of location-based emotions from photo platforms. In *Progress in Location-Based Services*; Krisp, J., Ed.; Springer: Munich, Germany, 2013.
30. Aiello, L.M.; Schifanella, R.; Quercia, D.; Aletta, F. Chatty maps: Constructing sound maps of urban areas from social media data. *R. Soc. Open Sci.* **2016**, *3*. [CrossRef] [PubMed]
31. Mody, R.; Willis, K.; Kerstein, R. Wimo: Location-Based Emotion Tagging. In Proceedings of the 8th International Conference on Mobile and Ubiquitous Multimedia, Cambridge, UK, 22–25 November 2009; ACM Press: New York, NY, USA, 2009; pp. 1–4.
32. Zeile, P.; Resch, B.; Dörrzapf, L.; Exner, J.-P.; Sagl, G.N.; Summa, A.; Sudmanns, M. Urban emotions—Tools of integrating people's perception into urban planning. In Proceedings of the REAL CORP: Conference on Urban Planning and Regional Development in the Information Society, Ghent, Belgium, 5–7 May 2015.
33. Nold, C. Emotional Cartography: Technologies of the Self. 2009. Available online: http://www.emotionalcartography.net/ (accessed on 11 September 2018).
34. Zeile, P.; Resch, B.; Loidl, M.; Petutschnig, A.; Dörrzapf, L. Urban emotions and cycling experience—Enriching traffic planning for cyclists with human sensor data. *GI Forum* **2016**, *1*, 204–216. [CrossRef]
35. Shoval, N.; Schvimer, Y.; Tamir, M. Tracking technologies and urban analysis: Adding the emotional dimension. *Cities* **2018**, *72*, 32–42. [CrossRef]
36. Dawson, E.M.; Schell, A.M.; Filion, D.L. The electrodermal system. In *Handbook of Psychophysiology*; Cambridge University Press: New York, NY, USA, 2007; pp. 200–223.
37. Boucsein, W.; Fowles, D.C.; Grimnes, S.; Ben-Shakhar, G.; Roth, W.T.; Dawson, M.E.; Filion, D.L. Publication standards for eda. *Psychophysiology* **2012**, *49*, 1017–1034. [PubMed]
38. Kreibig, S.D. Autonomic nervous system activity in emotion: A review. *Biol. Psychol.* **2010**, *84*, 394–421. [CrossRef] [PubMed]
39. Da Silva, A.N.R.; Zeile, P.; de Oliveira Aguiar, F.; Papastefanou, G.; Bergner, B.S. Smart sensoring and barrier free planning: Project outcomes and recent developments. In *Technologies for Urban and Spatial Planning: Virtual Cities and Territories*; Pinto, N.N., Tenedório, J.A., Antunes, A.P., Cladera, J.R., Eds.; IGI Global: Hershey, PA, USA, 2014; pp. 93–112.
40. Bakker, J.; Pechenizkiy, M.; Sidorova, N. What's your current stress level? Detection of stress patterns from gsr sensor data. In Proceedings of the 2011 IEEE 11th International Conference on Data Mining Workshops (ICDMW'11), Washington DC, USA, 11 December 2011; Spiliopoulou, M., Wang, H., Cook, D., Pei, J., Wang, W., Zaïane, O., Wu, X., Eds.; IEEE Computer Society: Washington, DC, USA, 2011; pp. 573–580.
41. MacKerron, G.; Mourato, S. Happiness is greater in natural environments. *Glob. Environ. Chang.* **2013**, *23*, 992–1000. [CrossRef]
42. Klettner, S.; Huang, H.; Schmidt, K.; Gartner, G. Crowdsourcing affective responses to space. *Kartographische Nachrichten* **2013**, *2*, 66–72.

43. Gabrys, J. Programming environments: Environmentality and citizen sensing in the smart city. *Environ. Plan. D Soc. Space* **2014**, *32*. [CrossRef]
44. Haklay, M. Beyond quantification: A role for citizen science and community science in a smart city. In Proceedings of the Data and City Workshop, Kildare, Ireland, 31 August–1 September 2015.
45. Niederer, S.; Priester, R. Smart citizens: Exploring the tools of the urban bottom-up movement. *Comput. Support. Coop. Work* **2016**, *25*, 137–152. [CrossRef]

© 2018 by the authors. Licensee MDPI, Basel, Switzerland. This article is an open access article distributed under the terms and conditions of the Creative Commons Attribution (CC BY) license (http://creativecommons.org/licenses/by/4.0/).

Article

Sharing and Riding: How the Dockless Bike Sharing Scheme in China Shapes the City

Yiyun Sun [1,2]

1. School of Management, Radboud University Nijmegen, 6525 HP Nijmegen, The Netherlands
2. School of Geography and Planning, Cardiff University, CF10 3AT Cardiff, UK; yiyunsun@163.com; Tel.: +86-134-262-88622

Received: 4 July 2018; Accepted: 31 July 2018; Published: 9 August 2018

Abstract: Over the last three years, the dockless bike sharing scheme has become prevalent in the context of the boom in the sharing economy, the wide use of mobile online payment, the increasing environmental awareness and the inherent market demand. This research takes Beijing as a case study, investigates the users' characteristics, their behaviour change, and perceptions of dockless bike sharing scheme by the quantitative survey, and then analyzes the reasons behind it and how it has changed the residents' life in Beijing. This new kind of dockless shared bikes, with great advantages of accessibility, flexibility, efficiency and affordability, helps to solve the 'last mile' problem, reduce the travel time, and seems to be very environmentally-friendly and sustainable. However, with the help of interview and document analysis, this research finds that the shared bikes are not the effective alternative for the frequent car-users. Nevertheless, it also has numerous negative consequences such as 'zombie' bikes blocking the sidewalks and vandalism to the bikes. The public is also worried about their quality and safety, especially the issues of 'right of way'. How to coordinate and solve these problems is not only related to the future direction of the dockless bike sharing scheme but also to the vital interests of the general public. Therefore, it is important to emphasize that governments, enterprises, and the public participate in multi-party cooperation and build synergic governance networks to carry forward the advantages and avoid the negative effects of the new bike sharing system.

Keywords: bike sharing; sustainable mobility; sharing economic; urban studies

1. Introduction

In recent years, growing concerns over climate change, deteriorating urban environment and unhealthy lifestyles have placed more attention on sustainable transportation alternatives such as bicycles. The bicycle, compared to other kinds of vehicles, has many advantages for both cyclists and society: it is a low-cost, low-polluting, health-improving way to travel [1]. In light of these benefits, cycling has become a major component of visions of sustainable urban transport systems in Europe, supported by market-based instruments, command-and-control approaches, as well as soft policy measures [2].

China, like many of other countries, has experienced a rapid growth of bicycles from the 1970s to the 1990s. However, after the mid-1990s, bicycle usage steadily decreased as a result of economic growth, increased urbanization, expanded city areas and a gradually deteriorating cycling environment [3]. At the beginning of the 21st century, the Chinese government realized that excessive dependence on cars has led to serious environmental pollution and resource constraints. To preserve the environment and achieve a harmonious balance of economic growth, population, resources and the environment, the Chinese government put forward the new urban development mode of 'a resource-conserving and environmentally-friendly society', and had a major shift from fossil fuels to renewable energy [4]. Nevertheless, a long history of bicycle usage in the country provides great potential for bicycles, a green form of travel, to be part of public and private transportation. Following the Chinese government's new approach, Chinese municipal governments have heavily subsidized the development of the Public Bike Sharing Program (PBSP) to encourage non-motorized transport and offer a flexible, convenient, and low-cost mobility option to the people.

Yang et al. used the real spatial location data of the public bicycle-sharing systems of Hangzhou and Ningbo in China, and discovered that the public bicycle-sharing systems can decrease the average trip time of passengers and increase the efficiency of an urban public transport network, as well as effectively improve the uneven level of traffic flow spatial distribution of an urban public transport network; they found that this will be helpful for smoothening the traffic flow and alleviating traffic congestion [5]. Zhang et al. found that bike-sharing systems have varying degrees of success based on the empirical study of five Chinese cities. The configurations which seem the most sustainable consider and integrate elements relating to transport planning, system design and choice of business model. PBSP, as a Product Service System, needs to be carefully developed to appreciate the quality and timely interplay between the physical design of the system and the provision of services being offered [6].

The first PBSP emerged in Beijing in 2005 when some touring-related firms started the bicycle rental operation to meet the needs of tourists, especially the overseas visitors who want to rent a bicycle to travel around Beijing. During the 2008 Beijing Olympic Games, the public bicycle rental market reached a peak. However, after one year, the public bicycle rental market encountered many problems. Some companies declared bankruptcy and were closed, others closed dozens of bicycle stations to reduce the operational costs. Some researchers summarized five reasons of failure of the first generation of PBSP in Beijing: unreasonable distribution of bicycle stations, lack of safety for cyclists, deteriorated conditions of public bicycle equipment, unattractive fare and inexplicit policy orientation [7].

One of the barriers that still hindered the traditional bike sharing services was the difficulty of access to docking stations [8]. Learning from the experience of PBSP, a successful dockless bike-sharing program may integrate the functions of docking stations directly into the shared bikes. In 2015, two start-up companies, Ofo and Mobike, initiated an innovative generation of fully Dockless Bike Sharing Scheme (DBSS) in China [9]. In mid-2017, the total amount of venture capital for the bicycle industry in China reached USD 2 billion, and more than 40 bike-sharing companies have been established, which makes the market tempting but fierce [10].

This new generation of bike sharing schemes is different from the traditional public bike system since it is easily accessible, flexible and cheap (Table 1). Before the existence of the DBSS, bikes needed to be docked at stations, whereas in the DBSS, bikes can be un-locked and paid for using a smartphone and can be picked up and left any parking area at users' convenience [11]. The DBSS becomes prevalent in the context of the boom in sharing economy, the wide use of smartphones, mobile Internet and online payment. Bike use dramatically increased within the recent years, when private companies started to combine digital technologies with sharing economy concepts. In July 2017, the total number of domestic shared bikes reached CNY 16 million, and the daily ride transaction of shared bikes reached CNY 50 million across China. The rapid development of the DBSS has created 100,000 new jobs in China [12].

Table 1. The comparison between the Dockless Bike Sharing Scheme (DBSS) and the Public Bike Sharing Program (PBSP).

Characteristics	Dockless Bike Sharing Scheme (DBSS)	Public Bike Sharing Program (PBSP)
Dock station	Dockless	Fixed docking stations
Location	Anywhere and can be found via apps	Near subway stations, bus stops and intersections
Usage	Scan the QR code with smartphone to unlock	Get a bicycle-rental card to unlock
Reservation	Can be reserved for 15 min	Cannot be reserved
Price	CNY 0.5~1 for 30 min	Usually free for the first 1 or 2 h
Deposit	Deposit can be returned anytime on apps	Refund deposit at the rental service branches

The DBSS has led a trend of 'green travel' in China. Based on the research, bike sharing in Shanghai saved 8358 t of petrol and decreased CO_2 emissions by 25,240 t in 2016 [11]. It seems that DBSS could significantly help China to achieve the declared goal in the Paris Convention of reducing the CO_2 emissions by 60–65% per GDP before 2030 [13]. On the other hand, DBSS with its great advantages of flexibility in short trips is just the one to deal with commuters' 'first mile/last mile' problem—the movement of people from a transportation hub to a final destination of the home or office. This new integrated transportation mode, namely the 'bike + bus/metro + bike' trip, has improved the efficiency of the traditional single type of vehicle mode.

The new generation of bike sharing services without docking stations is currently revolutionizing the traditional bike-sharing market as it dramatically expands in China and even around the world. However, many cities are not ready to welcome the mass of rubber and aluminum from blocking pedestrian walkways and piling up in the public space [14]. Though the DBSS is a fairly new trend, the concerns about the popularity, the benefits and potential harm behind it has prompted a hot debate among the public as well as the academic circle. However, there is still a gap between the descriptions of phenomenon and the assessment of the practice. It thus raises a pressing question—does DBSS, this new scheme, really help cities to move towards a more sustainable mobility mode?

In addition to the societal relevance, this study also has a scientific relevance. Firstly, although a range of empirical studies have already reported a wide variety of findings on bike sharing, it has often been argued that there are distinctive inconsistencies across studies due to study design limitation, measurement bias and cross-country variations. Particularly, a majority of research is drawn from the European and American cities, while very little research has been concentrated in Chinese cases with a rapid growth of PBSS [15]. To fill the gap in context-specific research, this paper takes Beijing as a case to investigate the bike sharing development in China. Secondly, there is a growing literature on the earlier breed of docked bike sharing schemes, there are very few critical academic studies of this new dockless bike sharing scheme [16]. This research seeks to contribute to social scientific debates on the new DBSS and its impacts. Thirdly, there is a lack of theoretical scientific knowledge and methods in existing research on DBSS. The current study of DBSS mostly uses the data provided by the operation companies, which include the basic bikes' and users' information plus GPS information about the route and parking place [11,17,18]. They normally focus more on the macroscopic usage of DBSS by big data mining and ArcGIS analysis. For example, Zhang and Mi discuss the environmental benefits from a spatiotemporal perspective, quantitatively evaluate environmental benefits of bike sharing using a large-scale bike-sharing dataset provided by the company Mobike, and estimate the impacts of bike sharing on energy use, carbon dioxide (CO_2) and nitrogen oxide (NO_x) emissions in Shanghai in 2016 [11]; Pan et al. conduct extensive experiments for hierarchical reinforcement pricing based on a real dataset from Mobike to propose a deep reinforcement learning framework for incentivizing users to rebalance dockless bike sharing systems [17]; Chang et al. take Beijing as a case study and present a framework design of the Faulty Bike-Sharing Recycling Problem optimization model to minimize the total recycling costs through the K-means clustering method that is used to divide the faulty bike-sharing into different service points [18]. Only Spinney and Lin studied the DBSS through a qualitative and societal perspective—by exploring the social, spatial and environmental relations produced by these new "hybrid mobiles", they explore the extent to which these systems represent more economically reproductive 'transactional' or disruptive and 'transformational' modalities of sharing [16].

This study however derives from the users' survey and is supported by experts' interviews. It tries to investigate people's perception and attitudes, while at the same time exploring the behaviour change of people's travel mode engendered by these disruptive forms of bike sharing, and by using a mixed quantitative and qualitative method.

From the above, the overall research aims can be summarized as below:

- To explore the reasons behind the popularity of the DBSS in China and investigate the users' characteristics and their behaviour change and perceptions of DBSS;
- To explore and critically assess the contribution of DBSS towards sustainable mobility in Beijing context;
- To propose recommendations for healthier DBSS development and governance in the future.

2. Materials and Methods

2.1. Case Study

The identification of the case to be studied is largely dependent on the researcher's interest. In this research, Beijing is the suitable and typical case worth studying. Beijing is suffering from strong air pollution, which is a serious threat against the health of the residents and the environment. Beijing, with its 21.5 million inhabitants, is one of the most crowded cities in the world, and the huge population has exacerbated the problem. To assess the contribution of DBSS to the city's sustainability and analyze the potential solutions for cities to cope with the challenges of the new bike boom, a single case study is adopted for both methodological and pragmatic reasons. First of all, Beijing was a pioneer in the new bike-sharing approach—by September 2017, there were 15 Shared bike bicycle enterprises, which comprised 2.35 million shared bikes. In addition, the two biggest operators, Ofo and Mobike, both chose to locate their headquarters in Beijing [14]. On the other hand, in September 2017, the Beijing Municipality just announced a new regulation to encourage the development of a standardized bicycle sharing system, to implement the holistic governance and control of the DBSS providers, and to keep a dynamic balance on the quantity of shared bikes that have been put into the market.

2.2. Data Collection and Analysis

In this study, the data is generally from three main sources: documentation, survey, and interview. To achieve the research aims, different methods are used to collect the targeted data (Table 2).

The analysis in this study is based on the primary data gathered from survey, interview and secondary data from other documentation. Analysis of survey data tends to be through the use of a computer utilizing a number of statistical analysis software packages. In this case, SPSS is used for descriptive, analytical and contextual analysis. The in-depth interviews were digitally recorded and fully transcribed. Afterward, the analysis of the transcripts involved three stages: familiarization, thematic analysis, and interpretations. All the data enrolled the triangulation to verify the validity and reliability.

Table 2. Targeted data and collecting methods.

Data from Survey			
Users' Characteristics	Travel Characteristics	Ride Characteristics	Users' Attitude
• Age • Gender • Income • Education • Occupation ……	• Commuting time • Commuting distance • Transport preference before and after the using DBSS ……	• Frequency of usage • Travel purpose • Travel length • Travel time • Reasons for using ……	• Satisfaction of bikes, infrastructures, parking, safety, • Influence on life and city ……
Data from Documentation and Interview			
Companies' Data and Documentation	Interview with Planners	Interview with Community Worker	Interview with Bike Hunter
• GPS location • Travel route • Travel mileage • Recycling and repairing • Policies and reports ……	• The sustainability of DBSS towards city • The impacts of DBSS towards city • The potential coordinating way ……	• The influence of DBSS on community • The responsibility of community • The coordination with other parties ……	• The operation and organization of the bike hunters' group • Daily job and self-reflection • The difficulties and solution ……

2.2.1. Survey

The survey in this study has four parts, and the full Internet survey is used to gather data. Firstly, the classification questions, namely the 'personal' section of the survey. Demographic information such as age, gender, income, education and occupation are collected in the beginning of the survey. Secondly, the survey asks respondents lifestyle and travel characteristics, for example the commuting time and distance, the transportation they choose for commuting, chores and entertainment. In this part, people need to answer the transportation mode they normally choose before the DBSS appeared and after to evaluate the behaviour change. Thirdly, the data of ride characteristics are collected, including the trip purpose, frequency, length and other related figures when people use the DBSS. Finally, the attitude scale form helps to assess the opinion and perception of users towards DBSS. There are also several open questions in the last part to give respondents greater freedom to answer in a way that suits their interpretation.

This study uses a non-probability sample, because the statistical accuracy may be less of a concern than being 'fir for purpose'. Purposeful sampling occurs where a selection is made according to a known characteristic, in this case—the Beijing citizens who regularly use the DBSS. Whilst the population in Beijing and the DBSS users are widely distributed, snowball sampling and convenience sampling are also helpful when obtaining substantial survey data. As for the sample size, in order to be able to measure differences or variability in the sample and to use these findings as estimates of the population, 260 samples are selected in this research. The number is calculated by the online sample size calculator, with the confidence level of 95% and confidence interval 6%. A population of 11,000,000 is cited by the registered DBSS users in Beijing in August 2017 [19]. The overall background range of samples is comprehensive and balanced, however the number is relatively small compared to the residents in Beijing, which might cause some bias of the research outcome.

Due to the limited time and budget, this study uses an online survey to collect data on DBSS users. There is a pilot survey phase before the formal distribution. Once the survey design was completed and prior to distribution to the sampling frame, a pilot study was undertaken on 15 people. The time-span of respondent recruitment is 2 weeks. In this study, once the recruitment postings had been made, the survey administration and recording of responses was self-running. The DBSS requires smartphone and online payment for operation, thus nearly all the users are smartphone holders, which means they could receive the link of the online survey by smartphone. Considering the above reasons, the survey is posted in the social media groups, and public pages, thus people who are interested in the topic, and satisfy the filter criteria of purposeful sampling could fill in the form whenever and wherever it is convenient. However, since the sample size is relatively small and the time-span is relatively short, the outcome may have some negative bias.

2.2.2. Documentation

In this study, both official documents and private documents are reviewed. The documentation in this research is from media and news reports relating to the growth, investment and impacts of DBSS in Beijing and China more broadly. For example, Mobike, one of the major companies that provides DBSS service, together with some academic institutions, has published certain reports that include a lot of useful information and users' travel data. Policies, government guidelines, as well as the data about infrastructures and transportation are collected from the government's yearbook and official website. For example, the various guidelines both from national government and Beijing municipality are carefully reviewed [20–24]; Meanwhile, the White Papers published by the Mobike company also contributed to this research [25,26].

2.2.3. Interview

To ensure the authenticity and availability of the information, two planners (experts in transportation), one local community worker from subdistrict office and one Mobike Hunter from the—Mobike Hunter's Volunteer Network agreed to participate in the semi-structured interview. The participants were asked about the problems they faced with cycling and development of the dockless bike sharing system in the city (see Table 2). Planners and community worker interviews are about their insights on the DBSS and its impact on the city's sustainable development and the potential approach for cities to cooperate with this new trend. The interview of Mobike Hunter is related to the research potential for solving the problems that DBSS has brought. Unfortunately, the operation companies refused to participate in the research, which means the perspectives from the market are missing.

2.3. Ethical Considerations

The topic of this thesis related to people's behaviour and attitudes, which did not involve any illegal behaviour. Ethical issues are carefully considered in this thesis. As regards the recruitment procedures, the target group in this project did not include any vulnerable groups. The project was spread by social media and conducted online. Meanwhile, all the interviewees who participated in the survey were asked for permission to conduct the interview and questionnaires. Besides this, all respondents were informed that they can withdraw from the study at any time and that the survey is entirely anonymous. The participation is voluntary and the data will only be used in this thesis. No observation was conducted. There was no potential risk for any respondent, neither physical nor psychological.

3. Results

3.1. Findings from the Survey

A total number of 260 survey respondents have been selected. Women and men are equally represented. Fifty-two percent of the participants are young (18–30), 48% are middle-aged (30–60) and there are very few senior participants (60+). The result implied that the DBSS users are popular in all age groups, particularly the active younger groups. Meanwhile, the majority of respondents had an academic background (75% had a bachelor's degree or above). Referring to the average monthly income in Beijing, which is CNY 7706 based on the Beijing Municipal Human Resources and Social Security Bureau, the participants were situated among various income levels apart from the no income group (15%); 44% had lower than the average wages, and 41% had higher wages than the Beijing average monthly income. As for the occupation, most of them are students or staff in public institutions or enterprises and professional workers who do not do too much manual labour. As for the participants' commuting figures, it can be observed that half of the participants commute under 40 min per day, and 58% commute less than 10 km (see Figure 1).

The survey shows that 38% users are frequent users of DBSS, and only 14% of participants never use the DBSS. People choose DBSS most because of its convenient and time-saving characteristics. For these non-users, however, their reasons to refuse the DBSS are mostly about their daily needs: to deposit money and to retain private information.

In most circumstances, the shared bikes are used for a short time and distance interval. Sixty percent of respondents finish their trip in less than 10 min and 91% in approximately 20 min. Two thirds of users use DBBS for 1–3 km distances. This means that the majority of the users use DBSS for their last mile of travel. The most common cycling time is 7:00–9:00 and 17:00–19:00 for commuting which equals to the rush hour in Beijing. Two thirds of trips are for commuting and one third is for leisure and everyday chores. It is also revealed that hybrid transportation modes were popular. Nearly half of the users always transfer to other modes of public transportation such as the metro (89%) and bus (54%).

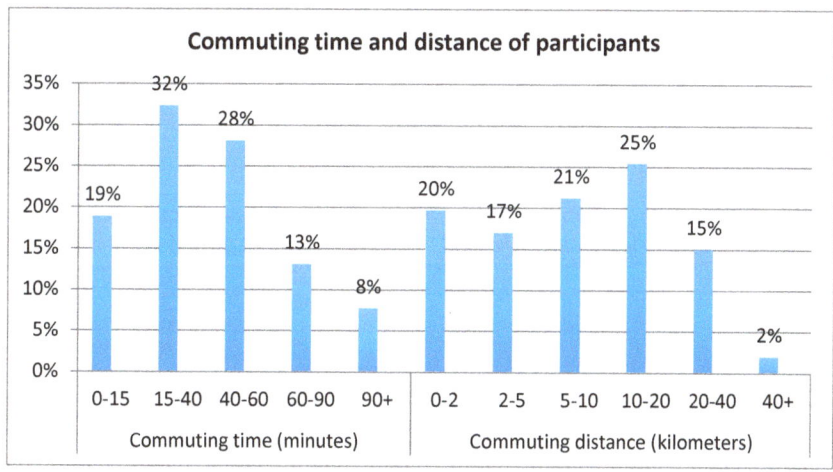

Figure 1. Commuting time and distance of participants.

3.1.1. How Does the DBSS Change People's Lives?

In the survey, people are asked to choose their transportation mode in the city for different purposes before and after the DBSS appeared. From Figure 2 below, we could find that the change of car-use and motorbike-use is not significant before and after the DBSS appeared. The usage of bikes as the mode of transportation for commuting purposes is doubled; meanwhile walking and the usage of public transport have slightly declined. The transportation mode change of chore purpose trip and entertainment purpose trip are similar to the commute purpose, which has the same increase in terms of bike use (more than doubled).

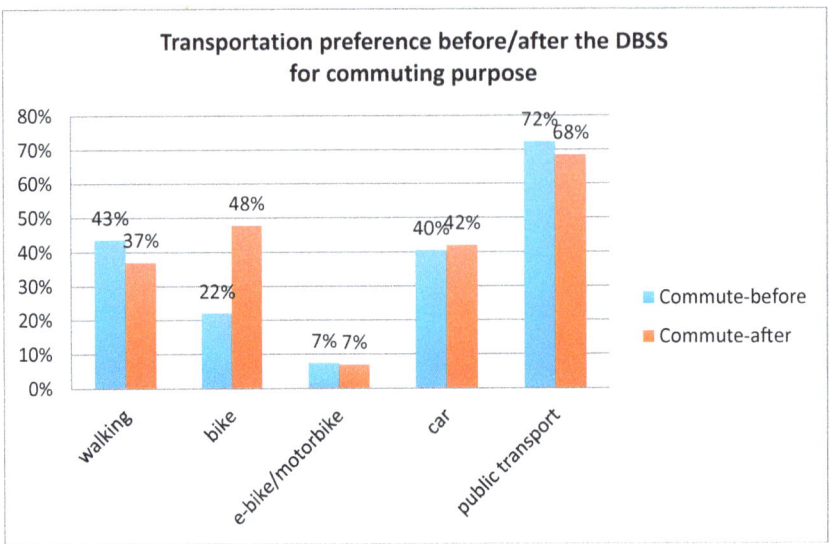

Figure 2. Transportation preference before/after the DBSS for commuting purposes.

'The cost of bike sharing is much lower than either buying a bicycle or taking the bus or taxi. It is more economical for me to share the bicycle, and at the same time, it is also beneficial to reduce the risk of it being stolen.' (Participant A, reflected from the survey)

However, most users indeed agree that the DBSS has changed their life (66%). Changes are reflected in the following aspects. Forty-four percent of users agree that the DBSS has extended their travel distance range, and users agree that the DBSS has reduced the time restriction (57%) and saved the travel time (76%) for going out. At the same time, 58% think the DBSS has reduced their travel budget.

3.1.2. Users' Satisfaction with DBSS in Different Aspects

Though the general satisfaction is relatively good (Figure 3), the DBSS companies need to pay more attention to the quality of the bikes since 30% of users express low or very low satisfaction about it. As for the factors that lead to dissatisfaction, 45% of users choose the 'pedals or the chain does not work properly', 35% blame the 'unsuitable seat', 35% reflect that 'the handle bar or the break doesn't work properly'. The channels for reporting the errors also need to be improved. Because over 63% respondents always see the broken or wrongly-parked shared bikes on the street, only 22% choose to report the error every time. Parking is another severe problem with which users are not satisfied.

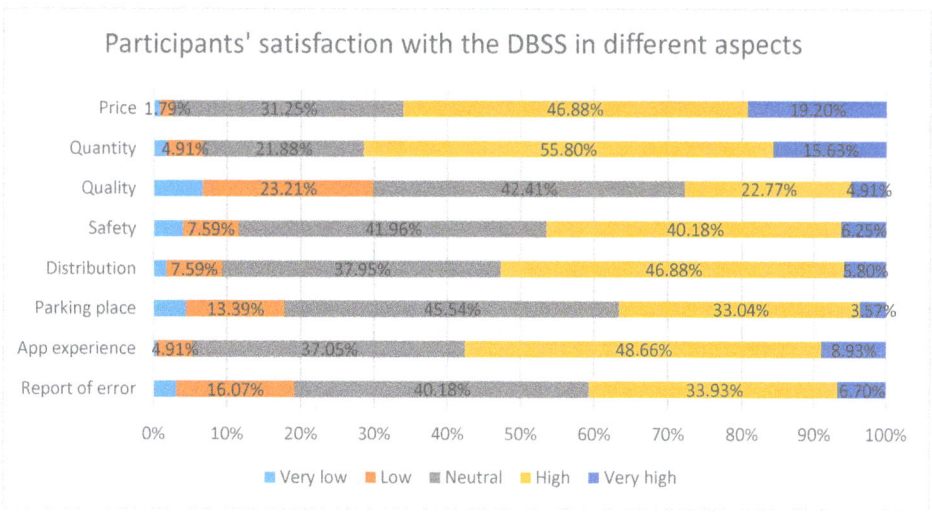

Figure 3. Participants' satisfaction with the DBSS in different aspects.

3.1.3. Users Perceptions towards DBSS in Different Aspects

'For... short-distance travel, the advantages of shared bikes are the flexibility and speed. Compared to driving or taking a taxi or bus in... rush hour in... large- and medium-sized cities, riding a shared bike could apparently save you time.' (Participant B, reflected from the survey)

'I don't need to look around for a parking place while finally arriving at my destination, because these bikes are "floating" without any dock. And I can always ride a bike when I'm too tired to walk while enjoying the street views at the same time.' (Participant C, reflected from the survey)

Before the DBSS, 52% of users thought the previous transportation could fulfil their needs, while after the launch of the DBSS, the number increased to 70%. Nevertheless, only 44% of users indicate that the bicycle lanes in Beijing could fulfil their needs, and for bicycle parking lots the number is even lower (40%). Sixty-four percent of users call for a special parking place for shared bikes, and the hottest spots they mentioned are around metro/bus stops, neighbourhoods, office buildings and shopping malls. People are overall optimistic in that more than 90% of participants think the DBSS helps to solve the 'last mile' problem; 65% agree it helps to improve the environment; 64% agree it mitigates the traffic congestion of the city.

3.2. The Contribution of DBSS towards Sustainable Mobility in Beijing

3.2.1. Environmental Impact

As reviewed in previous research studies, bicycles have their own advantages, especially in regard to their environmentally-friendly characteristics [26]. Therefore, as it stands, the DBSS should have helped with the improvement of the urban environment. However, the results of the survey and interviews raised some doubts about this assumption.

First of all, many people considered that the DBBS increased the cycling rate in the city and that it seems reasonable that fuel consumption and greenhouse emission have been reduced. Meanwhile, the DBSS companies also claimed that the DBSS has made great efforts in saving energy, reducing greenhouse gas emissions and saving the urban space [25].

'I helped the Mobike to conduct the research on Mobike White Paper. However, the company used their own conversion method and their users' data to write the Mobike White Paper. They simply replaced the *riding mileage with the driving mileage, and advertise how they contribute to the environment based on this figure (see Figure 4). This calculation is not scientific and reliable at all... because the hypothesis that people change their transport from car to shared bikes is not always truthful.'* (Mr. Wang, Planner)

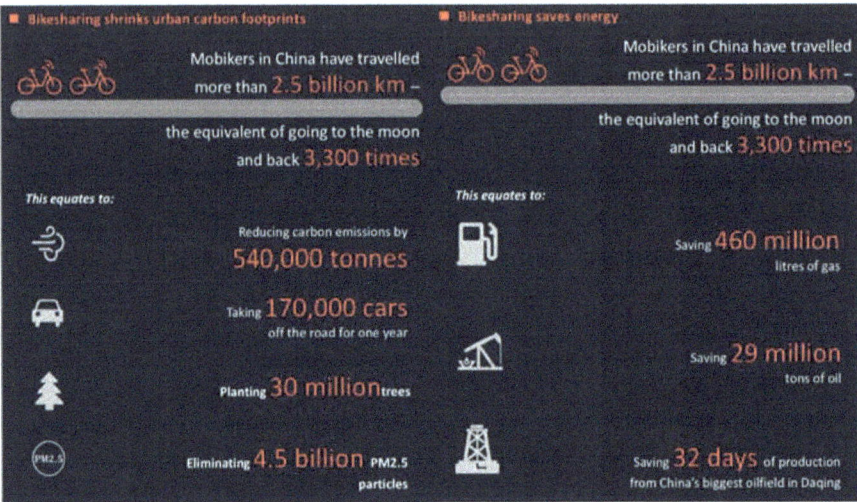

Figure 4. The statistics of bike sharing and its equitation to resource and environment data in Mobike White Paper [25].

The evidence can also be found from the survey—the results did not show that the residents replaced cars with bikes. From Figure 2, we could find that the change of car-use and motorbike-use was not significant before and after the DBSS appeared. The usage of bikes as the mode of transportation for commuting purposes is doubled; meanwhile, walking and the usage of public transport have slightly declined. The transportation mode change of chore purpose trip and entertainment purpose trip are similar to the commute purpose. This might imply that the DBSS is an additional transportation option for citizens to use, but it is unrealistic, at least in the short term, to control the usage of cars only by DBSS.

There is another critical voice arguing that the DBSS is not environmentally sustainable because it is neither a 'sharing economy' nor a 'circular economy'. The difference between the so-called 'bike-sharing' and the traditional sharing economy is that there are no spare resources in the shared bike model. All the bicycles are bought by the DBSS companies to meet market demand, which is different from the original intention of the sharing economy [27]. Moreover, some experts believe that the start-ups are too busy chasing territory and investment to focus on providing a good service: 'You see thousands of bikes parked everywhere around the city and many are not working because nobody takes care of them—the city's beauty has been destroyed' [9].

'Sometimes, government just drags away the wrongly-parked shared bikes to the shared bike... landfills without any warning. And if companies want to get these bikes back to the normal market, it is hard to negotiate with the government because of its low efficiency and high cost. Companies also pay more attention to the quantities rather than the qualities in the initial phase, because they need to occupy the local market and expand... fast. So those lack-of-care bikes become cities' foundling.' (Mr. Wang, Planner)

After some companies exit the market, the shared bikes they put on the street are abandoned and cause significant resource waste and environmental pollution. Bike vandalism and theft have also become a recurrent issue. Vandals have often targeted the bikes, placing them on trees or even destroying them by setting them on fire. Furthermore, currently, there is no efficient way to prevent these criminal activities. As Spinney and Lin discussed, 'on a conceptual level, the abandoning of bikes anywhere on the streets is emblematic of the maximization of private utility (saving time and effort) over collective utility (the ability of other users to easily use the public realm)' [16].

3.2.2. Economic Viability

Generally speaking, these new bike sharing services are a more advanced innovation with a valuable economic impact on cities' sustainable transportation development. The DBSS has expanded the scope of public transport services, allowing residents to choose from a wider range of lifestyles and work areas.

In China, the new DBSS, different from the traditional public bikes, is provided entirely by the private companies. The market gives the DBSS inherent advantages—efficiency. The DBSS compares to the public bikes provided by local government or joint venture between the government and private sectors, and provides a cheaper, more convenient, and more comprehensive service.

The survey result shows that 65% of the participants agree that the DBSS has changed their daily life; 56% think the DBSS reduces the time restriction for going out, and 76% think it saves traveling time. Meanwhile, more than half of the participants think the DBSS helps them to save on their traveling budget. The DBSS also has the obvious advantage of easing traffic congestion. From the report of Mobike White Paper [25], in Beijing, for trips shorter than 5 km, 92.9% of trips are quicker by shared bike plus public transport; for trips longer than 5 km, 23.7% of trips are faster by shared bike plus public transport.

In most cases, the DBSS is a good solution to the 'last mile problem' and has the significant feature of connecting to other public transportation. In Beijing, 81% of the Mobike trips start at the bus station and 44% of trips start near a metro station [25]. The DBSS has expanded the service scope of the metro stations and facilitated metro services to more citizens. If we set the distance range when the house rent is reduced to 80% as the so-called 'new metro area', the so-called 'new metro area' will extend from 900 m around the metro station to 1650 m from the year of 2013–2015 to 2016–2017 [28]. The expansion of this service range has naturally expanded the scope of the 'new metro area' and structural changes have taken place in the urban rental housing market. Furthermore, the DBSS as a basic transport facility spatially reconstructs our urban structure, which in turn affects our lives in more ways.

However, from the perspective of the DBSS companies, is this model economically sustainable? As an enterprise, to put shared bikes into the market is not a purely public welfare investment, and the final point is still for profit. In the beginning, the huge initial investment does not affect the recovery of its cost. Just like the previous car-hailing app, with the crazy money-burning mode, these new bike sharing apps quickly occupy the market. Most bike sharing apps require paying the deposit as a credit/mortgage to rent the bike, which constitutes a small part of the capital return. The bike sharing apps also bring web traffic that will attract advertisements. Moreover, the large-scale production and technological upgrade of the shared bikes reduces the production and repair cost.

> 'The companies are not about... sustainable transport, they are primarily about data mining. When the companies found that they cannot manage the data, then the investment is just pull[ed] out. The companies' actual business model itself is not sustainable and profitable. Operators intend to use the data to reshape the relationship between themselves and the municipality in ways that move further away from flat and cooperative power relations to more uneven relations.' (Mr. Spinney, planner)

From an explosive growth at the beginning of the year, to a series of bankruptcies by year's end, 2017 witnessed a roller coaster of China's bike-sharing business during the ups and downs. The industry boasted almost 60 bike-related start-ups over the last 18 months; nevertheless, by the end of November 2017, at least six well-known bike-sharing start-ups had shut down, and more than RMB 1 billion (USD 150 million) in deposits could not be refunded to users [29]. In the long run, with the wide spread of the new business mode, the recovery of funds is quite substantial. Hopefully, by optimising the cost and mining profit-points, bike sharing companies will gradually meet the profitability.

3.2.3. Social Profitability

From the social sustainability perspective, the DBSS gives residents another opportunity to go anywhere, anytime they want to go, without thinking about the long walking distance. This increases residents' frequency of travel and frequency of exchanges, improving the vitality and utilisation of the urban space. It also helps the health of the residents. The positive impact of the DBSS is to improve the access and reduce the exclusion, but the negative impact is that the DBSS has been shown to be relatively unequal and unsafe.

The DBSS has markedly improved the accessibility from door to door. After the introduction of the DBSS, users reported a decline in auto-rickshaw trips of 53%. The illegal auto-rickshaw is a common transport to deliver people from the metro station to their home. They are widely practiced despite repeated attempts by the government to stamp them out. Just take one instance of a metro station in Beijing, in spring 2016, just before the emergence of the DBSS: there were 200 auto-rickshaws, drivers each completing 40+ trips and earning up to 200+ RMB per day. However, after the growth in popularity of the DBSS, just 50–60 auto-rickshaws remain, and 70% of unlicensed drivers have changed jobs [25].

The inequality can be found both in terms of age and income. The senior citizens are hardly engaged in the DBSS, because the service is entirely based on the smartphone and online payment, and many older people do not have access to these new technologies. The relationship between income level and frequency of DBSS cycling was investigated by means of a regression test, and there was a strong correlation between the two variables ($p < 0.01$). This means that no-income or low-income groups tend to use the DBSS more frequently.

Safety is another big issue for the DBSS. Seventy-seven percent of respondents think that the drivers do not have the concession for riders, and they feel unsafe while riding the shared bikes. At the same time, many pedestrians also feel their walkways have been invaded by the moving or stopped bikes. Seventy-two percent of participants agree that the parking disorder has become the eyesore of the street and made the city messy, while 61% consider the shared bikes to take too much public space.

> *'In our sub-district, most streets are Hutong, so the alleys are very narrow. If the shared bikes are parked in the Hutong community, the streets will become even narrower. The bikes invade the residents' car-parking lots and walking pedestrians, and residents are angry about it. So, we have to hire the people from the property management company to clean up the inner Hutong, move the shared bikes into the vacant places, or at least put them in order.' (Ms. Sun, Community worker)*

There has been a major issue about the 'right-of-way' since the emergence of the DBSS. Ideally, motor vehicles, non-motor vehicles, and pedestrians should go their own ways, enjoy their respective rights in the corresponding areas, and other traffic participants should not infringe them. However, over the years, Chinese cities' urban planning has always placed the priority on car traffic. As motor vehicle ownership continues to grow, non-motorized vehicles and pedestrian access are severely squeezed. Many cyclists have negative experiences while riding the bikes. For example, there is a lack of isolation between motorized and non-motorized lanes, resulting in vehicles often passing by others' lane. Due to the limited place for riding, many cyclists have to ride on the sidewalk [30]. The mutual disrespect has led to chaos on the urban streets.

4. Discussion

The DBSS entered the public view at the end of 2016. Afterwards, it has become part of public transportation and public facilities. Due to low technical barriers, shared bikes have experienced savage growth in less than two years. Nevertheless, the DBSS comes with various disputes and queries. Nowadays, a large number of shared bikes with disorderly parking, serious damage and the over-supply has become a new urban management issue. Some cities have already begun to issue policy documents. However, this complicated problem still faces the challenges of refined management and scientific decision-making.

4.1. Government: Infrastructure and Regulation

According to the statistical data from the Beijing traffic department, the number of dockless shared bikes in Beijing soared from approximately 700,000 to 2,350,000 in four months from April 2017 to September 2017 [17]. However, problems such as disorderly parking, quality and safety have restricted the development of the industry. The lesson is that to avoid the 'tragedy of commons' and uncoordinated individualistic action in a transport network, we need the government interference [31]. The DBSS, as a 'disruptive innovation', does not absolve cities from the principles of sound city planning, street design, and realising the value of public spaces.

Due to historical reasons, the Chinese-style urban space and traffic planning mode of 'wide roads, big blocks and sparse roads' has been fixed [5]. Bicycles were regarded as inefficient mobility in the past, thus the transport planning did not pay much attention to the design of the bicycle infrastructures and facilities. However, with the rapid growth of the DBSS, the preparation of special plans for bicycles needs to be put on the agenda as soon as possible to ensure the construction of bicycle facilities. In the planning process, local authorities should set a clear quantitative target with the data support, and solve the specific problems faced with focal points by stages.

On the other hand, the government also plays a vital role in investment of bike infrastructure and supporting facilities such as bike lanes, parking lots, and bike signals to make citizens feel safe and comfort while cycling. Bicycle infrastructure construction needs to focus more on the daily travel environment in the city, especially cyclists' rights, dangerous points, and end-breaking roads, to achieve greater effectiveness.

> *'Sometimes, our government is too slow to react when facing a new disruptive innovation. They are afraid of changing, and sometimes shirk responsibility when something goes wrong. The lack of regulation and attention caused the barbaric growth of DBSS in the beginning and caused numerous problems that the government can no longer ignore. However, DBSS start-ups might lose their strength due to the governments' rough control and management. The DBSS is an insightful reflection for the contemporary urban planning and governance in China.' (Mr. Wang, planner)*

The Chinese government issued guidelines in August 2017 by the Ministry of Transport to regulate DBSS services, including forbidding children under the age of 12 from using the shared bikes; operators have to buy insurance for users; customers need to register with their real name, etc. [32]. On 15 September 2017, the Beijing Municipal Commission of Transport [21] released the 'Guidance for the development of standardized sharing bicycles in Beijing (Trial)'. Based on extensive investigations and studies and with the actual conditions in the municipality, the administrative departments of various districts, industry associations and DBSS enterprises have formulated the 'Technical Specifications for Bike Sharing Systems Technology and Services' and the 'Technology Guidelines for Bicycle Parking Area Settings' [23]. The policy documents provide a comprehensive, detailed, and solid policy guarantee and normative guidance to encourage the healthy development of the DBSS. Under new changes, the local Beijing government will order bike-sharing companies to be regulated and supervised by municipal authorities. The firms will also be made to pay accident insurance for users.

> *'It is not enough to publish these regulations. What is more important is how to implement them and supervise them.' (Mr. Wang, planner)*

4.2. Companies: Maintenance and Cooperation

The DBSS companies are now facing the trouble of the vicious competition within the industry. As for the current shared bike model, we can hardly see the improvement in bicycle utilisation efficiency. Instead, many companies mass-produce new bicycles and put them on the market. This commercial competition among companies is merely to expand the market and squeeze out other competitors. It has deviated from the good intention of 'sharing'. As a result, the number of bicycles is bound to significantly exceed the Pareto equilibrium level [33]. It could not improve the utilisation efficiency of social idle resources but causes a tremendous waste of resources. Recently, six out of 30+ operators recently went bankrupt, which might be a signal of the bubble bursting. Many of China's shared bike users have fallen as victims of defaults on their deposit refunds, after the operators went bankrupt. No party has claimed responsibility for refunding public deposits. From the survey, it can also be found that 70% of respondents think the providers could not maintain the shared bikes on time and caused an enormous waste resources.

Previously, some DBSS companies found that compared to repairing the bikes, producing new bikes was even cheaper. For this reason, they would rather let the 'zombie bikes' spread on the street and blindly produce new bikes [34]. The new guidance released in September 2017 clearly defined the standard on the shared bike recovery and maintenance. This prompts enterprises to regularly recondition the shared bikes and keep the shared bikes' serviceability rate above 95%. Shared bikes should generally be put in use for three years and then they should be updated or scrapped; DBSS enterprises should own or rent parking spaces to meet the needs of vehicle turnover and maintenance [21].

Beijing has also controlled the total amount of shared bikes in the city. The promulgation of this policy precisely led enterprises to devote more energy and investment to maintenance and management rather than manufacturing. Thus, some experts believe that if companies adjust their business focus to the quality and maintenance of the bikes, the overall burden will not increase too much.

> *'It's good to see companies start to share their data with institutions for research purpose, because they are valuable for transport planning. But the business model is about mining and selling the data. So, I'd like to see more cooperation between companies and government, though I think government should buy it. However, privacy is a big issue when using this data.' (Mr. Spinney, planner)*

On the other hand, the result revealed that there is fear of social exclusion in the current DBSS; to include marginalised low-income groups who cannot afford smartphones, those who cannot work with smartphones or those who even prefer not to have smartphones, the DBSS requires more comprehensive software. New tools such as fingerprint recognition programs or urban transport cards can help.

4.3. Citizens: Culture and Participation

Education and various activities could help to encourage good behaviour and cultivate a cyclists-friendly environment. These can be initiated by the government, market, civil society, or a combination of all. It is not enough to rely solely on infrastructure to enhance the attractiveness of bicycles. Bicycles are closely linked to the social symbolic effect and the level of income. With the rise of residents' income levels, bicycles often embody the 'cheapness', which hinders the social acceptance and popularity of bicycles. We also interviewed some non-users of the DBSS and asked them why they rejected this service. Many of them said they did not know how to ride the bikes or that the bike is not a need in their life. Therefore, to encourage more people to cycle and to enable the cyclists to feel proud and satisfied as the car groups, large-scale publicity and education need to be carried out, so as to change people's view and make the bicycle become a part of the daily life style and the organic component of the city image. On the other hand, to guide the safe and right cycling/driving behaviour, and create a bike-friendly environment, schools, NGOs and local communities could help with the supervision and education.

For instance, the vandalism acts towards shared bikes led to the formation of a spontaneous civic group—'bike hunters':

'We use the APP GPS information to retrieve those illegal placed, abandoned, or stolen bikes. By reporting the violations of out-of-service or damaged bikes through the APP, the bike hunters could gain some rewards and at the same time, assist the orderly operation.' (Mr. Zhao, Mobike Hunter)

Moreover, some shared bike operators have already set a credit system to encourage a better behaviour by rewarding users' credits for reporting broken or illegally parked bikes, and demerits for correspondingly bad behaviour. If your score drops too low, your next ride could become much more expensive [35].

'We regard bike hunting as a treasure hunting game. We enjoy the procedure of finding the stranded and damaged bikes, reporting them. It seems that we could contribute to the urban environment and society in our own way. The reward from the APP is not the main reason for us. The hunters in our volunteer groups become good friends and even become couples.' (Mr. Zhao, Mobike Hunter)

4.4. Hybrid Governance

The national guideline put forward must adhere to the principle of multi-party governance and give full play to the joint efforts of the government, enterprises, social organisations, and the public. There must be coordination on three levels to achieve the continuous innovation for the DBSS [36].

- Synergy of the transportation mode

The DBSS alone itself cannot achieve the revival of bicycles. To promote the bicycles, the holistic green traffic solution should be provided to the public through the optimization of the connection and integration between the bicycles and various public transports.

'Many Chinese cities have issued guidance on the regulation of shared bike services, setting up a "black list for riding", piloting geo-fences, planning of banned parking areas, and enforcing real-name registrations to standardise the development of shared bikes, but with little success. Cycling brands have responded with the introduction of their own governance, such as developing geo-fences and artificial data platforms, etc., which have certain results in the short term. In the long run, if there is no unified control and standard, old problems cannot be eradicated. Therefore, a unified management governance system platform should be established to achieve accurate management of bicycle placement and operation.' (Mr. Wang, planner)

For example, local authorities could incorporate the infrastructure investment with private sector companies. In the past, each DBSS company was basically independently managed and did not communicate with other players. As a result, the number of bicycles in the parking area was excessive and not properly divided. The establishment of a systematic DBSS management platform could enable the unified management of different brands of shared bikes. Its back-end system platform can also be open to all DBSS companies. In this way, shared bikes can be put into places where people gather and flow, such as bus stations, large squares, and stations near subways. If the number of bicycles exceeds the standard or the bikes are in short supply, they can use the backstage management system to conduct scientific and directional and effective operation and maintenance.

- Synergy of information

It is also helpful to promote comprehensive research on multi-source multidimensional data (open data, data sharing and public crowdsourcing data). Combining the traditional data and new data could support the process of decision-making.

Since according to the new guideline, all shared bikes have to be equipped with the GPS chips, the companies could share their transportation data on where people ride their bikes to, and where they park. With the help of the empirical data, the government could make a better decision on where to build the new bike tracks, parking lots and public realm improvements [37]. In practice, Mobike and the Beijing Institute of Urban Planning and Design have signed a cooperation agreement. The big data will support the planning of Beijing's pedestrian and bicycle lanes during the 13th Five-Year Plan period. It will also assist with the planning of parking lots and parking spots and select and support Beijing 3200 km bike lanes' construction [38].

- Synergy of participants

Encourage all stakeholders including enterprises, government, the public, social organisations and so on in the process to achieve the win-win cooperation.

'We have different WeChat groups to discuss how to improve the dockless bike sharing system in different cities. There are officers from the Mobike Company, experts, users, and general people who are interested in helping with the issues in this online discussion group, so that our voices can be heard by the company. We also submitted our opinions and suggestions to relevant departments of city government, at the stage of releasing the trial requirements for comments. Actually, our final goal is that, one day in the future, we won't have any bikes to hunt.' (Mr. Zhao, Mobike Hunter)

The participation of the public in urban DBSS management can, on the one hand, improve the public's awareness, quality and ability of democratic participation, self-management, and self-service; on the other hand, it can also promote the transformation of urban government functions and ensure the democratic and scientific public decision-making. It is conducive to the construction of a public service-oriented government that combines the concepts of responsibility, service, and the rule of law. In addition, the public participation in management also facilitates the implementation of government policies and accelerates the standardisation of the DBSS [39].

5. Conclusions

5.1. Brief Summary

With the emergence of the sharing economy, the popularity of the mobile payment, the environment awareness and the inherent market demand, the DBSS has led a trend of bicycle revival in Beijing, which is becoming a role model for all of China. These new kind of dockless shared bikes with great advantages in terms of flexibility during short trips are just the ones that could solve the commuters' 'last mile' problem. However, people are still worried about its safety and quality. Considering sustainability criteria, the DBSS was expected to have positive impacts on the reduction of greenhouse gas emission, elimination of pollution and health risks. However, the result of the survey shows that the shared bikes are not an alternative for the frequent car-users. Nevertheless, it has also yielded negative consequences such as blocked sidewalks and vandalism of the bikes. Oversupply has led to graveyards of bikes, and deep concerns about quality control, maintenance, and management of these systems. If there is no efficient way to avoid the bad treatment towards shared bikes and abasement of public space, it may be more of a curse than a blessing. Moreover, though the DBSS has increased the accessibility within the urban mobility framework to a great extent, the seasonal and tidal phenomenon calls for a more efficient way to dispatch and distribute the bikes. Furthermore, the business model of the DBSS companies seems to be not very sustainable or profitable. The public is also worried about their quality and safety, especially the issues of 'right of way'. How to coordinate and solve these problems is not only related to the future direction of the DBSS, but also related to the vital interests of the general public. Therefore, it is the general trend to emphasise that governments, enterprises, and the public participate in multi-party cooperation and build synergic governance networks to carry forward the advantages and avoid the negative effects of the new bike sharing system.

The city government should improve the construction of the bicycle traffic network, standardise the parking place setting of bicycles, and strengthen the supervision and law enforcement of illegal activities. Operators should implement the responsibility of DBSS parking management, popularise and apply technologies such as geo-fencing, take comprehensive measures such as economic rewards and punishments and credit records, and guide users to regulate parking. At the same time, it is important to strengthen the publicity and education to guide mutual respect among drivers, cyclists and pedestrians through public service advertisements, theme education and volunteering activities. Users themselves are encouraged to enhance their awareness of the cycling etiquette, abide by traffic regulations, and abide by social ethics. The three-level coordination, namely the synergy of transportation mode, information and participants is recommended for the DBSS's future healthy development and efficient hybrid governance.

5.2. Limitations and Recommendations for Future Study

In this research, since surveys constitute a general method for collecting large amounts of data, profound and comprehensive views from specific users are lacking. The online sampling and distribution method may also cause the bias in this research. Future research may fill the gap by conducting in-depth interviews with various background users and generate more ideas from their perspective by qualitative methods. Moreover, though the actual performance of DBSS is being criticised assessed in this research, there are still many issues that had not been solved prior to evaluating the DBSS's sustainable mobility. For instance, directions for further studies may include the research about the quantified index, which could measure the performance of the DBSS towards sustainability in different cities.

In this research, only four interviewees agreed to join the research, and representatives from companies or local authorities are excluded. So, the research lacks direct views from the government and company perspective. Thus, more detailed operations and management advice needs to be proposed in future research. For example: how regulations could be improved and implemented more efficiently, how to utilise the companies' technology and data to better shape the city, etc.

Since, this research only focuses on Beijing as the single case study, there might be other cases that could be studied and compared to reveal the differences in DBSS's contribution at a different city scale. Moreover, with the expansion of DBSS companies to other parts of the world, appropriate coordination between the local government and the private firms to avoid potential chaotic situations is required. By observing the Chinese experience presented in this research, further studies may focus on how to develop the DBSS in cities worldwide, as well as on researching the obstacles that the DBSS is facing and how to solve them in different contexts. DBSS and its healthy development and governance need more valuable investigation in future research.

Funding: This research received no external funding.

Acknowledgments: This research work is supported by Erasmus Mundus PLANET Europe program EPMC scholarship funded by the Education, Audiovisual & Culture Executive Agency (EACEA) of the Commission of the European Communities.

Conflicts of Interest: The authors declare no conflict of interest.

References

1. Handy, S.; Wee, V.B.; Kroesen, M. Promoting cycling for transport: Research needs and challenges. *Transp. Rev.* **2017**, *34*, 4–24. [CrossRef]
2. Gössling, S.; Choi, A.S. Transport transitions in Copenhagen: Comparing the cost of cars and bicycles. *Ecol. Econ.* **2015**, *113*, 106–113. [CrossRef]
3. Zhang, H.; Shaheen, S.A.; Chen, X. Bicycle evolution in China: From the 1900s to the present. *Int. J. Sustain. Transp.* **2014**, *8*, 317–335. [CrossRef]
4. Feng, Z.; Yan, N. Putting a circular economy into practice in China. *Sustain. Sci.* **2007**, *2*, 95–101.
5. Yang, X.H.; Cheng, Z.; Chen, G.; Wang, L.; Ruan, Z.Y.; Zheng, Y.J. The impact of a public bicycle-sharing system on urban public transport networks. *Transp. Res. Part A Policy Pract.* **2018**, *107*, 246–256. [CrossRef]
6. Zhang, L.; Zhang, J.; Duan, Z.; Bryde, D. Sustainable bike-sharing systems: Characteristics and commonalities across cases in urban China. *J. Clean. Prod.* **2015**, *6*, 124–133. [CrossRef]

7. Liu, Z.; Jia, X.; Cheng, W. Solving the last mile problem: Ensure the success of public bicycle system in Beijing. *Procedia Soc. Behav. Sci.* **2012**, *43*, 73–78. [CrossRef]
8. Fishman, E.; Washington, S.; Haworth, N. Bike share: A synthesis of the literature. *Transp. Rev.* **2013**, *33*, 148–165. [CrossRef]
9. Uber for Bikes: How 'Dockless' Cycles Flooded China—And Are Heading Overseas. 2018. Available online: https://www.theguardian.com/cities/2017/mar/22/bike-wars-dockless-china-millions-bicycles-hangzhou (accessed on 10 May 2018).
10. Consumer News and Business Channel (CNBC). Bike-Sharing Boom in China Pedals to New Heights. Available online: https://www.cnbc.com/2017/07/18/bike-sharing-boom-in-china-pedals-to-new-heights.html (accessed on 10 May 2018).
11. Zhang, Y.; Mi, Z. Environmental benefits of bike sharing: A big data-based analysis. *Appl. Energy* **2018**, *220*, 296–301. [CrossRef]
12. Chinese National Information Center. Bike Sharing Industry Employment Research Report. Available online: http://www.sic.gov.cn/News/250/8452.htm (accessed on 5 April 2018).
13. Gao, Y. China's response to climate change issues after Paris Climate Change Conference. *Adv. Clim. Chang. Res.* **2017**, *7*, 235–240. [CrossRef]
14. Quartz. Chinese Cities Are Saying "Enough Already" to Bike-Sharing Services Run Rampant. Available online: https://qz.com/1058438/chinese-cities-saying-enough-already-to-chaos-generated-by-bike-sharing-services-like-ofo-and-mobike/ (accessed on 5 April 2018).
15. Fishman, E. Bikeshare: A review of recent literature. *Transp. Rev.* **2016**, *36*, 92–113. [CrossRef]
16. Spinney, J.; Lin, W.I. Are you being shared? Mobility, data and social relations in Shanghai's Public Bike Sharing 2.0 sector. *Appl. Mob.* **2018**, *3*, 66–83. [CrossRef]
17. Pan, L.; Cai, Q.; Fang, Z.; Tang, P.; Huang, L. Rebalancing Dockless Bike Sharing Systems. *arXiv* **2018**.
18. Chang, S.; Song, R.; He, S.; Qiu, G. Innovative bike-sharing in China: Solving faulty bike-sharing recycling problem. *J. Adv. Transp.* **2018**, *2018*, 4941029. [CrossRef]
19. Sohu. How Many Shared Bicycles Are Needed in Beijing: Currently There Is a Shortage of Nearly One Million? Available online: http://www.sohu.com/a/165830743_161062 (accessed on 8 April 2018).
20. Central Ministry of Transport. Guiding Opinions on Encouraging and Regulating the Development of Internet Rental Bicycles. August 2017. Available online: http://www.gov.cn/xinwen/2017-08/03/content_5215640.htm (accessed on 10 April 2018).
21. Beijing Municipal Traffic Commission. The Normative Guidance for Encouraging the Development of Shared Bicycles in Beijing Municipality (Trial). Available online: http://zhengce.beijing.gov.cn/library/192/33/50/438650/1283011/ (accessed on 10 April 2018).
22. Beijing Municipal Traffic Commission. Shared Bike System Technology and Service Specification. Available online: https://www.weibo.com/ttarticle/p/show?id=2309404153633913591745 (accessed on 10 April 2018).
23. Beijing Municipal Traffic Commission. Technical Guidelines for Setting Parking Areas for Bicycles. Available online: https://www.weibo.com/ttarticle/p/show?id=2309404153633913591745 (accessed on 10 April 2018).
24. Mobike. The Mobike White Paper: Bike-Share in the City. Available online: https://mobike.com/sg/blog/post/mobikewhitepaper (accessed on 10 April 2018).
25. Mobike. The Mobike Second White Paper: How Cycling Changes Cities. Available online: https://mobike.com/sg/blog/post/cycling-changes-cities (accessed on 10 April 2018).
26. Cahill, M. Transport, environment and society. In *Environmental Impacts*; McGraw-Hill Education: London, UK, 2010.
27. China Europe International Business School. Bike-Sharing Is a Pseudo-Sharing Economic and the Turning Point Has Arrived. Available online: http://news.hexun.com/2017-11-17/191679081.html (accessed on 10 May 2018).
28. Metro Data Team. Bike-Sharing Redefined the "Subway Room"? Available online: http://www.sohu.com/a/193031969_274982 (accessed on 10 May 2018).
29. Zhao, P.; Li, S. Bicycle-metro integration in a growing city: The determinants of cycling as a transfer mode in metro station areas in Beijing. *Transp. Res. Part A Policy Pract.* **2017**, *99*, 46–60. [CrossRef]
30. First Financial. Crime and Punishment of the Bike-Sharing. Available online: http://www.yicai.com/news/5191474.html (accessed on 10 May 2018).

31. Ruan, Y.; Hang, C.C.; Wang, Y.M. Government's role in disruptive innovation and industry emergence: The case of the electric bike in China. *Technovation* **2014**, *34*, 785–796. [CrossRef]
32. CNET. Bike Sharing Is Going Global but Regulations Could Tie it down. Available online: https://www.cnet.com/news/inside-chinas-stranglehold-on-bike-sharing/ (accessed on 5 June 2018).
33. Bullock, C.; Brereton, F.; Bailey, S. The economic contribution of public bike-share to the sustainability and efficient functioning of cities. *Sustain. Cities Soc.* **2017**, *28*, 76–87. [CrossRef]
34. ABC News. China's Oversupply of Shared Bikes Creating Piles of Broken, Unused Bicycles on City Streets. Available online: http://www.abc.net.au/news/2017-05-21/chinas-oversupply-of-shared-bikes-clogging-up-city-streets/8543720 (accessed on 10 May 2018).
35. China Is Introducing a New Bike-Share System in Cities around the World. But Not Everyone's Thrilled. 2018. Available online: https://www.washingtonpost.com/world/asia_pacific/china-exports-its-bike-sharing-revolution-to-the-us-and-the-world/2017/08/31/474c822a-87f4-11e7-9ce7-9e175d8953fa_story.html (accessed on 10 May 2018).
36. Li, H.; Wu, Y.; Liang, J.; Duan, B.; Wang, P. Return Bicycles to Cities: From Bike-Sharing to Data Ecosystems. Available online: http://www.bikehome.cc/news/20171028/566752_1.html (accessed on 10 May 2018).
37. Transport Futures. Dockless Bike Sharing and Relearning. Available online: https://transportfutures.co/dockless-bike-sharing-and-relearning-ebd60359d507 (accessed on 10 May 2018).
38. Mobike Launches Urban Mobility Institute. 2018. Available online: http://www.chinadaily.com.cn/china/2017-04/12/content_28900644.htm (accessed on 10 May 2018).
39. Xiong, J. Chaos of "Sharing bikes"and its multi-center cooperative governance. *Leg. Syst. Soc.* **2017**, *25*, 146–147.

© 2018 by the author. Licensee MDPI, Basel, Switzerland. This article is an open access article distributed under the terms and conditions of the Creative Commons Attribution (CC BY) license (http://creativecommons.org/licenses/by/4.0/).

Article

Producing Opportunities Together: Sharing-Based Policy Approaches for Marginal Mobilities in Bogotá

Giovanni Vecchio

Department of Architecture and Urban Studies, Politecnico di Milano, 20133 Milan, Italy; giovanni.vecchio@polimi.it

Received: 1 June 2018; Accepted: 29 June 2018; Published: 2 July 2018

Abstract: Everyday mobility practices are increasingly an element of interest for urban policy, as well as for suggesting alternative solutions to urban issues. Amongst their manifold contributions, practices can be relevant for securing individuals' access to places and opportunities. They can do so by promoting services and behaviours based on resources that individuals may share between themselves. This role could be significant especially for those settings where the traditional provision of transport services and infrastructures is more difficult, such as in the informal settlements of the urban South. Drawing on these assumption, this paper intends to investigate policy solutions based on mobility practices, as a suitable way to enhance the access to urban opportunities from informal settlements. Policy approaches focused on mobility supply and demand are explored, addressing options such as the coproduction of mobility services and behavioural approaches based on demand matchmaking. A possible operationalization of such approaches is explored in the marginal informal neighbourhoods of Bogotá, considering their accessibility issues, how shared use mobility policies may tackle them, and what features are necessary for the implementation of such measures. The proposed policy measures emerge as suitable operational options that nonetheless require recognition and support by the institutions responsible for urban mobility planning.

Keywords: sharing; coproduction; matchmaking; urban mobility; mobility policy; accessibility; informality

1. Introduction

Increasingly, everyday mobility practices are an element of interest for urban policy, as well as for suggesting alternative solutions for urban issues. Practices are here considered as the forms in which each person shapes and uses mobility to achieve their own aims. These express new forms of mobility and reflect the spatio-temporal transformations of contemporary societies, which involve unprecedented territorial scales, temporal dimensions and modal choices [1]. Practices are based on the mobilization of manifold individual resources, which each person uses to achieve specific aims: mobility in fact is fundamental for overcoming spatial friction, accessing significant opportunities, and taking part in valued activities [2]. Given that the mobility potentials available to each person are different, individuals shape and appropriate mobility according to their personal characteristics and aims [3]. Practices are thus a relevant knowledge tool to examine how individuals use the resource of individual mobility and how collective flows affect the spatio-temporal organisation of a territory. However, practices do not simply act as a knowledge tool, but may also contribute to the social production of goods and services [4]. Practices could be significant also for urban mobility policy since they make use of existing services in unforeseen ways and create innovative solutions [5] that reflect individual mobility needs and mobilize unprecedented resources.

Within a rich debate that has extensively analysed the variegated forms, spaces and subjects of mobility practices [6], this paper focuses on the *everyday* forms in which each person shapes and uses mobility. A practice is what any person does, intentionally or not, within a structured field [7] (p. 48), but the main thinkers who have dealt with this concept have privileged an everyday life perspective [8]. In the case of urban mobility, a practice is thus what a subject does to move, within a field structured by material and immaterial elements (such as infrastructures or service timetables). Practices can be recursive, that is, they can be repeatedly deployed to deal with similar needs and wants. In this sense, these become a *habitus* of the individual, which can be defined as a disposition of the individual that results from organizing actions and personal predispositions [9] (p. 206).

Focusing on recursive forms of everyday mobility, the relatively short trips occurring within the living areas become relevant, thus excluding non-reversible movements like relocations or migrations [10]. However, practices are not exclusively individual but may imply a collective dimension: in case these involve individual activities whose exercise generates specific social relationships, practices originate communities distinguished by the continuative deployment of an activity [11]. In terms of urban mobility policy, practices are thus significant for at least three reasons. First, they are deployed daily in urban settings, involving the spatial and temporal dimensions with which planning and policy approaches usually deal. Second, practices involve individuals and their "process of choice construction in contemporary societies" [12] (p. 17), a dimension that could be *nudged* [13] to direct individual choices toward better collective outcomes. Third, collectivities and their decisions may also be tackled, as the existence of communities of practices demonstrates.

Amongst the policy measures that practices could suggest, sharing-based approaches may contribute to address urban mobility issues. In the field of mobility, sharing is usually related to shared use mobility, that is, "travel alternatives that try to maximise the utilisation levels of the finite mobility resources that a society can realistically afford to have by disengaging their usage from ownership-bound limitations" [14] (p. 11). These may include services whose business model is based on the access to (rather than ownership of) vehicles, such as bikesharing, carsharing or ridesharing. However, the concept of shared use mobility may assume a specific meaning referring to practices: this would refer to unprecedented initiatives in which individuals share material assets (e.g., vehicles, money) and immaterial resources (e.g., individual skills, free time slots) between themselves to provide needed services or to coordinate individual needs, in order to enhance the access to places and the valued opportunities they offer. The focus on practices is in line with some distinguishing features of shared use mobility [14] (p. 11), such as providing a wider range of mobility choices, delivering first- and last-mile solutions to help riders connect with other forms of transport, cutting down transportation costs for individuals and households, and even establishing an ethos of sharing resources on an as-needed basis within communities. Furthermore, practices focus on a small part of the extensive and sometimes ambiguous field of shared use mobility, also providing a better representation of the shared-mobility users' behaviour, an element required for also improving urban transport analysis [15] (p. 408).

The interest in sharing arises from practices that, in a given territory, show recurrent individual needs, attractive places and mobility practices: many subjects need to accomplish similar tasks but they do so individually, even if the places to reach and the activities to realize are often the same for different people. To develop devoted policy solutions, shared use mobility approaches can rely on practices in two senses. First, these are knowledge tools for ongoing forms of mobilities, showing what needs are recurring and what similar resources are mobilised by individuals. Second, these can become policy tools, for example through behavioural approaches that address individuals' choices, behaviours, and their reflection on mobility practices. Practices can thus be relevant for securing individuals' access to places and opportunities, by promoting services and behaviours shaped by and coordinated through communities.

Drawing on these assumption, this paper intends to investigate policy solutions based on mobility practices, which could complement the traditional provision of mobility infrastructures and services. As the next sections explain, the proposed discussion is limited to a specific setting (informal settlements) and a precise mobility issue (the lack of accessibility to valued urban functions).

The discussion focuses on a specific setting and draws on a survey on everyday mobility practices, to detect recurring features and emerging valuable resources for unprecedented policy measures. This paper's discussion considers four research questions in particular: (1) what are the recurrent needs and latent resources highlighted by mobility practices; (2) what shared use mobility measures may originate from practices; (3) what policy features are required to operationalise such measures; (4) what are the opportunities and the issues that shared use mobility measures raise from an institutional perspective? In doing so, the expected outcome is a policy framework, which considers how practices may be treated as knowledge and policy tools in the various stages of a policymaking cycle. Even if the findings will be place-specific, the paper intends to contribute to further research and practice on shared use mobility policy, by offering a framework that may be adopted when approaching other settings.

While shared use mobility measures based on practices are increasingly considered in relation to many settings and mobility issues [16], this paper focuses on informal settlements and the improvement of the accessibility available to them. Increasingly, mobility planning and policy are distancing themselves from the simple provision of infrastructures and services [17,18], and this change of paradigm is even more significant for the marginal areas of the urban South. These areas in fact suffer historically from scarce access to urban opportunities, due to their spatial distribution (a matter of land use planning) and a scarce availability of transport connections (an issue of mobility planning). Furthermore, their unplanned origin and the features of the urban fabric impede the possibility of simply providing public transport services or road infrastructures. Nonetheless, the issues of access in informal settlements are crucial to fighting against the prevailing poverty of their inhabitants [19] or the high rates of urban criminality [20] (p. 77), as well as to promote a more democratic participation in urban life [21] (p. 1). Amongst the approaches that may enhance access to urban opportunities from informal settlements in the urban South, behavioural approaches (based on mobility demand) and service coproduction (based on mobility supply) are explored. On the one hand, behavioural measures address mobility demand and allow the possibility of considering individuals' preferences and needs as reflected in their travel choices, making practices themselves a policy tool [5]. On the other hand, coproduction addresses transport supply and offers an alternative way of providing mobility services, which also proves to be more viable when the available financial resources are scarce [22]. The discussion of this paper draws specifically on research on urban mobility and individual capabilities led in Bogotá: the city was chosen due to its celebrated public transport strategies, which aimed at improving access to the city for all but were only partially able to do so for the huge marginal areas of the city [23–25].

Moving from these assumptions, the discussion of the paper is structured as follows. First, a short theoretical discussion considers why urban mobility planning should secure access to urban opportunities and examines significant shared use mobility approaches addressing both supply and demand (Section 2). Then, a possible operationalization of such an approach is explored in the setting of Bogotá, focusing on marginal informal neighbourhoods and drawing on a qualitative survey involving local inhabitants. Section 3 succinctly explains why the case of Bogotá is interesting and describes the adopted methodology. The proposed approach is then discussed referring to three stages of a policy making cycle [26] (p. 210):

- *problem setting*: defining which areas are more in need of interventions that improve their access to urban opportunities and what mobility practices are already in place (Section 4);
- *policy design*: defining how behavioural and coproduction initiatives may be articulated in these settings (Section 5);
- *policy implementation*: discussing the conditions for realizing such initiatives and considering the necessary interactions with the current mobility policies of a city (Section 6).

2. Toward Sharing-Based Policies for Urban Accessibility: Service Coproduction and Demand Matchmaking

Sharing-based practices can contribute to improving access to urban opportunities through interventions adoptable in a short temporal term. Accessibility in fact is emerging as a priority for mobility planning and policy, being crucial for the achievement of opportunities that are decisive for individuals' wellbeing and quality of life [27]. However, accessibility is primarily defined by the interplay of consolidated features such as land use and transport systems, which define where people live, where opportunities are located, and what forms of mobility are available to make them interact [28]. Insufficient access may be addressed with long-term actions, providing new infrastructures or intervening on land-use. However, in adopting a shorter temporal threshold, other courses of action may also improve the access to opportunities. Three options would be available in this sense: enhancing the usability of existing connections to existing opportunities, providing closer opportunities, and introducing new services to reach existing opportunities. In relation to the latter, new forms of intervention on both mobility offer supply and demand may be relevant.

Two options emerge as suitable operational avenues, to be further explored: the coproduction of mobility services may address the lack of required connections, while a suitable operational take on mobility demands is conveyed by matchmaking and behavioural approaches to mobility. The coproduction of services and the matchmaking of needs act complementarily: coproduction addresses the side of supply, while matchmaking and behavioural approaches deal with the demand side. Sharing is a condition that makes both options necessary and feasible. On the one hand, coproduced services may be promoted by different kinds of resources brought together by individuals who live in the same area and experience similar mobility issues. On the other hand, matchmaking relies on similar needs expressed by individuals who may share their own practices for enhancing the achievement of valued opportunities. The following sections briefly introduce coproduction and matchmaking.

2.1. Producing New Opportunities: The Coproduction of Services

Coproduction refers to "the process through which inputs used to produce a good or service are contributed by individuals who are not 'in' the same organization" [29] (p. 1073). In settings characterised by the absence of needed services and scarce available resources to provide them, alternative forms of provision could be significant. In fact, coproduction approaches provide several advantages when compared to traditional forms of service provisions, but their main contribution is probably the focus on individuals and the value they may bring in the production processes. In fact, "the central idea in co-production is that people who use services are hidden resources, not drains on the system, and that no service that ignores this resource can be efficient" [30] (p. 11). The value provided by individuals consists of the manifold resources they may share for coproducing services, from monetary resources to the human resources necessary for running a service. In the field of mobility, coproduced initiatives may involve public transport services designed, financed (at least partially) and sometimes even run by individuals [30]. Coproduction may even involve private car sharing initiatives made possible by different vehicle owners who bring together their own vehicles [31].

The involvement of people better conveys individual needs and includes the eventual resources, both material and immaterial, available to them. In this way, equivalent services—i.e., services that meet the same goals, but in a more efficient way [32]—can be provided with alternative production processes, or informal services may be included within regular public transport networks [33]. These processes can also overcome those governance and logistical limitations that may impede the effective delivery of services, due to complex environments or lacking resources [31]. However, bottom-up initiatives and local involvement imply that these subjects should help themselves create those services that other citizens already receive in traditional ways, "dissolving any expectation that the contract between state and society should extend to the poor, now in any case reconfigured as the resourceful" [34] (p. 484) (see also [35] for a brief review of critical voices). Therefore, it becomes crucial that coproduction approaches are proposed and evaluated according to the real improvement they can provide to overall accessibility and individual opportunities, avoiding bottom-up solutions that are not beneficial.

2.2. Matching Existing Needs: A Behavioural Approach to Urban Mobility

Matchmaking refers to the possibility of helping two or more categories of customers find each other and engage in mutually beneficial interactions [36]. These matches could be favoured by addressing the behavioural aspects that define individual choices and defining different mobility profiles [37–40]. Forms of matchmaking drawing on behavioural elements could also be significant in settings where services are currently missing and could be the result of devoted coproduction initiatives. Behavioural elements would in fact work on the motivations that may facilitate the individuals' engagement in such measures: for example, engaging in a fulfilling activity [41], appreciating cooperation with others [42], and being involved in an activity useful for one's own and collective purposes [43]. Matchmaking examples may include private ridesharing circuits, involving neighbours or colleagues heading to nearby destinations. Another example is that of time banks, definable as time-based exchange systems between individuals accomplishing tasks on behalf of someone else.

However, behavioural approaches are subject to criticism, due to elements that may affect their effectiveness and relevance. First, behaviour-based approaches must deal with established habits, one of the main barriers for the promotion of alternative choices [44,45]. Moreover, behavioural measures may simply conceptualize citizens as passive users or consumers, rather than focusing on their self-realization as human beings: these approaches lean toward 'forced choices' assuming "the idea that rational maximization is what people should do" [46] (p. 23). This is an aspect particularly critical in urban South contexts where it may be assumed that "it is the behavioural weakness of the poor that has to be corrected" [47] (p. 580).

3. Methodology

3.1. The Setting

This paper bases its discussion on the setting of Bogotá (Colombia). The city has promoted significant public transport infrastructural investments inspired by an explicit social commitment, intending to address its significant social imbalances. Bogotá in fact has grown disorderly in the last decades and nowadays hosts approximately 8 million inhabitants; their distribution is strongly imbalanced, since the huge informal settlements in the southern areas of the city are those with the highest residential densities and the worst socio-economic conditions. The public transport strategy of Bogotá dates almost two decades, since its most significant intervention—a bus rapid transit system called TransMilenio—started its operations in the year 2000. The buses serve some of the main road corridors of the city, offering a fast service accessible to approximately half of the city inhabitants [25]. An effective and relatively economical measure that brought significant improvements to the mobility of Bogotá, TransMilenio, has been praised and imitated worldwide [48]. However, the contribution of this public transport system to the improvement of social inclusion has been partial, especially for marginal areas and the worst-off populations. Such issues have been highlighted by analyses referring to the accessibility that the city transport system provides to relevant urban opportunities [22,23].

Analyses that define what areas suffer from scarce levels of accessibility are context-dependent, since according to the examined setting the opportunities that "are assumed to be necessary to prevent households from social exclusion" [49] (p. 482), the prevailing modal choices, and the distance thresholds that determine what opportunities are available or not are different. In the research on which this paper draws, accessibility to job opportunities by public transport was estimated by assuming travel time thresholds of 30 and 60 min (see [50] for an in-depth description of the methodology). Drawing on these analyses, areas suffering from scarce levels of accessibility were defined, including a significant share of the city's marginal settlements. Amongst them, two areas in the southern part of Bogotá were chosen for a deeper analysis (see Figure 1): the neighbourhoods of La Merced del

Sur and La Torre. In the perspective assumed by the paper, these areas are relevant for their low socioeconomic conditions and their poor performances in terms of accessibility to urban opportunities. It must be noted that these areas were chosen also due to the availability of local contacts (and the consequent possibility to reach these areas and interact with their inhabitants). Both neighbourhoods are in mountainous areas and occupy an unfavourable position in relation to the job opportunities of the city (see Figure 2), but their locations and the available public transport services define a different time geography of access for the two neighbourhoods (see Figure 3).

Figure 1. Position of the two examined neighbourhoods (source: [50]).

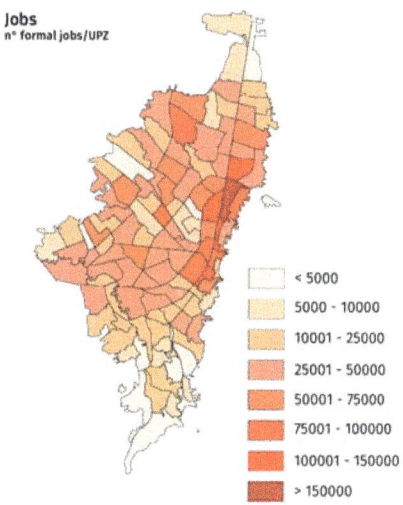

Figure 2. Job opportunities in Bogotá (source: [25]).

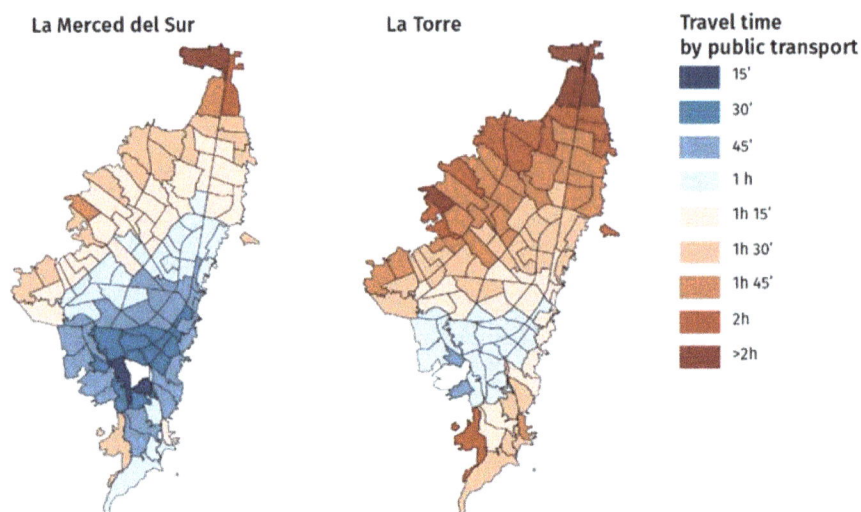

Figure 3. Travel time by public transport for the two examined neighbourhoods (source: [50]).

La Merced del Sur is in the southern part of Bogotá and was established between the Forties and the Fifties, when immigrants from other regions of Colombia arrived, attracted by the presence of productive activities such as mines and furnaces. Today the neighbourhood is a consolidated settlement, with two or three-story houses, but it still lacks paved streets, and it hosts prevalently low-income inhabitants. As part of the consolidated informal city, the neighbourhood does not suffer from severe forms of isolation from the rest of the city, but it lacks any form of formal or informal public transport. La Torre instead is located at the southern margin of Bogotá and was recently originated by the arrival of refugees from other Colombian regions, fleeing the violent civil war. Its expansion continues every year, so that the steep and unpaved streets of the neighbourhood pass by consolidated brick houses and new born shacks built with recycled objects. The socioeconomic conditions of its population are amongst the worse in the city. However, the very position of the neighbourhood is a perfect summary of what it means to be marginal in the city: the settlement is in an elevated position, has no public transport service, and can only be reached by climbing a long stairway or using an informal transfer.

3.2. Data Collection

In the chosen areas, an interview-based qualitative survey was led to detect what opportunities people value, where and when these activities occur, and what mobility practices are deployed to achieve them. Thanks to the help of two local charities, ten subjects in each neighbourhood were involved. These were mainly inhabitants (8 in La Torre, 9 in La Merced del Sur) with the additional presence of social workers (2 in la Torre, 1 in La Merced del Sur); the interviews, which lasted on average half an hour, were anonymised, audio recorded, transcribed in Spanish and then translated in English. The interviews were collected during working hours, so that the sample does not reflect exactly the social composition of the two neighbourhoods. The focus on two specific settlements allowed the involvement of a relatively small number of interviewees, which was assumed to be sufficient to grasp the constitutive features of the everyday mobilities and opportunities experienced in these areas. Microstories were collected through semi-structured interviews, realized between September 2016 and January 2017, in individual conversations with the interviewees. The interviews revolved around three elements: 1. subjects (conveying their social, economic, gender and age features; six questions); 2. valued activities (classifying them according to activity typology and frequency; two questions, repeated for each activity) and places (where activities occur; two questions, repeated for each activity); and 3. mobility practices (what mobility practices are necessary to reach places, and what are their features—in terms of modal option, services, travel times and costs; eleven questions, repeated for each activity).

3.3. Thematic Analysis of Data

Thematic analysis was used to examine the data previously collected. The data were originally collected as part of research on urban mobility and individual capabilities in Bogotá. While interviews were transcribed, the answers related to valued activities and places were also mapped. Following the framework from [51], the features of the analysis can be summarised as follows:

- a realist method, "which reports experiences, meanings and the reality of participants" [51] (p. 81), was used to grasp the everyday mobility experiences of inhabitants;
- codes for analysing data were defined in view of four issues: destinations, activities pursued there, frequencies of the trips to the destination, and modal choices (for example, codes for modal choices included walking, going by public transport, going by informal transport, bicycling, going by car, and going by motorbike);
- themes were detected in view of the places mentioned by at least two people.

Given the initial interest in mobility and capabilities, the thematic analysis enabled a focus on the emergence of recurrent mobility practices as a base for shared use mobility policy measures. In fact, interviews did not explicitly refer to such feature, but rather the active role of the researcher highlighted such recurrent patterns and considered their possible policy relevance.

4. Problem Setting: Recurring Accessibility Issues in Marginal Settlements

To deploy shared use mobility measures for enhancing accessibility, it is necessary to set the problem to be faced by such policy. In fact, problem setting "is a process in which, interactively, we name the things to which we will attend and frame the context in which we will attend to them" [52] (pp. 39–40). To 'name the things', three elements are here necessary. First, define what areas are suffering from scarce levels of accessibility (as shown in Section 3.1). Second, examine the opportunities valued by local inhabitants and the mobility practices deployed to achieve them. Third, assess if favourable conditions for shared use mobility initiatives are present.

In the chosen areas, interviewees highlight several opportunities significant for them and their beloved ones. Apart from jobs, these mainly include activities necessary for the fulfilment of everyday needs, such as shopping and relational activities (that is, those related to the management of the needs of one's closest relatives). Other relevant typologies are instead differentiated according to the neighbourhood, with a prevalence of education-related activities in La Merced and care-related activities in La Torre. Most respondents tended to move by public transport, despite highlighting the scarce quality of the available services. A good explanation is provided by one respondent, who mentioned that "the public transport is the only alternative. The only skill you need is to plan the travel in advance, so that you can reach the hospital on time for your appointment" (D., La Torre). Only few respondents could not afford to pay the bus fare or, on the contrary, they could move by using private vehicles. Instead, the deriving geography of accessible areas and available opportunities was similar (see Figure 4): while people in La Merced del Sur were able to reach a few surrounding neighbourhoods and even some central areas, the inhabitants of La Torre mainly remained confined to a portion of southern Bogotá.

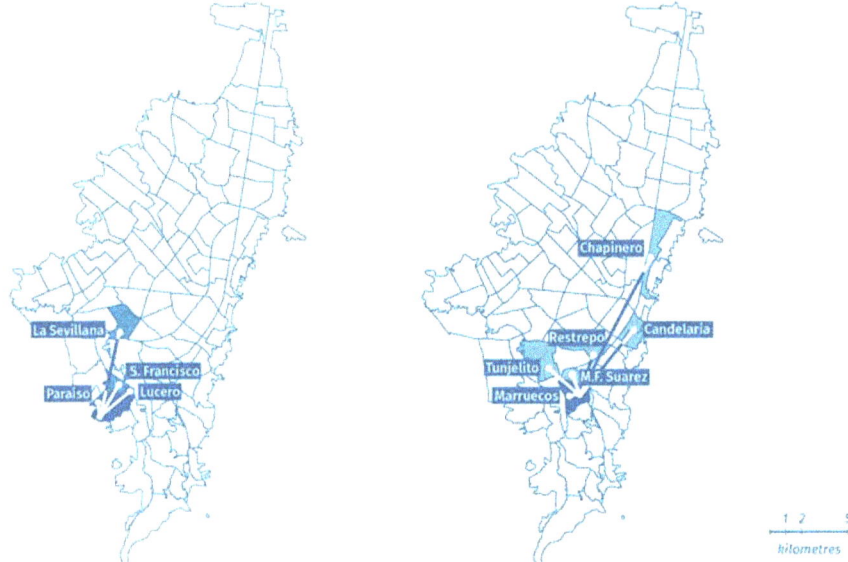

Figure 4. Principal areas of interaction for the neighbourhoods of La Torre (**left**) and La Merced del Sur (**right**) (source: [50]).

From the interviews conducted in the two marginal neighbourhoods, inhabitants confirmed the low level of accessibility available to them, highlighting features that may pave the way for shared use mobility policy measures. In fact, most of the respondents agreed that they can reach the places they need: as stated by one of them, "I can reach all the places I need for me and my family" (M., La Torre). They also recognized overall mobility issues, as in the case of V. (La Merced del Sur) who stated: "For me it is quite difficult [to move], because I only walk to the places I need; often there is no transport, or it is too expensive for me and my children". In particular, some common features emerge. First, a recurrence of needs, places and mobility practices emerge: many subjects need to accomplish similar tasks with similar frequencies, but they do so individually, even if the places to reach and the activities to realize are often the same for different people. Such recurrence is particularly visible at the local scale (see Figure 5), where local polarities emerge in relation to basic needs such as shopping, care and relational activities (for example, schools attended by children or health care facilities needed by elderly relatives). Second, a prevalence of trips by public transport emerge but respondents also extensively mention the low quality of the existing services: the scarcity of routes, their low frequencies, and their limited ability to reach desired places are recurrent elements in the interviews.

In relation to possible shared use mobility measures, this short insight on the two neighbourhoods already offers some elements of interest. The interviewees express similar needs that they currently achieve *despite* the poor modal alternatives available to them. However, to do so they must invest significant personal resources, coping with huge efforts, monetary expenses, and temporal costs. As G. (La Merced del Sur) admitted, "I can reach most of the places I need, but if transport was better (more routes, better travel conditions), for sure I would be able to move more and do more activities in different places". Given that institutions in Bogotá struggle to provide infrastructures or services in traditional forms [25] (pp. 11–12), shared use mobility measures could prove a viable alternative for enhancing the accessibility available in marginal areas.

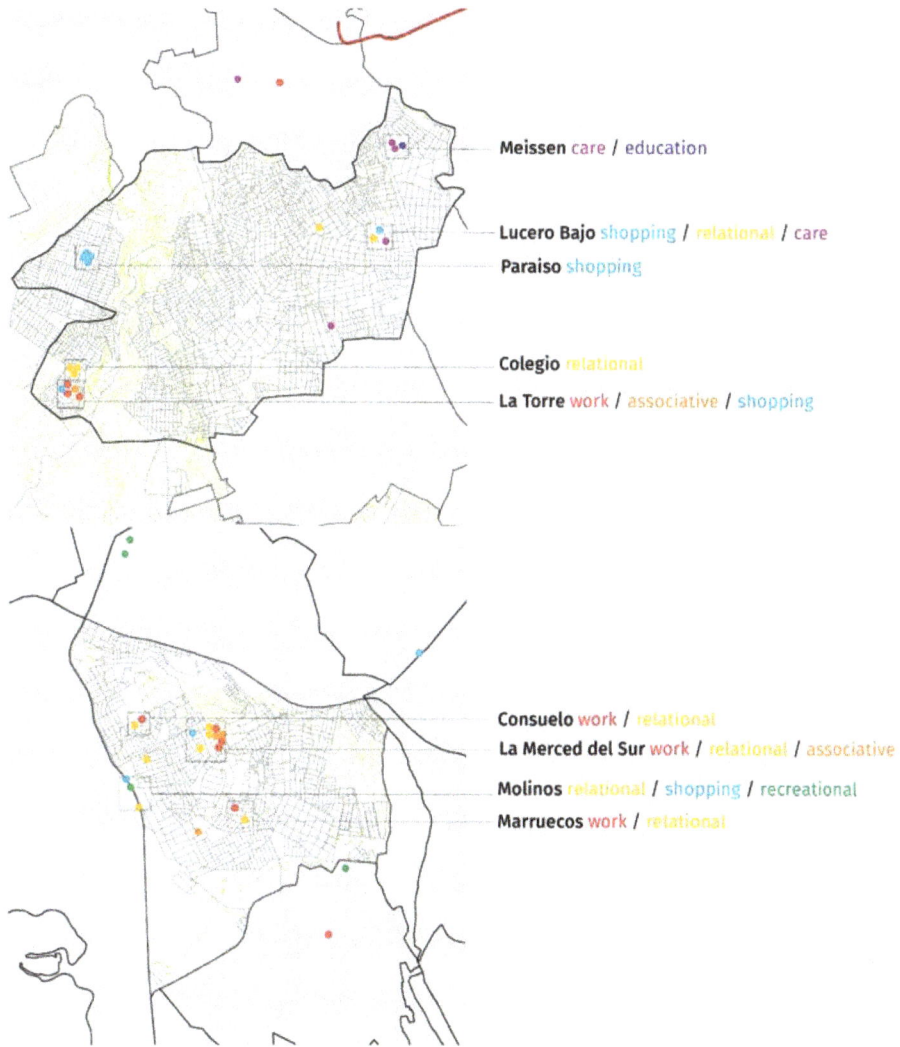

Figure 5. Locations and typologies of the activities at the neighbourhood scale, as mentioned in the interviews (source: [50]).

5. Policy Design: Operationalizing Coproduction and Matchmaking

The individual needs and the mobility issues highlighted in the previous section can contribute to the design of shared use mobility policy measures, in relation to both demand and supply. Policy design in fact is directed to define policy instruments and implementation tools for solving the problem previously set. The features of these interventions, the evaluation of their benefits and costs, and a realistic assessment of their feasibility are here discussed.

If the available modal choices remain unaltered, matchmaking provides a first operational option. In fact, inhabitants undertake recurrent activities in the same locations and with similar frequencies, suggesting the coordination of their mobility needs. As shown in Figure 5, some local polarities emerge: for La Merced del Sur, the area of Molinos (a commercial polarity near a TransMilenio station, along the trafficked Avenida Caracas); for La Torre, the areas of Paraiso (for shopping reasons), Lucero Bajo (with commercial and care activities, in a dense neighbourhood) and Meissen (attractive because of schools and a hospital). Some recurring activities may be accomplished by a smaller number of subjects acting on behalf of a larger number of inhabitants, establishing for example a time bank (the author discussed the proposal with a local charity, which confirmed the suitability of such an initiative). Figure 6 provides a representation of how this initiative may work, assuming of course the presence of effective forms of coordination between the needs and the practices of different subjects. F. (La Torre) mentioned that some subjects need the contribution of other people to achieve some tasks: "I agree with my daughter who has the experience of travelling with an elderly and with children. If you are with these people, or if you must carry the food you just bought, travel can be very unpleasant. Moreover, you also have long travel times as well as waiting times". Such shared accomplishment of significant tasks may nonetheless prove to be insufficient for improving the available access to valued opportunities, for which new mobility services could be significant. These may be the result of coproduction initiatives, in which inhabitants share resources of their own (be they economic, human or other) to provide a service that is currently absent.

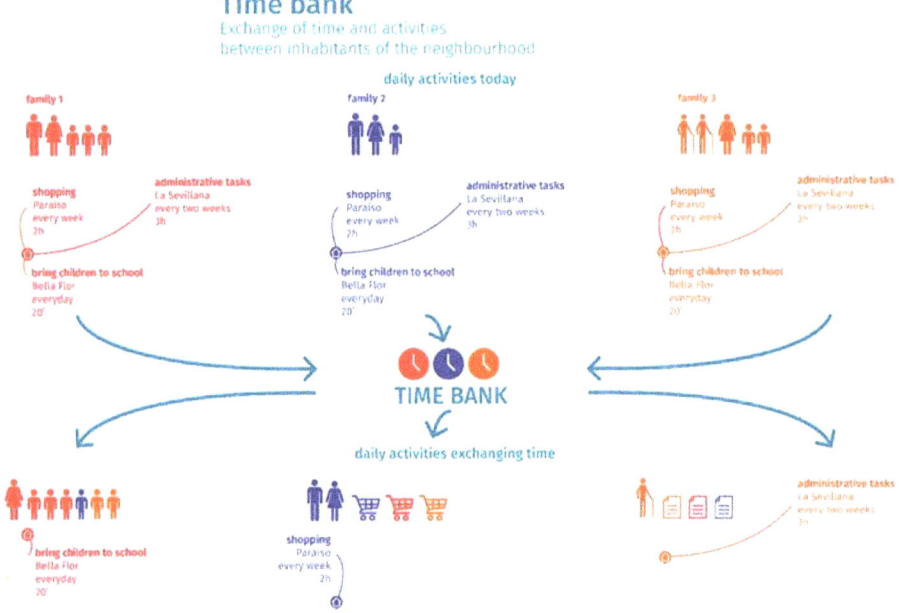

Figure 6. A suitable matchmaking example: Functioning of a local time bank for the La Torre neighbourhood (source: [50]).

Coproduction and matchmaking may contribute to the achievement of similar aims. Considering, for example, the inhabitants of La Torre going to the Paraiso neighbourhood for their shopping (as shown in Figure 5), most inhabitants currently walk to the area on a weekly basis, while going back with an informal bus if they need to carry heavy items. They may first establish a matchmaking mechanism, so that only a few of them would be responsible for groceries. Others instead would accomplish other significant activities in other areas. If this option proved ineffective, a devoted service connecting La Torre to Paraiso could be coproduced by inhabitants, who would benefit of the new connection as well as of the occasion of employment it may provide to some locals.

The neighbourhood of La Torre proves a good example to observe how the two options may also be developed in relation to other forms of intervention. Many inhabitants rely on few public transport options, so that the locations and opportunities they can reach are in many cases limited. For example, the attractive and near area of Lucero Bajo can usually be reached with at least one transfer. Improving the comfort and usability of existing public transport services may make them more usable, for example facilitating the understanding of how the public transport routes work. A matchmaking system would instead allow for the use of existing mobility practices to satisfy the needs of a wider number of local inhabitants. If these actions prove insufficient for improving accessibility due to the persisting lack of services, coproduced services may provide a possible solution, offering a required connection by using currently unused bottom-up resources. Both public and private transport providers in fact often refuse to serve these areas "They always promised us to bring a bus line to the neighbourhood, where not even taxi drivers like to come. They say that roads are unsafe due to their poor maintenance and to the presence of criminals" (J., La Merced del Sur).

Coproduction could thus be more efficient and effective than traditional courses of action. In fact, it would assess different ways of improving existing services before investing additional resources for providing new ones. Furthermore, the evaluation of each option considers the need for accessing valued opportunities, guaranteeing the effectiveness of the measures in responding to the specific accessibility needs of an area and its inhabitants. According to this perspective, institutions should provide new public transport services or new facilities only in case there is no room to improve existing equipment. The discussion here provided thus offers a preliminary but significant insight on suitable priority interventions for areas suffering from low levels of accessibility. In doing so, the proposed approach expands a set of options often limited to the public provision of infrastructures and services.

An evaluation of the benefits and costs for each measure is less straightforward, though. Assuming the provision of sufficient accessibility as the main aim of urban mobility planning and policy [27], this would be the target that a measure should be able to achieve. The benefits of a measure would thus depend on the number of people who would see an improvement to the accessibility available to them, eventually assuming that the generated benefit is inversely proportional to the current socioeconomic condition of the person. The benefits may be tentatively quantified attaching a monetary value to saved travel time, or to each additional new opportunity that can be reached. Nonetheless, this money-based approach is prone to limitations and should also consider the diminishing marginal value of increased accessibility [53]. In case a varied set of feasible measures could improve the accessibility available to the targeted area or population, the evaluation would consider their costs. For example, if both a coproduced bus line and a new cableway infrastructure were able to improve the basic accessibility available to La Torre, the former, cheaper option would probably be preferable.

However, the policy measures previously proposed are prone to limitations. The proposed approach is in fact not sufficient for addressing individual and collective mobility needs, especially when considering their operational implications. Other elements that influence the functioning of urban mobility require traditional approaches: for example, this is the case for the spatial distribution of significant activities to be reached, or for the infrastructures that convey huge mobility flows. The case of Bogotá and its peripheral settlements suggests that a few issues need to be faced in parallel with the provision of new services. Neighbourhoods of informal origins show difficult spatial conditions (for example, their orography) and a lack of adequate infrastructures (like roads) that function as obstacles to the provision of ordinary services. The same inhabitants acknowledge this: "In general, the inhabitants here lack a lot of basic services (water, gas, electricity ...) as well as public equipment (like parks and sport grounds). Nonetheless, I think that the situation will improve, especially if the TransMiCable (e.g., a cableway connecting to the nearest us terminal) will be built" (L., La Torre).

Furthermore, significant conditions for the development of the discussed options must face unwelcoming local conditions. For example, subjects other than public institutions have consistent power on the peripheral settlements and often exercise it with violence. Finally, Bogotá would require a drastic change in the current approaches to urban planning and policy. Despite an explicitly declared interest in improving access to urban opportunities for the worst-off inhabitants, these aims have only been partially pursued. Furthermore, the construction of new infrastructures is still the main strategy to address the urban mobility needs [54], while the public transport system is suffering severe financial restrictions. The approaches previously discussed may thus contribute to the economic sustainability of the existing (public) transport system of Bogotá, mobilizing additional resources to provide needed services and increasing their use by nudging individual travel choices.

6. Policy Implementation: Roles and Issues for Institutions

In the implementation phase, the policy defined in the previous stages is given form and effect, being put into practice and delivered to the public. Institutions are fundamental for implementing shared use mobility policy measures for urban mobility, having a twofold role. On the one hand, they need to recognize which areas and populations require priority interventions for enhancing accessibility. On the other hand, they should recognize what benefits would be generated by different measures and assess if the preconditions for their implementation are present. In relation to settings where such measures may be developed, institutional actors may act as facilitators, providing the conditions that would allow the creation and the growth of such initiatives.

Institutions should recognize those areas and communities that may potentially host initiatives such as service coproduction and demand matchmaking. Different forms of capital would be required: monetary resources to invest (economic capital), skilled people to run the service (human capital) and even the trust and sense of community that may inspire and sustain similar initiatives (social capital). For example, in the case of coproduced services, the necessary human resources would refer to "the human power needed to plan, manage, operate, and support local public transport systems" [55] (p. 4). In the case of matchmaking schemes, these resources would imply instead the managerial skills to run the initiative as well as the fundamental trust bounds required to keep beneficiaries together. While the social and human capital to be mobilized may also be promoted by public institutions [56], it is more suitable to address areas where local subjects (associations, community organizations, charities) are already active.

Once promising settings are recognised, institutions may have a double role as facilitators of the mentioned initiatives. First, they may provide trained figures to sustain such processes, such as 'coproduction development officers' [35] in charge of supporting and accompanying local coproduction initiatives. Moreover, institutions should also intervene on a normative dimension, providing the frameworks of rules within which such initiatives may develop. The explored options often challenge existing norms, leading to the "need to reconceptualise service provision as a process of social construction in which actors in self-organizing systems negotiate rules, norms and institutional frameworks rather than taking the rules of the game as given" [35] (p. 858). For example, new legal subjects may be necessary. The mentioned initiatives in fact imply that more complex forms of engagement may then be relevant, involving users in the definition of desired services as well as in their provision. This would foster the creation of community enterprises devoted to transport services. Definable as "organizations that promote innovate solutions for development, autoregulation, and management of spaces and services for local communities" [57], community enterprises may actively involve local users in the provision of needed mobility services, tailored on the exigencies directly expressed by users.

Normative frameworks are not neutral and rather directly involve a political dimension, though. A first political element implied by the mentioned options refers to their shaping. This element is highlighted by coproduction initiatives. The very interest in coproducing services and goods may appear as a political action: in fact, "while many of the collective activities undertaken by Southern residents may not involve direct political claims, nevertheless through their focus on state services (as well as other kinds of resource) they involve some engagement with the state and the realm of politics" [58] (p. 343). Moreover, the interactions between the involved actors imply the typical dynamics of policy processes, shaping not only the desired outcome, but also the relationships between the subjects, and the subjects themselves. Such processes in fact require a mutual adjustment of expectations [59] and contribute to the formation of values and meanings [60]. However, a possibly ambiguous role of institutions emerges: institutional subjects need to have an enabling role to guarantee the success of such initiatives [61], but the political dimension of these processes implies that, anyway, they are ordinary actors deploying their own tactics and strategies. The involved subjects and the interactions they establish between themselves are thus crucial for the shaping of shared use mobility policy approaches. Nonetheless, such elements necessarily refer to small-scale initiatives, where the involved communities and areas are easily definable and can be involved within specific interactions.

A second political element refers instead to the adoption and the acceptance of the mentioned initiatives. Innovative solutions cannot be simply technically feasible but need to be recognized as socially useful, and they require that institutions support their development [62]. For example, in the case of Bogotá, the adoption of initiatives of this kind may be more suitable in peripheral settings, especially when characterized by high degrees of informality. On the one hand, the setting conditions (in terms of spatial features as well as of existing mobility demands) often do not allow the provision of traditional services, due to their infrastructural requirements (e.g., road conditions) or entry conditions (e.g., high fares, complex system functioning). On the other hand, institutions at different levels (with the municipality playing a leading role) still tend to privilege the provision of infrastructures, as the recent project for a cableway serving one of the peripheral areas investigated in this work demonstrates [63]. The presence of different institutional subjects also raises governance issues related to the cooperation between different bodies, an aspect that is generally critical in relation to urban mobility issues. Apparently, these conditions do not match with the experimentation of innovative solutions involving a wide range of actors as protagonists; nonetheless, as proven by other coproduction experiences [61], these initiatives may and should contribute to institutional change, redesigning existing institutions.

A third significant dimension refers to the acceptability that such initiatives may receive from the bottom. A first dimension refers to the actual will that local inhabitants may have to engage in such initiatives, sharing their own practices or participating in the provision of needed services. Such form of community action in fact depends on specific features of places and individuals, making it difficult to recognize replicable models [64]. Consequently, mobility practices that show similar needs and forms are simply a starting point for the eventual design of shared use mobility policy measures. Communities may thus be considered as developers of policy initiatives not a priori, but rather according to the specific inclinations they may show. A second dimension refers instead to the presence of other ongoing informal initiatives, that may base their existence also on the exploitation of current imbalances. For example, the neighbourhood of La Torre is served by an informal van connection that simply provides access to the nearest public transport stop, reachable only with a steep route. However, the violence used by the subjects operating such services impeded the provision of additional services, so that the municipality for example refused to bring a planned bus route to the neighbourhood because of the many threats received. Shared use mobility measures may thus be considered feasible when considering ongoing mobility practices but features of the local settings are crucial to determine their actual degree of feasibility.

Finally, a fourth political issue refers to the real benefits and costs generated by the discussed policy approaches, and the consequent social legitimacy of implemented measures directly involving their beneficiaries. While transport involves a specific form of justice due to the impact it has on individuals' quality of life [27], the definition of the subjects who should provide it is less straightforward. Public institutions have been traditionally in charge of planning and providing public transport services, but other actors may be relevant too. In fact, "it may be that the capabilitarian ideal society is better reached by a coordinated commitment to individual action or by relying on market mechanisms" [65] (p. 7). Nonetheless, the setting of Bogotá requires a realistic assessment of the actors who may contribute to the enhancement of the accessibility available in informal settlements through shared use mobility measures.

At least three actors may be involved in the development of these initiatives: inhabitants, institutions and private companies. Local inhabitants may be involved only if these initiatives prove to be feasible (that is, local resources are available and can be mobilised) and beneficial (for example, providing also unprecedented employment and entrepreneurial occasions). In the perspective of the inhabitants, the benefits of these measures should then go beyond the simple mobility sphere and obviously exceed costs. Institutions should be responsible for assessing what areas need accessibility improvements and, if so, under what conditions shared use mobility initiatives may be relevant. Additionally, a supportive role actively promoting the development of initiatives would be necessary. In this perspective, and contrarily to what has been feared by some scholars [33,34], institutions would not retreat from the necessary provision of sufficient levels of accessibility to areas or populations in need but would rather have a wider range of operational options at their disposal. Additionally, non-local actors may potentially intervene in the development of similar initiatives, for example in the case of private companies offering transport services. However, the settings here presented show low levels of profitability (as the current absence of significant transport services demonstrates) and, even if new initiatives were to be introduced, the benefits provided by enhanced accessibility should be realistically compared with the costs that inhabitants should pay. Considering the fundamental role of accessibility for the wellbeing of the targeted populations and the priority attributed to measures contributing in this sense [27], institutions may act as controllers of such eventual private initiatives.

7. Conclusions

The feasibility of shared use mobility policies and their significance for enhancing accessibility to urban opportunities has been observed throughout the stages of the policy making cycle. To foster their development, institutions should define areas and populations requiring priority interventions for enhancing accessibility and consequently act as facilitators for the deployment of differentiated courses of action. Interestingly, coproduction and matchmaking acquire new meanings in the marginal settings here examined. Coproduction goes beyond participation in design, but rather gives a leading role to local inhabitants for the provision of needed services. Matchmaking instead configures new forms of sharing for mobility, which do not simply imply the presence of technology-based companies offering inedited services but rather make people put their own everyday practices together.

The proposed approach seems to configure several advantages for institutions intervening on urban mobility. On the one hand, the coproduction of services may be able to mobilise additional resources by involving local communities and their economic, social and human forms of capital. On the other hand, the matchmaking of mobility demands allows the more efficient use of existent resources by intercepting and coordinating potential users who could benefit from their use. Moreover, considering local subjects as potential protagonists of mobility service provisions, it may be possible not only to respond to local mobility needs but also to offer further occasions for local development, for example, offering new employment and entrepreneurial opportunities. The new mobility opportunities would thus actively involve individuals "in shaping their own destiny" [66] (p. 53). However, the positive outcomes would involve not only the expansion of individual opportunities required to guarantee societal development [67] but also the provision of novel resources and the generation of new behaviours that may have positive collective externalities [30].

However, these approaches should be intended as complementary to traditional takes on urban mobility, promoting alternative courses of action where usual options are not viable (e.g., construction of new infrastructures or provision of new services). Some experiences from other Latin American settings [68] have proved effective in this sense. A first requirement refers to the territorialisation of these measures, defining analytical tools to define which urban settings and populations may be more in need of similar actions, as well as those areas and subjects that present conditions favourable for the implementation of such measures (e.g., the presence of various forms of capital required to coproduce services). Switching from an emphasis on transport goods provisions to their actual use, behavioural measures may instead usefully promote the use of specific infrastructures and services, reducing the risks of realizing underused 'white elephants' [69]. Therefore, even the overall implications of such measures may be relevant: for example, the development of behavioural approaches may change some dynamics underlying urban mobility modelling, introducing new variables and possibly leading to different results when simulating the outcomes of planning and policy measures.

In conclusion, a focus on individual opportunities appears to be a suitable source for new policy approaches to urban issues. The discussion provided in this paper recognizes the need for proposing shared use mobility policy approaches and assesses their significance in the various settings where they could be significant, considering the local specificities that may make a focus on opportunities more relevant. Nonetheless, the main element of interest seems to be the possibility to consider sharing not only in those settings where it is already an established option for mobility, but even to address through it the urgent need for accessibility in marginal settlements.

Conflicts of Interest: The author declares no conflict of interest.

References

1. Viry, G.; Kaufmann, V. *High Mobility in Europe. Work and Personal Life*; Palgrave Macmillan: London, UK, 2015.
2. Cass, N.; Shove, E.; Urry, J. Social exclusion, mobility and access. *Sociol. Rev.* **2005**, *53*, 539–555. [CrossRef]
3. Kaufmann, V.; Bergmann, M.; Joye, D. Motility: Mobility as Capital. *Int. J. Urban Reg. Res.* **2004**, *28*, 745–756. [CrossRef]
4. Donolo, C. Dalle politiche pubbliche alle pratiche sociali nella produzione di beni pubblici? Osservazioni su una nuova generazione di policies. *Stato e Mercato* **2005**, *73*, 33–65.
5. Pucci, P. Mobility practices as a knowledge and design tool for urban policy. In *Understanding Mobilities for Designing Contemporary Cities*; Pucci, P., Colleoni, M., Eds.; Springer: Berlin, Germany, 2016.
6. Cresswell, T.; Merriman, P. (Eds.) *Geographies of Mobilities: Practices, Spaces, Subjects*; Ashgate: Abingdon, UK, 2011.
7. Pasqui, G. *Città, Popolazioni, Politiche*; Jaca Book: Milan, Italy, 2008.
8. De Certeau, M. *The Practice of Everyday Life*; University of California Press: Berkeley, CA, USA, 1984.
9. Bourdieu, P. *Outline of a Theory of Practice*; Cambridge University Press: Cambridge, UK, 1977.
10. Kaufmann, V. *Re-Thinking Mobility*; Ashgate: Farnham, UK, 2002.
11. Wenger, E. *Communities of Practice: Learning, Meaning and Identity*; Cambruidge University Press: Cambridge, UK, 1998.
12. Bourdin, A. Les mobilités et le programme de la sociologie. *Cah. Int. Soc.* **2005**, *118*, 5–21. [CrossRef]
13. Thaler, R.H.; Sustein, C.R. *Nudge, Improving Decisions about Health, Wealth and Happiness*; Yale University Press: Yale, CT, USA, 2008.
14. Nikitas, A.; Kougias, I.; Alyavina, E.; Njoya Tchouamou, E. How Can Autonomous and Connected Vehicles, Electromobility, BRT, Hyperloop, Shared Use Mobility and Mobility-As-A-Service Shape Transport Futures for the Context of Smart Cities? *Urban Sci.* **2017**, *1*, 36. [CrossRef]
15. Le Vine, S.; Polak, J. Introduction to special issue: New directions in shared-mobility research. *Transportation* **2015**, *42*, 407–411. [CrossRef]
16. Cohen, B.; Kietzmann, J. Ride On! Mobility Business Models for the Sharing Economy. *Organ. Environ.* **2014**, *27*, 279–296. [CrossRef]
17. Martens, K. Basing Transport Planning on Principles of Social Justice. *Berkeley Plan. J.* **2006**, *19*, 1–17.
18. Shaw, J.; Hesse, M. Transport, geography and the 'new' mobilities. *Trans. Inst. Br. Geogr.* **2010**, *35*, 305–312. [CrossRef]
19. World Bank. *Cities on the Move: World Bank Urban Transport Strategy Review*; The World Bank: Washington, DC, USA, 2002.
20. Gouverneur, D. *Diseño de Nuevos Asentamientos Informales*; Fondo Editorial Universidad Eafit, Ediciones Unisalle: Medellín, CA, USA, 2016.
21. United Nations Human Settlements Programme. *Planning and Design for Sustainable Urban Mobility*; Routledge: Abingdon, UK, 2013.
22. Joshi, A.; Moore, M. Institutionalised Co-production: Unorthodox Public Service Delivery in Challenging Environments. *J. Dev. Stud.* **2004**, *40*, 31–49. [CrossRef]

23. Bocarejo, J.P.; Oviedo, D. Transport accessibility and social inequities: A tool for identification of mobility needs and evaluation of transport investments. *J. Transp. Geogr.* **2012**, *24*, 142–154. [CrossRef]
24. Ardila-Gómez, A. Transit Planning in Curitiba and Bogotá. Roles in Interaction, Risk, and Change. Ph.D. Thesis, Massachusetts Institute of Technology, Cambridge, UK, 2004.
25. Vecchio, G. Democracy on the move? Bogotá's urban transport strategies and the access to the city. *City Territ. Archit.* **2017**, *4*, 15. [CrossRef]
26. Marsden, G.; Reardon, L. Questions of governance: Rethinking the study of transportation policy. *Transp. Res. Part A Policy Pract.* **2017**, *101*, 238–251. [CrossRef]
27. Martens, K. *Transport Justice: Designing Fair Transportation Systems*; Routledge: London, UK, 2017.
28. Geurs, K.T.; Van Wee, B. Accessibility evaluation of land-use and transport strategies: Review and research directions. *J. Transp. Geogr.* **2004**, *12*, 127–140. [CrossRef]
29. Ostrom, E. Crossing the Great Divide: Synergy, and Development. *World Dev.* **1996**, *24*, 1073–1087. [CrossRef]
30. Boyle, D.; Harris, M. *The Challenge of Co-Production*; New Economics Foundation: London, UK, 2009.
31. Kudo, H. Co-design, Co-creation, and Co-production of Smart Mobility System. In *Cross-Cultural Design*; Rau, P.L., Ed.; Springer: Berlin, Germany, 2016; pp. 551–562.
32. Diamond, R.; Shove, E. Defining Efficiency: What Is 'Equivalent Service' and Why Does It Matter? 2015. Available online: http://www.demand.ac.uk/05/10/2015/article-defining-efficiency-what-is-equivalent-service-and-why-does-it-matter/ (accessed on 21 September 2016).
33. Cervero, R. *Informal Transport in the Developing World*; United Nations Centre for Human Settlements (Habitat): Nairobi, Kenya, 2000.
34. Amin, A. Telescopic urbanism and the poor. *City* **2013**, *17*, 476–492. [CrossRef]
35. Bovaird, T. Beyond engagement and participation: User and community coproduction of public services. *Public Adm. Rev.* **2007**, *67*, 846–860. [CrossRef]
36. Evans, D.S.; Schmalensee, R. *Matchmakers: The New Economics of Multisided Platforms*; Harvard University Press: Cambridge, MA, USA, 2016.
37. Anable, J. 'Complacent Car Addicts'; or 'Aspiring Environmentalists'? Identifying travel behaviour segments using attitude theory. *Transp. Policy* **2005**, *12*, 65–78. [CrossRef]
38. Cao, X.; Mokhtarian, P.L. How do individuals adapt their personal travel? Objective and subjective influences on the consideration of travel-related strategies for San Francisco Bay Area commuters. *Transp. Policy* **2005**, *12*, 291–302. [CrossRef]
39. Cairns, S.; Sloman, L.; Newson, C.; Anable, J.; Kirkbridge, A.; Goodwin, P. Smarter choices: Assessing the potential to achieve traffic reductions using 'soft measures'. *Transp. Rev.* **2008**, *28*, 593–618. [CrossRef]
40. Kazhamiakin, R.; Marconi, A.; Perillo, M.; Pistore, M.; Valetto, G.; Piras, L.; Avesani, F.; Perri, N. Using Gamification to Incentivize Sustainable Urban Mobility Using Gamification to Incentivize Sustainable Urban Mobility. In Proceedings of the 1st IEEE International Smart Cities Conference, Guadalajara, Mexico, 25–28 October 2015.
41. Schwanen, T. Beyond instrument: Smartphone app and sustainable mobility. *Eur. J. Transp. Infrastruct. Res.* **2015**, *15*, 675–690.
42. Hirschman, A.O. *Shifting Involvements: Private Interest and Public Action*; Princeton University Press: Princeton, NJ, USA, 1982.
43. Sennett, R. *Together: The Rituals, Pleasures, and Politics of Cooperation*; Yale University Press: New Haven, CT, USA, 2012.
44. Hirschman, A.O. *Getting Ahead Collectively: Grassroots Experiences in Latin America*; Pergamon Press: New York, NY, USA, 1984.
45. Te Brömmelstroet, M. Sometimes you want people to make the right choices for the right reasons: Potential perversity and jeopardy of behavioural change campaigns in the mobility domain. *J. Transp. Geogr.* **2014**, *39*, 141–144. [CrossRef]
46. Berndt, C.; Boeckler, M. Behave, global south! Economics, experiments, evidence. *Geoforum* **2016**, *70*, 22–24. [CrossRef]
47. Berndt, C. Behavioural economics, experimentalism and the marketization of development. *Econ. Soc.* **2015**, *44*, 567–591. [CrossRef]
48. Wood, A. The Politics of Policy Circulation: Unpacking the Relationship between South African and South American Cities in the Adoption of Bus Rapid Transit. *Antipode* **2015**, *47*, 1062–1079. [CrossRef]

49. Lucas, K.; van Wee, B.; Maat, K. A method to evaluate equitable accessibility: Combining ethical theories and accessibility-based approaches. *Transportation* **2016**, *43*, 473–490. [CrossRef]
50. Vecchio, G. Urban Mobility as Human Capability. Bridging the Gap between Transport Planning and Individual Opportunities. Ph.D. Thesis, Politecnico di Milano, Milan, Italy, 2018.
51. Braun, V.; Clarke, V. Using thematic analysis in psychology. *Qual. Res. Psychol.* **2016**, *3*, 77–101. [CrossRef]
52. Schön, D. *The Reflective Practitioner*; Basic Books: New York, NY, USA, 1983.
53. Martens, K.; Di Ciommo, F.; Papanikolau, A. Incorporating equity into transport planning: Utility, priority and sufficiency approaches. In Proceedings of the XVIII Congreso Panamericano de Ingeniería de Tránsito, Transporte y Logística, Santander, Spain, 11–13 June 2014.
54. Alcaldía Mayor de Bogotá. El Metro de Bogotá. Available online: http://es.presidencia.gov.co/Documents/MetroRuedaPrensa2016917.pdf#search=transmilenio80%25 (accessed on 17 May 2017).
55. Fukumoto, M.; Kato, H. An Empirical Study on Sustainable Formation of Local Public Transport Systems by Participation of Community. In Proceedings of the 13th World Conference on Transport Research Conference, Rio de Janeiro, Brazil, 15–18 July 2013.
56. Evans, P. Government Action, Social Capital and Development: Reviewing the Evidence on Synergy. *World Dev.* **1996**, *24*, 1119–1132. [CrossRef]
57. Tricarico, L. *Imprese di Comunità Nelle Politiche di Rigenerazione Urbana: Definire ed Inquadrare il Contesto Italiano*; Euricse: Trento, Italy, 2014.
58. Mitlin, D. With and beyond the state—Co-production as a route to political influence, power and transformation for grassroots organizations. *Environ. Urban.* **2008**, *20*, 339–360. [CrossRef]
59. Whiaker, G.P. Coproduction: Citizen Participation in Service Delivery. *Public Adm. Rev.* **1980**, *40*, 240–246. [CrossRef]
60. Deneulin, S.; McGregor, J.A. The capability approach and the politics of a social conception of wellbeing. *Eur. J. Soc. Theory* **2010**, *13*, 501–519. [CrossRef]
61. Shand, W. *Exploring Institutional Change. The Contribution of co-Production to Shaping Institutions*; IIED: London, UK, 2015.
62. Feitelson, E.; Samuelson, I. The Political Economy of Transport Innovations. In *Transport Developments and Innovations in an Evolving World*; Beuthe, M., Himanen, V., Reggiani, A., Zamparini, L., Eds.; Springer: Berlin, Germany, 2004.
63. Guerrero Arciniegas, C. *Todo Listo Para el Cable a Ciudad Bolívar*; El Espectador: Bogotá, CA, USA, 2016.
64. Tricarico, L. Community action: Value or instrument? An ethics and planning critical review. *J. Archit. Urban.* **2017**, *41*, 221–233. [CrossRef]
65. Robeyins, I. Capabilitarianism. *J. Hum. Dev. Capab.* **2016**, *17*, 397–414. [CrossRef]
66. Sen, A.K. *Development as Freedom*; Oxford University Press: Oxford, UK, 1999.
67. Sen, A.K. Individual freedom as social commitment. *India Int. Cent. Q.* **1990**, *17*, 101–115.
68. Forni, F.H.; Longo, M.E. Desde la sociedad civil a fortalecer el Estado y a compensar los costos del mercado: Reflexiones acerca del sector informal. *Lavboratorio* **2007**, *8*, 38–44.
69. Flyvbjerg, B. Machiavellian Megaprojects. *Antipode* **2005**, *37*, 18–22. [CrossRef]

© 2018 by the author. Licensee MDPI, Basel, Switzerland. This article is an open access article distributed under the terms and conditions of the Creative Commons Attribution (CC BY) license (http://creativecommons.org/licenses/by/4.0/).

MDPI
St. Alban-Anlage 66
4052 Basel
Switzerland
Tel. +41 61 683 77 34
Fax +41 61 302 89 18
www.mdpi.com

Urban Science Editorial Office
E-mail: urbansci@mdpi.com
www.mdpi.com/journal/urbansci

www.ingramcontent.com/pod-product-compliance
Lightning Source LLC
Chambersburg PA
CBHW040225040426
42333CB00052B/3358